The Death of Progressive Education

The Death of Progressive Education is the first authoritative survey of the changing politics of the classroom since the Second World War. It charts the process by which society moved away from being one in which teachers decided both the content of the school curriculum and how it would be taught towards the present situation in which a host of external influences dictates the nature of the educational experience.

The book identifies the key social and political developments which made this transformation inevitable and, at the same time, raises the question of how far the loss of control by teachers has also meant a shift away from progressive, child-centred education. Key issues covered include:

- The post-War debate on the school curriculum as well as the extent to which it was fiercely contested
- The Black Paper Movement of the early 1970s
- The ways in which radical right rhetoric has come to dominate the politics of education and the educational press
- How the term 'progressive education' has been subtly reworked, so that those claiming to reform education now focus on measurable outcomes and the answerability of schools to parental and government pressure
- An historical analysis of the ways in which the 'Thatcher revolution' in schools has been taken forward and developed under both John Major and Tony Blair.

This ground-breaking analysis of how we have arrived at the present situation in our schools will be of interest to all students of education and to all those who wish to learn more about the changes that have taken place in our education system over the past sixty years. It helps us understand why they happened and, in so doing, raises profound questions about the aspirations of modern society and the role of the schools in shaping it.

Roy Lowe has an OBE for his services to education and is Visiting Professor at the Institute of Education, University of London, UK.

The Death of Progressive Education

How teachers lost control of the classroom

Roy Lowe

Routledge
Taylor & Francis Group

LONDON AND NEW YORK

For Kathy

First published 2007
by Routledge
2 Park Square, Milton Park, Abingdon, Oxon OX14 4RN

Simultaneously published in the USA and Canada
by Routledge
270 Madison Ave, New York, NY 10016

Routledge is an imprint of the Taylor & Francis Group, an informa business

© 2007 Roy Lowe

Typeset in Times by
GreenGate Publishing Services, Tonbridge, Kent
Printed and bound in Great Britain by
TJ International Ltd, Padstow, Cornwall

British Library Cataloguing in Publication Data
A catalogue record for this book is available from the British Library

Library of Congress Cataloging in Publication Data
Lowe, Roy.
  The death of progressive education : how teachers lost control of the classroom /
Roy Lowe.
     p. cm.
  Includes bibliographical references.
  ISBN 978-0-415-35971-9 (hardback) -- ISBN 978-0-415-35972-6 (pbk.) 1.
Educational sociology--England--History--20th century. 2. Progressive
education--England--History--20th century. 3. Education--Political aspects--
England--History--20th century. 4. Education--Social aspects--England--History-
-20th century. 5. Education and state--England--History--20th century. I. Title.
  LC191.8.G72E5355 2007
  379.41--dc22
                                                2007001040

ISBN-10: 0–415–35971–6 (hbk)
ISBN-10: 0–415–35972–4 (pbk)
ISBN-10: 0–203–94595–6 (ebk)

ISBN-13: 978-0-415–35971–9 (hbk)
ISBN-13: 978–0-415–35972–6 (pbk)
ISBN-13: 978–0-203–94595–7 (ebk)

Contents

Acknowledgements

There are several people whom I have to thank. First, my friend Maurice Whitehead, who, a few years ago, suggested that I might write a book on the theme of the control of popular education since the Second World War. Without his initial encouragement I doubt that I would have embarked on the lengthy process of researching and writing this book. It has been a fascinating quest and I am grateful for the first shove in the right direction.

Second, I want to thank my colleagues at the Institute of Education, who, without necessarily realising it, through their warmth, encouragement and kindness, and a preparedness to exchange ideas, made the whole business far easier than it might have been. Gary McCulloch, David Crook, Richard Aldrich, Vincent Carpentier, Tom Woodin, Dennis Dean, John White and, more recently, Jane Martin have each played a part and I thank them too.

Third, as ever, the staff of the various libraries and archives in which I have worked have been unfailingly helpful, courteous and unsparing in their efforts to ensure that I had access to the material I needed. Much of my time has been spent at the Public Record Office, at the Institute of Education library and at the library of the University of Birmingham. I owe a particular debt to those staff at each of these places who helped me.

As has been the case with all of my previous books, my publisher is Routledge. I thank them for the chance to pursue this research. In particular Anna Clarkson remains, as ever, a great facilitator. I owe a particular debt to Amy Crowle, who helped me restore several chapters after the kind of computer glitch which my generation is prone to and who was also helpful at every turn.

Also, I thank my wife and best friend, Kathy, who was a schoolteacher during much of the period covered by this book and who subjected each chapter to close critical scrutiny. I am grateful for her help and also for her forbearance, encouragement and understanding. Being married to an author is not the easiest row to hoe and there is a self-focus about writing which will challenge any relationship. I am truly appreciative. Without her this book would not have been finished.

Finally, I thank my wider family of three daughters, two sons-in-law and six grandchildren for their love and encouragement and for giving me a sense of perspective throughout the whole enterprise. I told my oldest grandson, Finn, aged seven, that I was writing a book on schools. He thought for a moment or two and then asked, 'Why on earth are you doing that, Granddad?' I was lost for an answer. I hope that what follows provides some kind of belated response, both to him and to the wider readership.

Roy Lowe
Birmingham
November 2006

List of abbreviations

AMMA	Assistant Masters' and Mistresses' Association
APU	Assessment of Performance Unit
A/S Examination	Advanced Subsidiary Level Examination
BBC	British Broadcasting Corporation
BERA	British Education Research Association
CBI	Confederation of British Industry
CEO	Chief Education Officer
CPS	Centre for Policy Studies
CPVE	Certificate of Pre-Vocational Education
CSE	Certificate of Secondary Education
DES	Department for Education and Skills
ESRC	Economic and Social Research Council
GCE	General Certificate of Education
GCSE	General Certificate of Secondary Education
GEC	General Electric Company
GLC	Greater London Council
GMTV	Good Morning television programme
GTTR	Graduate Teacher Training Registry
HMI	His (or Her) Majesty's Inspectorate (also used individually)
HORSA	Hutting Operation for the Raising of the School Leaving Age
IAHM	Incorporated Association of Head Masters
ILEA	Inner London Education Authority
IMF	International Monetary Fund
IPPR	Institute for Public Policy Research
ITA	Initial Teaching Alphabet
LEA	Local Education Authority
LMS	Local Management of Schools
MSC	Manpower Services Commission
NAHT	National Association of Head Teachers
NASUWT	National Association of Schoolmasters and Union of Women Teachers
NCC	National Curriculum Council
NFER	National Foundation for Educational Research

NUT	National Union of Teachers
OFSTED	Office for Standards in Education
OPEC	Organisation of Petroleum Exporting Countries
ORACLE	Observation and Classroom Learning Evaluation Project
PFI	Private Finance Initiative
PGCE	Postgraduate Certificate in Education
PRO	Public Record Office
QCA	Qualifications and Curriculum Authority
RIBA	Royal Institute of British Architects
RNR	Royal Naval Reserve
SATS	Standardised Assessment Tasks
SCAA	School Curriculum and Assessment Authority
SEAC	School Examinations and Assessment Council
SHA	Secondary Heads Association
SSRC	Social Science Research Council
TES	*Times Educational Supplement*
TGAT	Task Group on Assessment and Testing
TTA	Teacher Training Agency
UMIST	University of Manchester Institute of Science and Technology
UNESCO	United Nations Educational, Scientific and Cultural Organisation
YTS	Youth Training Scheme

Introduction

This book is an attempt to describe and explain the process by which, since the Second World War, teachers in England have lost control of what they do in the classroom. It is written in the belief that, as government, the State and external agencies have steadily assumed more control over what goes on in schools, there have been significant changes in educational practice, in terms of both what is taught and how it is taught. In the pages that follow I will be attempting to trace the intricate, complex and changing relationships between pedagogic practice and the politics of education. In charting the slow retreat from progressive education, I will necessarily be concerned with several interrelated underlying questions. Who should determine what is taught to a child in school? What exactly is the best way to provide that education? How is it best organised? How is it best conducted? What should it involve? These are central questions for any society concerned with the schooling of its young citizens. They are particularly salient for the United Kingdom at the present time, and my hope is that, by offering some insights into the political and social context within which the schools have operated during the recent period, and trying to show how these factors have influenced educators and educational practice, I might be able to throw a little light on the question of where (as a society committed to the provision of formal education for its children) we might go from here; what is possible, what is likely and what is desirable.

This attempt at historical analysis will also, necessarily, draw on my own perceptions during the half century that I have been involved in education, first as a schoolchild who entered an all-age elementary school in 1944, progressing through a rural grammar school and a new university to pursue my own career in education. I began that career as a teacher in comprehensive and grammar schools and went on to spend many years in teacher education. Inevitably, I have developed views on the nature of the changes that have taken place in the profession during that time. But this is not intended as some kind of autobiography, nor as the nostalgic reflections of someone looking back to a lost golden age. Whilst this book necessarily draws on and is to some degree reflective of my own experience, it is rather an attempt to unravel what seems to me to be one of the historical puzzles which still hangs over these years, and that puzzle concerns the complex links between the aspirations of educators, the politics of education and what actually goes on in the classrooms.

Perhaps the problem is best identified by reference to a few salient bench-marks which are easily identified at the outset and which have given rise to what is little short of an historical orthodoxy in the way these events are perceived. First, the 1940s saw a major Education Act in 1944 (the only domestic legislation to reach the statute book during the War), followed by a massive reconstruction effort with the rebuilding of the education system as one key element. The Act itself was silent on the subject of the curriculum (the word did not appear any-where in the legislation) because, as a succession of commentators have pointed out, it was universally assumed that the details of what went on in the classroom were either too obvious to need spelling out or were the sole responsibility of the teachers themselves. The post-War reconstruction placed a great emphasis on the provision of school places, the supply of teachers and, to a lesser extent (although increasingly so into the 1950s), the structure of the system. Political debates on class size, on the training of teachers and on selection did not tend to dwell on questions of pedagogy if they were mentioned at all. Looking back, it seems almost as though the question of what teachers actually did (or should be doing) was taken for granted.

In the 1950s new issues began to emerge which clearly had some curricular ramifications, although these were still not what drove these debates. Rather, the continuing viability of the secondary modern and technical schools and the grow-ing demands for comprehensivisation came to the fore, as did discussions of the cost of state schooling to the taxpayer, and the changing needs of a quickly chang-ing economy. Regarding the new GCE examinations introduced in 1951, discussion focused far more on which students should sit them than on what form they might take. It was only in March 1960, in the Commons debate on the Crowther Report, that David Eccles commented memorably that it was perhaps time for central government to take an interest in what he referred to as 'the secret garden of the curriculum'.

All this was to change in the 1960s. A new generation of young teachers, for the most part committed to some degree or other of change in pedagogy (at both primary and secondary levels), was one important catalyst. Another was the active promotion by the LEAs of teacher involvement in curriculum reform, with local teachers' centres and the newly formed Schools Council as key agen-cies. This generated debate on both the structure of the curriculum and teaching method which was more public and more overt than had ever previously been the case. During this decade the question of examination reform also came to the fore. Major reports such as those from the Newsom (1963) and Plowden (1967) committees also fuelled a sense that things were changing in the class-rooms. But these were still discussions which were monopolised by the profession itself. Politicians remained focused in the main on the vexed ques-tions of selection for secondary schooling and the growing need for an expansion of opportunity at post-school level.

Prime Minister Callaghan's October 1967 Ruskin speech is widely seen as the hinge point, the moment at which government began to take a close interest in the day-by-day detail of schooling. Insisting that educational expenditure by the State would not go beyond the annual figure of six billion pounds, Callaghan appealed for 'value for money' and made it clear that it was the right (and even the responsibility) of central government to see that this was delivered by those within the education system. From this moment onwards a succession of initiatives, first from that Labour government, then, within a few years, from Thatcher's Conservative administration, and most recently from New Labour, have ensured that the control of what went on in the schools was no longer to be the sole responsibility of the teaching profession. The semi-permanent weakening of the teaching profession by the industrial action of 1985–6, followed by the draconian 1988 Education Reform Act, resulted not only in a national curriculum, but in the establishment of testing at ages seven, eleven and fourteen and in the publication of league tables of school performance as well as of the reports on school inspections. Virtually at a stroke, teachers were made answerable to their political masters and to their wider publics. The developments of the 1990s and of the first years of the twenty-first century have served only to confirm this new settlement. There is no sign of any administration in the foreseeable future which would wish to turn the clock back. The recent emphasis on target-setting has worked only to take control of pedagogic practice further away from the teaching profession.

As these developments have worked their way through the system, there have also been subtle changes in classroom practice, in part the result of the changing social and economic context within which teachers work, but in part too as a direct result of this new answerability, which sees the profession, as never before, obliged to justify its practices and to conform to directives and regulations which impose, ever more directly, the details of the classroom regime. To what extent has this meant the marginalisation, or even ending, of so-called 'progressive' approaches to teaching? That is one of the key questions which I will attempt to unravel in this book.

This focus means that necessarily this book is not a straightforward history of curriculum change. Rather, it is an attempt to establish an argument and an explanation. Consequently, I am forced in the attempt to adhere to my central theme to say very little about special needs education, which merits its own history for these years and which is of itself a major issue. Nor do I have much to say about gender contrasts in educational performance and the ways in which questions of sexual identity impinged on the curriculum debate. These are the two most salient omissions. Doubtless there are more.

But what I do attempt to do is to flesh out the brief, caricatured account of curriculum change since 1945, which I have outlined above, to pursue the question of how accurate it really is. I am attempting to tease out some of the deep-seated changes in society which help explain how and why the teaching profession is no longer in control of its own destiny. I seek also to identify those underlying political tensions which are constant throughout the period and which suggest a deeper reality to the politics of education in the period since the Second World War. In doing so, I am trying to raise the question of what we might learn from our own recent history about the best approaches to the teaching of our children and our grandchildren as we move into the twenty-first century. In what ways can insights into the delicate relationship between the teachers, their public and the politicians inform us as we approach the vexed question of how best to educate a child? These are the issues at the heart of this book and I hope that what follows helps to throw at least a little light on these complex questions.

1 Popular education in England
The historical legacy

In England the State began to take an interest in the provision of education during the nineteenth century. From the outset there were contested views as to who should determine what went on in the schools and precisely what was the best way to educate a child within a formal school setting. This was hardly surprising, since there were then, as there have been ever since, contrasting views on the nature of childhood, on the needs of the child and on the purposes and functions of schooling.

First, the nature of childhood itself was not fully understood and was certainly contested. On the one hand, running through European literature and underpinning much Christian thinking, was the view that the child was from birth intrinsically evil and in need of redemption and improvement. Only through the intervention of adults could the growing child be moulded, reformed, disciplined or saved, depending on the particular world-view in play in any particular situation. This view necessarily involved the belief that children needed to be 'schooled' and that schooling should be directed towards particular ends. On the other hand, there were those who took a much more idealistic view of childhood, seeing it as a period of innocence which was slowly eroded by the realities of growing up. One version of this view was expressed by the poet Wordsworth, who subscribed to a neo-Platonist view that it was possible to look back to an age of innocence during which various insights into the nature of being were possible in ways that were denied the corrupted adult. He wrote:

> There was a time when meadow, grove, and stream,
> The earth, and every common sight,
> To me did seem
> Apparelled in celestial light,
> The glory and the freshness of a dream.
> It is not now as it hath been of yore –
> Turn wheresoe'er I may,
> By night or day,
> The things which I have seen I now can see no more.

In his *Ode* 'Intimations of Immortality from Recollections of Early Childhood', Wordsworth was coming close to the view of childhood expressed not many years earlier by Rousseau in his novel *Emile*. So, differing views of the nature of child-hood and of the needs of the child have been, and remain still, one reason for the ongoing contest over the nature of schooling.

The constraints on popular education

These contrasting views of the nature of childhood were only one of many influ-ences on the development of popular education. Another was the political and social intentions of educators and those involved in setting up the schools. It has been well-established by historians of education over many years that, when the State began to involve itself in the provision of schooling, it did so for particular purposes and in a particular style. The churches were anxious not to lose the ever-increasing numbers of working poor in the growing industrial towns and cities of the nineteenth century. Thus the question of religion and its place in the school-room loomed large throughout the century. Linked to this was an ongoing fear of revolution, which never entirely went away after the French Revolution. Industrialists were anxious to ensure that there was a supply of labour into their factories. For much of the nineteenth century this involved only a minimal educa-tion and a sense of discipline, a readiness to accept the rhythms and timing of the working day. Hence the sense of order instilled in the classroom was seen as a preparation for life in the factory.

At the heart of this was a determination to establish what Richard Johnson identified many years ago as 'social control'. Writing in *Past and Present* in 1970, he concluded that

> the early Victorian obsession with the education of the poor is best under-stood as a concern about authority, about power, about the assertion (or the re-assertion?) of control. This concern was expressed in an enormously ambitious attempt to determine, through the capture of educational means, the patterns of thought, sentiment and behaviour of the working class. Supervised by its trusty teacher, surrounded by its playground wall, the school was to raise a new race of working people – respectful, cheerful, hard-working, loyal, pacific and religious.[1]

Several things followed from this. First, it was clear from the start for most providers, that popular education must, necessarily, be circumscribed and limited in its scope. Second, it must also involve a regime which imparted social order and discipline. Equally, it was the role of government, through its inspectorate, to ensure that these conditions were met. There was no question about where power lay in determining the nature and content of popular education. These were to become key characteristics of the operation of the nineteenth-century elementary school and they generated a set of assumptions around schooling which have largely survived down to the present.

All this has been well-established by a generation of historians of education and a few very familiar quotations will suffice to underline the point. It is worth recalling the well-known remarks of Davies Giddy in the Commons in 1807, responding to Whitbread's Parochial Schools Bill, which was intended to set up rate-aided parish schools. In what was nothing short of an out-and-out rejection of popular schooling Giddy said:

> However specious in theory the project might be of giving education to the labouring classes of the poor, it would be prejudicial to their morals and happiness: it would teach them to despise their lot in life, instead of making them good servants in agriculture and other laborious employments. Instead of teaching them subordination, it would render them fractious and refractory ... it would enable them to read seditious pamphlets, vicious books and publications against Christianity; it would render them insolent to their superiors; and, in a few years, the legislature would find it necessary to direct the strong arm of power towards them.[2]

This view coloured the provision of popular education for much of the nineteenth century, although it was necessarily modified as the schools came to impart basic literacy and numeracy. By 1861 it was possible for James Fraser, an Assistant Commissioner to the Newcastle Committee which had been set up to report on popular education, to state in his evidence:

> Even if it were possible, I doubt whether it would be desirable, with a view to the real interests of the peasant boy, to keep him at school till he was 14 or 15 years of age. But it is not possible. We must make up our minds to see the last of him ... at ten or eleven ... I venture to maintain that it is possible to teach a child, soundly and thoroughly, in a way that he shall not forget it, all that it is necessary for him to possess in the shape of intellectual attainment, by the time he is ten years old ... He shall be able to spell correctly the words that he will ordinarily have to use; he shall read a common narrative ... with sufficient ease to be a pleasure to himself and to convey information to listeners; if gone to live at a distance from home, he shall write his mother a letter that shall be both legible and intelligible; he knows enough of ciphering to ... test the correctness of a common shop bill; if he hears talk of foreign countries he has some notions as to the parts of the habitable globe in which they lie; and, underlying all ... he has acquaintance enough with the Holy Scriptures to follow the allusions and the arguments of a plain Saxon sermon, and a sufficient recollection of the truths taught him in his catechism, to know what are the duties required of him towards his maker and his fellow man. I have no brighter view of the future or the possibilities of an English elementary education floating before my eyes than this. If I had ever dreamt more sanguine dreams what I have seen in the last six months would have effectually and for ever dissipated them.[3]

In this context, it is hardly surprising that, a year later, introducing the Revised Code, which was to determine what went on in the elementary schools until the end of the century, Robert Lowe told the Commons:

> I cannot promise the House that this system will be an economical one and I cannot promise that it will be an efficient one, but I can promise that it shall be one or the other. If it is not cheap it shall be efficient; if it is not efficient it shall be cheap.[4]

By introducing payment by results, and making the pay of elementary school teachers dependent on the results of the annual visit of the schools' inspector, this Code ensured that the curriculum remained focused on reading, writing and arithmetic and that what was to be taught and how it was taught remained firmly under the control of the government of the day. This precedent, together with the fact that class sizes never fell to a level at which real innovation was a possibility, meant that the elementary sector, through which most English children passed, remained limited in its scope and style until it was rolled into the new system of primary education introduced by the 1944 Education Act. This goes far to explain the nature of the schooling I received in an all-age elementary school in the late 1940s which is described in the next chapter (the 1944 Act was not fully implemented until the early 1960s, so many children went through one or other variant of the old system for years after the Act came into force). In brief, elementary schooling for most English children meant a heavy dosage of the three Rs and, as a direct result of classes which in many cases contained over fifty pupils, a reliance on recitation, copying, and teacher-centred lessons with only very limited use of even question and answer. My grandmother was an elementary schoolteacher throughout the first forty years of the twentieth century in an industrial township in the West Midlands. I asked her once how she kept order in a class of sixty pupils. She replied that it was easy. On her desk she had a bell. If the noise level became too great she rang the bell. If the pupils failed to respond she went among them with a cane. I suspect that this was common practice for much of the period that she was a teacher. It suggests that the very limited aspirations spelt out by James Fraser in 1861 were shared by many within the elementary sector up to a century later.

The secondary schools had quite different origins from those in the elementary sector, and, until 1944 at least, a separate clientele. Established to provide a sound education for the sons of the middle and upper classes, secondary schools had differing aspirations from those in the elementary sector and developed a slightly different set of traditions of organisation and teaching. Their purpose was to prepare their pupils for the universities or for employment in the professions, and, since they were not directly funded by the State they were less directly answerable to government. Classes were smaller than those in elementary schools and the curriculum rather broader. Towards the end of the nineteenth century a growing number of girls' secondary grammar schools appeared and, after 1902, when the local authorities began to assume some responsibility for secondary education, a large number of municipal secondary schools were set up, many of them for girls.

But in this sector, too, there were strong forces which placed limits on the power of the teachers to innovate. First, the growing influence of external examinations, be it the dead hand of Oxbridge entry, or the School Certificate introduced in 1917, meant that there was considerable uniformity of curriculum across the country. Indeed, the 1904 Regulations for Secondary Schools introduced by Robert Morant ensured that the curriculum of all schools in receipt of government grants would conform closely to the model that had been established by the public schools during the late nineteenth century. These regulations insisted that instruction must be 'general' and must be 'complete'. Its details were closely specified:

> the course should provide for instruction in the English Language and Literature, at least one language other than English, Geography, History, Mathematics, Science and Drawing, with due provision for Manual Work and Physical Exercises, and, in a girls' school, for Housewifery. Not less than four and a half hours a week must be allotted to English, Geography and History: not less than three and a half hours to the Language where only one is taken or less than six where two are taken; and not less than seven and a half hours to Science and Mathematics, of which at least three must be for Science. The instruction in Science must be both theoretical and practical.[5]

Beyond this, the appearance during the late-Victorian and Edwardian period of sets of thirty and more textbooks, to be followed for the school year in each subject, provided a template from which few teachers strayed, even determining the literary tastes and experience of a generation of English schoolboys. Thus, in sum, what had emerged in England in the century before the passage of the 1944 Act were two separate but increasingly interlinked systems of schooling, each with its own traditions and practices, but both deeply conformist in the ways they went about their work because of the constraints upon them.

The emergence of progressivism

Despite the persistence of these pressures and constraints, which put a straightjacket on the provision of education in England, there were, from the outset, those who took a more sanguine view of what was possible in a school. For the sake of convenience we will call them 'progressives' although, as authors such as Kevin Brehony have shown, this risks bundling together such disparate voices and intentions as to make the term opaque at best,[6] while one American commentator has described 'progressivism', as applied to education, as 'a vacuous and mischievous concept'.[7]

On the one side there were the major figures whose thinking and precepts had an impact on schooling right across the industrialising world. Among the best known was Pestalozzi. His belief that complex issues could be pared down to their basics in the schoolroom, his advocacy of object lessons and his unswerving belief in the inherent goodness of the child led to Pestalozzi being visited at Yverdun by a host of educational pioneers, many of them from England. Andrew Bell, Robert

Owen, Maria Edgeworth and Henry Brougham all made the journey. But the two educational reformers who did most to disseminate Pestalozzi's ideas in the United Kingdom were James Pierrepoint Greaves, who became secretary of the Infant School Society on his return from Yverdun and the Reverend Charles Mayo, who made his school at Cheam 'the most famous Pestalozzian school in England'.[8]

Frequently in opposition to the followers of Pestalozzi were those Froebelians who worked tirelessly from the mid-nineteenth century to spread the gospel of the kindergarten and of carefully defined methods for the instruction of young children. Bertha Meyer Ronge, a refugee from Germany, co-founded with her husband the first Froebelian school to be set up in Britain in Tavistock Place in 1854. Under her influence, the Manchester Kindergarten Society was set up in 1873, and two years later the London Froebel Society.[9] One London teacher, Louisa Walker of the Fleet Road Board School, introduced Froebelian methods in the infant section and was described in contemporary journal *The practical teacher* as being 'at the fountain head of the modern implementation of the kindergarten principle'.[10]

Another influential figure was Maria Montessori, whose followers have been described by Kevin Brehony as

> the most prominent advocates of individual instruction in England ... By pro-
> viding instruction in a prepared environment that was mainly individual, but
> at the same time was given in the presence of other pupils, Montessori offers
> to the teachers of young children in public elementary schools an alternative
> to whole-class teaching.[11]

Brehony has shown that well-known authorities such as Sir John Adams gave publicity to Montessori's ideas. Adams was the influential Principal of the London Day Training College and London's first Professor of Education. His book *The new teaching* claimed that Montessori 'had claimed to have sounded class teaching's death knell'.[12] Some elementary school teachers, such as Lily Hutchinson of the Upper Hornsey Road School in London, set about implementing her system, although the inspectorate tended to pour cold water on Montessorian methods whenever they came across them in the state sector.[13] In brief, it is clear that the names of Pestallozi, Froebel and later Montessori were not unknown to those teaching in state schools in England (certainly by the early years of the twentieth century) and that there were some sporadic, individualistic efforts to implement their ideas, despite the context in which teachers found themselves.

Beyond this, there is ample evidence of individuals who, either in private schools or occasionally in the state sector, sought to offer a version of schooling which went beyond the limited visions of many parliamentarians. Robert Owen made the schoolroom central to his model community at New Lanark. His son, Robert Dale Owen, wrote *An outline of the system of education at New Lanark*. In it he pointed out that the course of mental arithmetic taught to the older classes was

similar to that adapted by Mr. Pestalozzi ... In this, as in every other department of instruction, the pupils are taught to understand what they are doing ...
and in what ways the knowledge they are acquiring may be beneficially
employed in later life.[14]

Owenite schools became a key feature of the cooperative movement during the
nineteenth century and were established in several locations. Thus in 1839, following the precept that 'the character of man is formed for him, not by him',
middle-class members of the Liverpool Rational School Society set about the
establishment of a school to promote

> the full development and temperate exercise of all the physical and moral
> powers ... All will be trained in the same manner and to the same extent with-
> out any distinction except what is rendered necessary from the peculiar
> natural organisation of each child.[15]

Similar principles were taken on board in the numerous Chartist Halls of Science
which appeared a few years later.

One of the best known individuals who set about the provision of a broader,
more child-centred education within the developing elementary sector, was
Richard Dawes, rector of King's Somborne in Hampshire. In 1842 Dawes found
himself involved in the establishment of an elementary school for this parish.
Apparently uninfluenced by either Continental or domestic theories of education
Dawes wrote that 'the task I set myself was to make the schools so good that the
parents might see that there was no question about the fact that their children were
better for attending'. Accordingly, as W. A. C. Stewart explained,

> he immediately distinguished the teaching given in his school from the mon-
> itorial instruction in the three R's that was common in all but a few of the ...
> village schools of the time. He sought to make the children think and reason
> rather than master facts, and he modified the usual curriculum in order to
> bring it closer to everyday life, and in particular to include a good deal of sci-
> ence. Above all he realised that children learned more rapidly and effectively
> when solving problems that related directly to their own experience.[16]

At the school the children were regularly involved in field visits which incorporated both botanical and scientific experimentation.

As the nineteenth century progressed it is possible to identify much broader
movements which had an influence, if only peripheral, on work in a number of
schools and particularly on what went on in the teacher training colleges. First,
there was the child study movement which developed during the second half of
the century and began to look increasingly like a crusade. The British Child Study
Association was set up in 1894 and two years later the Childhood Society was
founded. The two organisations, although representing differing approaches to the
study of childhood, merged in 1907 to become the Child Study Society. Although

not directly concerned with teaching method, these organisations had a profound
influence on the origins of child psychology in Britain and on many who went on
to become teacher educators.

This was all evidence of the late nineteenth-century quest for a science of education. Dick Selleck has identified the years from 1870 to 1914 as those when
efforts were made to identify and introduce 'the new education' based on far more
rigorous scientific principles than any previous educational initiatives. Selleck
saw this new education as

> calling upon the teacher to free himself from the limitations of the system of
> payment by results ... .it brought many prophets besides those who wished to
> put education on a scientific basis: eager and dedicated Herbartians; ... gen-
> tle and sometimes sentimental kindergarteners trying to make an Englishman
> out of Froebel; advocates of manual training or heuristic science, who
> believed that the future of education was assured if their version of 'learning
> by doing' became accepted; advocates of physical education, of school
> meals, of medical inspection, who believed that the task of training the
> child's mind had to wait on the task of improving his health; advocates of
> moral instruction, who put the formation of character before all.[17]

During the Edwardian period there is some evidence that this lobbying began to
have an impact on official policy. In 1905, for example, the Board of Education's
official *Handbook of suggestions* stated that

> the only uniformity of practice that the Board of Education desire to see in
> the teaching of the public elementary schools is that each teacher shall think
> for himself, and work out for himself such methods of teaching as may use
> his powers to the best advantage and be best suited to the particular needs and
> conditions of the school.[18]

Although there may be a major question mark over the impact this policy statement had in practice, it heralded a long period in which the classroom teacher
was seen as being autonomous in terms of both teaching method and the details
of the curriculum.

A few years later, in 1911, Edmund Holmes, a recently retired schools' inspector, published *What is and what might be*, a blistering critique of the elementary
system within which he had worked for many years. His arguments involved deep
scepticism about the three Rs. He derided a fixed syllabus and was scathing on
the question of the influence of examinations. Some of his observations speak to
us today and have a direct bearing on issues that are still contested. He commented that

> the Western belief in the efficacy of examinations is a symptom of a wide-
> spread and deep-seated tendency ... to judge according to the appearance of
> things, to attach supreme importance to visible 'results', to measure inward

worth by outward standards, to estimate progress in terms of what the 'world' reveres as 'success'.

He made a major distinction between what he called the externals and the internals of education:

> the tendency of the Western teacher to mistake the externals of education for the essentials ... gives rise to many misconceptions, one of the principal of which is the current confusion between information and knowledge ... It frequently happens that one who has a retentive memory is able to impart information glibly and correctly without possessing any real knowledge of the subject in question.

For Holmes, it followed from all this that,

> things being as they are ... it is inevitable that the education given in many of our elementary schools should be based ... on complete distrust of the child ... He must not express what he really feels or sees for if he does the results will probably fall short of the standards of neatness, cleanness and correctness which an examiner might expect ... The experiment is much too risky to be tried ... But to forbid a child to use his own perceptive faculties is to arrest the whole process of his growth.[19]

In the spirit of Holmes' remarks, a few teachers at this time set about using the Dalton Plan, an American scheme for a child-centred approach to the curriculum, based on individual work rather than whole-class teaching. Some of these enthusiasts were elementary school teachers such as A. J. Lynch, a headmaster who in 1924 wrote a book extolling the virtues of the Dalton Plan.[20] Another educationalist, Helen Parkhurst, devised a plan of individual pupil assignments on the Dalton model and publicised it through the New Education Fellowship, another organisation which was lobbying for a fresh approach to teaching at this time. Thus there is clear evidence of a groundswell of opinion which was far from comfortable with existing practice in the elementary sector particularly, although it is not clear whether this had any significant practical impact on the majority of schools.

During the inter-War years the chorus of voices calling for reform of classroom practice grew, with several leading figures in teacher education being identified as 'progressives' and polemicising for change. They included Percy Nunn, an idealist whose book, *Education, its data and first principles*, was in print throughout the period. It placed individuality, freedom and growth at the heart of classroom practice. Similarly, Susan Isaacs, a psychologist whose important research was done at the Malting House School, produced numerous books and articles arguing for discovery methods and pupil activity in the classroom.[21] Increasingly, this kind of thinking began to percolate through policy documents. Perhaps most famously the 1931 Hadow Report insisted that 'the curriculum is to be thought of in terms of activity and experience rather than knowledge to be acquired and facts to be stored'.[22]

Thus, there is clear evidence of a long-term advocacy of alternative strategies in the classroom, and we are indebted to historians such as Dick Selleck,[23] Peter Cunningham,[24] Kevin Brehony[25] and Bill Marsden[26] in particular for teasing out in their writings some of the complexities of this movement as well as a picture of the extent to which it impinged on day-by-day practice in the majority of schools. Their work has highlighted the long-term tension between 'traditionalists' and 'progressives' and sets the scene for any account of the developing politics of the curriculum after the Second World War. Has the period since 1945 simply witnessed another increment in a struggle whose main characteristics are little changed over a century? Or is it the case that the social and political changes which have occurred since 1945 are so deep-seated that it would have been impossible for the battle for the control of the school curriculum to be nothing more than a replication of earlier struggles? These are the central questions which underpin my account in the chapters which follow.

2   The post-War educational settlement

A conservative revolution

What is wrong with people nowadays? Why do they all seem to think they are qualified to do things far above their capabilities? This is all to do with the learning culture in schools. It is a consequence of a child-centred learning emphasis which admits of no failure and an education system which tells people they can become pop stars, high court judges or brilliant TV presenters or infinitely more competent heads of state without ever putting in the necessary work or having the natural ability. It is a result of a social utopianism which believes humanity can be genetically engineered to contradict the lessons of history.

> Prince Charles, the Prince of Wales, in a written memorandum cited at an employment tribunal in Croydon, *The Guardian*, 18 November 2004, p. 1

There are numerous reasons why questions of pedagogy did not loom large for educational planners in the years immediately following the Second World War. The issues of exactly what the young people of Britain should be taught and how they should be taught it were not seen as unimportant, but were largely eclipsed and subsumed by more pressing issues. To explain and make sense of this claim it is necessary first to explain something of the educational context of the late 1940s.

First, for those working in the old elementary schools, soon to become the primary sector under the terms of the 1944 Education Act, both the curriculum and pedagogic practice seemed to be the almost inevitable result of a century of evolution and a teaching context which made thought of innovation and change appear fanciful. The three Rs continued to dominate the curriculum and classroom practice continued to rely heavily on drill, on repetition and recitation, on the chanting of multiplication tables, with the teacher firmly in control and at the centre of everything that went on. The size of classes, the continuing prevalence of benches in many schools, the overcrowded and gloomy environment of many old elementary school buildings and the fairly cursory training of most teachers preordained that this was so.

The 1931 Hadow Report[1] which had famously suggested that the curriculum was to be thought of in terms of activity and experience rather than facts to be learned and knowledge to be stored may have had some limited impact upon the minority of children lucky enough to find themselves in the newer suburban schools built during the inter-War years. But for the vast majority of English elementary schoolchildren what went on in the classroom remained remarkably redolent of the late-Victorian era. I attended an all-age school in the late 1940s and was well aware that the paraphernalia for object lessons which my teacher kept on top of the cupboard had been there since before the First World War, was rarely used, and that my lot was a staple diet of handwriting practice, recitation of multiplication tables, spelling tests and rote learning. I had no reason then and have none now to think that my experience was all that unusual.

Meanwhile, at secondary level, the situation was equally unpropitious. Here the grammar schools dominated everything. The reforms of the late nineteenth century had seen some expansion of the curriculum but this had come to an end with the 1904 Secondary School Regulations promoted by Robert Morant. Although in force for only three years these had the effect of stabilising the curriculum of the secondary school for much of the twentieth century. Indeed, some commentators pointed out that, when the national curriculum introduced by the 1988 Education Reform Act was announced, at secondary level, barring one or two changes of nomenclature, it bore an uncanny resemblance to those 1904 Regulations. There were other long-term factors which conspired to ensure that what went on in secondary classrooms remained relatively unchanging too. The popularity of set texts, the dead hand of the School Certificate Examination and the marketing of well-tried class readers across a range of subjects all meant that, up and down the country, secondary schoolchildren had remarkably similar experiences in the classroom. This was only intensified by the particular kind of subject-specialist training which most grammar school teachers received in the universities.

If this suggests something of the longer-term context, the particular circumstances of the Second World War also ensured that the return to peacetime conditions would mean no immediate revolution in the classrooms of Britain. Rather, the quest was for a return to the tried and known. First, the War had involved massive disruption of the education service. Most strikingly, evacuation had impacted both on its subjects and on the host communities. Few schoolchildren in England had escaped its touch. Historians have detailed the social class tensions provoked by evacuation, as well as the longer-term psychological impact which generated a sense that children deserved better and which was one of the motors of the post-War neonatalist movement. All this made the re-establishment of what had been lost appear a primary need. In the major cities many schools had either been requisitioned for wartime use for military purposes or in many cases been severely damaged in the bombing raids. The teaching profession itself had suffered massive disruption too. As teachers went off to war they were replaced in many cases by women or by those previously retired. Stabilisation of this situation also meant a return to what had been known before.

Perhaps even more significant was the agenda created by the 1944 Education Act. The requirements that a new primary sector would be created, that all pupils would proceed to secondary education and that the raising of the school leaving age (which had been postponed at the outbreak of the War) would be implemented at the earliest opportunity posed a major challenge to the planners. In this situation curriculum reform was hardly likely to find itself at the top of any serious list of priorities.

This was compounded by the simple fact that these provisions meant that the country would need an unprecedented number of teachers during the next few years. The proposed solution was the Emergency Training Scheme, which, while it did succeed in getting over 35,000 extra entrants into the profession, did so at the cost of any protracted teacher training. These recruits to teaching were obliged to focus on class control and on classroom organisation and were hardly likely to become the standard-bearers in a campaign to revolutionise classroom practice.

Planning the New Jerusalem

But there was a deeper consideration which also deflected the debate away from pedagogy. So pressing were the practical needs of this immediate post-War situation that the focus was almost exclusively on the structures of the education system rather than its day-by-day working. This had been anticipated in two major reports from the Board of Education's Consultative Committee: the 1938 Spens Report and the 1943 Norwood Report. These both called for an education system which would acknowledge and accommodate 'types of mind'. Deeply influenced by the current fad of the educational psychologists (who were an increasingly influential lobby), the planners were driven to think largely in terms of first identifying and then providing schools for pupils who were believed to fall into one of three main categories: academic, technical or practical. While this proposal clearly did have curricular implications the first emphasis was simply upon the provision of places and there was, in the event, very little discussion of the detail of exactly how the curriculum should differ in each of the three types of school.

This concentration on access, on who would go to which type of school, derived in part from the historic split of schooling in England into elementary and secondary sectors, with the bulk of the population being excluded from the secondary schools. This imbalance had led to a sense of injustice and denial which became one of the underpinnings of the evolving education policy of the Labour Party. The establishment of 'secondary education for all' as the rallying cry of the party during the 1920s meant that, de facto, a widespread aspiration to what the grammar schools had to offer (both in terms of life chances and curriculum) became the dream of many working-class families. Although in the past many working-class children had turned down grammar school places, either because they could not afford the ancillary costs or because they thought they would be better off in one of the new higher elementary schools, politicians continued to see the grammar school as the ideal to be aimed for. After the 1945 election this was hardly surprising since the vast majority of the parliamentary Labour Party were themselves products of the grammar schools and had got where they were partly because of the start in life which the grammar schools had given them.

Popular hostility to elite forms of education was also eroded by the War itself. The Army Bureau of Current Affairs helped spread a new idealism among the armed forces. Popular radio programmes such as the BBC Brains Trust, the New Left Book Club as well as the 'specials' which began to appear under the Penguin label: all worked to spread the sense that a new meritocracy was sweeping away privilege. All of this led both politicians and educationalists to focus increasingly on access as the key educational issue. It is significant that, for example, when the *Picture Post* ran a special edition in January 1941 proposing its 'Plan for Britain', the article on education, authored by A. D. Lindsay ('one of the leaders of progress in educational ideals') said nothing about the curriculum. Identifying the four pressing needs of the English education system Lindsay focused on the fact that there was still 'one system for the poor and another for the rich'. He reflected what was seen as the best wisdom of his age when he stressed that the educational ladder and the fact that the education of the poor ended too early were the key issues. He called for a closer integration of the public schools with the state system. In a telling aside, reflecting a widely-held view, he remarked that

> the great variety of types of secondary school is not an evil. The evil is a different one. The decision as to which boys should go to which schools ... depends not on ability or fitness, but on wealth and class. The social division thus created is the outstanding evil.[2]

This neat summary of the contemporary wisdom explains in a nutshell why, after the Second World War, questions of access rather than the precise content of the curriculum became the primary focus of political debate.

This emphasis carried with it another implication. What was happening at this time was a gradual and inexorable shift of political attention away from the old elementary sector (the new primary schools) towards the secondary. A system which stressed types of mind and the need to differentiate was increasingly one which focused on the fairness of selection at eleven-plus. This was reflected neatly in the Ministry of Education's own 1948 publication, *The nation's schools*, which emphasised that it was innate differences between children, widening as they grew older, which necessitated selection for an appropriate schooling. But the overwhelming majority of those calling for a new education before the Second World War had been identified with the elementary sector. That debate was coming to be seen as increasingly passé and irrelevant to the needs of the moment.

In the event, once in power after the 1945 election, the Labour government found itself dealing with what seemed to be nothing more nor less than a constant ongoing crisis. Full employment belied the realities of a desperate economic situation, particularly in terms of external trade. The bleak winter of 1947 brought the country to its knees; problems of supply meant that rationing continued in force until the early 1950s. As if this were not enough, the returning soldiery made their own contribution to the challenges confronting the education system by ensuring that in 1947 the birth rate reached an unprecedented level, forcing the planners to focus their attention on the supply of places, on the provision of temporary classrooms and making teacher supply an ongoing issue into the post-War era. In this context it is fully understandable that the incoming Labour government toyed briefly with the idea of postponing the raising of the school-leaving age (planned for implementation in 1947), and equally understandable that it took the view that such a move would be an unthinkable betrayal of those who had put them in power. But, in confirming the decision to go ahead, the government put another nail in the coffin of 'the new education' ensuring that short term practical exigencies would dominate the politics of education for years to come rather than any radical rethinking of classroom practice.

The progressive lobby

Despite this gloomy context, there were still a number of individuals who were ready to argue for a more innovative approach to classroom practice. Some of them had been involved in the pre-War debates; others were new to the scene; but in sum they generated a vocal chorus and several of them were in positions of influence.

First, there was a small number of chief education officers all at work in the years immediately following the Second World War who had themselves been influenced by movements such as the New Education Fellowship during the inter-War years and who were ready to encourage at least some degree of experimentation in the schools under their charge.[3] Perhaps most notable among them was Alec Clegg. An ex-grammar school teacher who had trained at the London Day Training College, Clegg was appointed to the West Riding in 1945, becoming Chief Education Officer before the end of the year. Peter Cunningham has deftly summarised his influence in Yorkshire, commenting that 'progressive principles such as child-centredness, curriculum integration and concern for the school environment, ran through his administration, colouring its development and innovations'.[4] But it is worth noting too that all of the initiatives which Cunningham and others have attributed to his influence (the focus on art education, the encouragement of teachers to experiment, the backing of 'informal' teaching) were all to bear fruit later in his regime, during the 1950s and 1960s.

In contrast, there is some evidence that another reforming administrator, Stewart Mason, appointed CEO of Leicestershire in 1947, had an immediate impact. Insisting from the outset on a regime of advice rather than inspection, Mason succeeded in transforming the atmosphere, if not the day-by-day practice, of many Leicestershire schools. One of his first appointments, as adviser for infant education, was Dorothea Fleming, a Froebelian and 'a great protagonist of the English Nursery School Association'. One returning teacher commented in 1947:

> I came back to the new and exciting atmosphere created by Miss Fleming ... The main noticeable change was the freedom of movement children had in their classrooms. Previously they came in, sat down, and didn't move and the teacher was a person apart from the children. You had to make the children write with their right hands ... by 1947 you left them alone ... allowing a few kids to go into a corner and pick up a book, compared with them all having to go at the same speed: these are great improvements.[5]

Fleming was not averse to using the educational press to polemicise her views. In 1949, in a letter to the *Times Educational Supplement*, she set out her credo:

> I believe that much of the reluctance to break away from the old formal methods of teaching on board, chalk and talk lines is due to ignorance, fear and distrust rather than to large classes or to an avowed intelligent decision that such methods are not in the best interests of the children ... in the hands of a sincere teacher of average competence there is nothing to prevent work of this kind being carried out with a class of fifty ... there is a danger prevalent in some quarters to over-emphasize the obstructive power of poor buildings, size of classes and inadequate space ... the right people and the right attitudes can triumph gloriously over material obstacles.[6]

In Hertfordshire, John Newsom's approach to innovative teaching was through the classroom environment and he had a major impact on the design of school buildings and on classroom space. Appointed as CEO in 1940, a friend and disciple of Henry Morris who had been responsible for the Cambridgeshire Village colleges, Newsom found himself in the late 1940s on the receiving end of the London overspill population which was being housed in the new towns, four of which were in Hertfordshire. Stuart Maclure has commented on Newsom's belief 'that the child was educated by the whole environment in which he or she was taught'. Newsom wanted 'schools which elevated the spirit and ennobled the mind'.[7] He had already surrounded himself by a team of architects immersed in the modern movement, but was unable initially to pre-empt the worst effects of the Ministry's post-War Hutting Operation for the Raising of the School Leaving Age: despite Newsom's reservations, between 1947 and 1950 Hertfordshire erected over 600 prefabricated HORSA units. Yet, alongside all this, some innovation was possible. In 1951 one of the new Hertfordshire primary schools became the first prefabricated building of any kind to win a medal from the RIBA as Newsom's team strove to adapt prefabrication to the needs of the pupils. Interestingly, what all three of these eminent local administrators shared was a belief in the formative power of art education, and all three set about the provision of works of art in the state schools under their charge as well as the development of art education itself.

Similarly influential were a few members of the Schools' Inspectorate, some of whom were also in tune with contemporary thinking. The best known, rightly, is Christian Schiller whose career is a not untypical example of an 'establishment' figure with a background in the one of the progressive schools in the private sector who went on to exercise a massive influence over practice in England's state primary schools. A Cambridge mathematics graduate who trained, like Clegg, under Percy Nunn at the London Day Training College, Schiller began his teaching career with one of his own teachers, J. H. Simpson, who had moved on from Gresham's to be head of Rendcomb School in Gloucestershire, a progressive private school. Here Schiller became caught up in the reform of geometry teaching and was recruited to the Mathematical Association's committee on the teaching of geometry in preparatory schools. This led naturally to an appointment in the Schools' Inspectorate, where in Gloucestershire during the inter-War years he worked alongside Alec Clegg. In 1946 he became the first Staff Inspector for Primary Education, and it was at this point in his career that he began to play a major part in the debate on teaching method. Coming to believe increasingly that novel approaches to mathematics, to art and to movement were the keys to improved learning in the primary schools he set about the establishment of small in-service courses for selected teachers, many of whom went on themselves to become apostles of a revolution in primary education later in their careers. In 1956 this led him to leave the Inspectorate for a senior lecturership at the London Institute of Education where he extended his proselytising work, although his refusal to consider formal examination of his courses was to lead him into conflict within a system increasingly obsessed with accreditation and this clouded his later career.

Schiller's close ally during the post-War period was Robin Tanner, a graduate of Goldsmiths' College which was another hotbed of art education. After a teaching career Tanner became an HMI in 1935 working in Leeds, Gloucestershire and later Oxfordshire. In this last position Tanner worked alongside and became a close ally of Edith Moorhouse, appointed in 1946 as a schools' adviser to the county. She was to go on to play a major part in the dissemination of ideas on child-centred education during the 1960s and 1970s. In this connection he too came into contact with Clegg and became well-known to Schiller who collaborated with him in the establishment of some of the earlier in-service courses for teachers. Tanner believed that the study of natural things, as well as the exploration of arts and crafts, music and poetry were essential for the full realisation of human potential. He was himself an artist and was frequently involved in setting up displays which included his own output at Woolley Hall, the teachers' in-service centre set up by Clegg just outside Wakefield.

Another primary schools adviser in Oxfordshire was J. C. Gagg, who moved into the advisory service after working as a teacher-educator at Eastbourne College of education. His book for primary teachers, *Commonsense in the primary school*, was intended to 'suggest ways in which you can make use of the progressive ideas which are abroad'.[8] At the same time, Gagg was anxious to ensure that changes in classroom method did not mean a complete rejection of what had gone before. In a letter to the *Times Educational Supplement* in 1947 he congratulated the editors:

> it was most refreshing to read the case for compromise in your journal. There is little doubt that the rarity of freer methods in the primary schools is due to the over-enthusiasm of their supporters. Advocates of activity, projects, centres of interest, call them what you will, have sailed so furiously into print in the past that the fifty per class teachers have been left gasping for breath in the wind of their passing. Now, no-one seriously suggests that the whole of school time should be devoted to activity. Yet, with one recent exception, books on activity methods have certainly given the impression that the normal timetable should be completely scrapped. The real answer would seem to lie in compromise.[9]

Gagg was one of a fairly tight network of like-minded educationalists within the Inspectorate who, during the years immediately following the Second World War, were instrumental in promoting the debate on teaching method, particularly for the primary sector.

The third strand of this professional lobby was to be found increasingly in the expanding teacher-training sector. Although a three-year course of training was not introduced until 1960, the demand for more teachers meant that numerous new colleges were set up and those which existed already felt the impact of swift expansion. Many of the tutors recruited to these posts were sympathetic to the reform of classroom teaching, and, even if they were not of that bent on appointment, they quickly found themselves in an environment in which an uncontrite defence of existing practice was at best unfashionable and at worst seen as obstructionist.

Prominent among them was Mary Atkinson, a tutor in the University Education Department at Newcastle, who encouraged primary schoolteachers in the North-East to collaborate to produce *Basic requirements of the junior school* arguing that 'the traditional conception of the purpose of the junior school is the greatest stumbling block to reform'.[10] Another teacher-educator, W. K. Richmond, argued in his *Purpose in the junior school* that after the War schools were settling back into the old pattern and that there was a crying need for activity methods.[11] Other notable authors and polemicists included M. V. Daniel and Nancy Catty. Daniel was the author of the influential *Activity in the primary school* and Principal of Hereford Training College. She sought 'to give encouragement to those fearful of breaking new ground' and much of her book was given over to detailed descriptions of activity methods in practice.[12] Nancy Catty had retired from Goldsmiths' College in 1928 and had been one of those responsible for the college's emphasis on art education. She remained active long after her retirement and her *Learning and teaching in the junior school* (1941) influenced a generation of teachers after the War.[13] Another significant voice was that of Dorothy Gardner, a tutor at the London Institute who collaborated with A. H. Halsey to investigate working-class access to the grammar schools. She argued in the *Times Educational Supplement* in 1950 that research must underpin the transition to new styles of teaching. She saw 'a research method' as central to what went on in the junior school, adding that 'junior teachers who have the courage to put the deeper needs of the children in the first place often astonish their more cautious colleagues by the standard of knowledge and attainment achieved by allowing children to learn in natural ways'.[14]

The educational press was increasingly ready to air the views of these and like-minded colleagues. *Education*, the *Journal of Education* and *New Era* were all prepared to give voice to a progressive ideology at this time, and qualified support came from the *Times Educational Supplement* itself, although, as we will see, the *TES* was also more than ready to publicise, without adverse comment or criticism, the ideas of those who were violently antagonistic to any change in classroom practice. The availability of these outlets for publicity was to prove very significant, for they undoubtedly gave a general impression that any changes taking place in classroom practice were more widespread and more radical than was actually the case, making it easier for critics to play on a sense of crisis. Thus, inadvertently, the debate on classroom practice began to take on political undertones.

What is significant in our context is that almost all of this advocacy of a new approach (or of new approaches) was focused on the primary sector. But the realities of austerity, the rise in the birth rate and the shortage of qualified teachers meant that this sector was under particular pressures, with the result that this dialogue of the experts fell largely on deaf ears, at least for the immediate post-War period.

Meanwhile, those at work in the secondary sector were marching to a different drum. Here the implementation of universal secondary schooling meant the establishment of schools of different types, aimed at differing kinds of mind, all underpinned by a rigorous system of examining and diagnosis and a plea for 'parity of esteem'. The extent to which it proved impossible to break out of this political straightjacket is perhaps best demonstrated by quoting at length from the Ministry's own *The new secondary education* (1947) which hammered home the need for that tripartism first spelt out in the Spens and Norwood reports some years before:

Experience has shown that the majority of children learn most easily by dealing with concrete things and following a course rooted in their own day-to-day experience. At the age of 11 few of them will have disclosed particular interests and aptitudes well enough marked for them to require any other course. The majority will do best in a school which provides a good all round education in an atmosphere which enables them to develop freely along their own lines. Such a school will give them the chance to sample a variety of 'subjects' and skills and to pursue those which attract them most. It is for this majority that this secondary *modern* school will cater.

Some children, on the other hand, will have decided at quite an early age to make their careers in branches of industry or agriculture requiring a special kind of aptitude in science or mathematics. Others may need a course more exacting than that provided in the modern school, with a particular emphasis on commercial subjects, music or art. All these boys and girls will find their best outlet in the secondary *technical* school.

Finally there will be a proportion whose ability and aptitude require the kind of course with the emphasis on books and ideas that is provided at a secondary *grammar* school. They are attracted by the abstract approach to learning and should normally be prepared to stay at school long enough to benefit from the 'sixth form' work which is the most characteristic feature of the grammar school.

Both 'books' and 'activities' are essential in all three types of secondary course; no school can afford to base its work exclusively on one or the other.[15]

That, in a nutshell, was the Ministry's summary of the curricular implications of the coming of universal secondary education. It meant, of course, that the grammar school remained paramount and, as we will see, this was to prove of vital significance as the debate on teaching method unfolded during the next few years.

The curriculum debate: maverick voices

Yet, at just the time that the emergence of this 'progressive lobby' might have given the impression to onlookers that a consensus was developing on the school curriculum in the years following the Second World War, it is possible to find evidence of the existence of much more quirkish, random and wide-ranging opinions across the country. The 1944 Act had remained silent on the subject of the curriculum. As a host of historians have pointed out, what went on in the classrooms was widely seen as being largely, if not exclusively, the province of the professionals. It was a topic on which both government and civil service remained silent.

This silence was not shared by the people of England. Perhaps sparked by the evasiveness of the legislation, perhaps spurred on by the coming of universal secondary education, a growing number of citizens took it upon themselves to write in to the new Ministry to offer their own proposals for the school curriculum. There is no evidence that they were encouraged in this. But what is left to us in three surviving copious files at the Public Record Office[16] provides a glimpse of a society which housed a wide variety of often ill-coordinated, frequently maverick and strikingly individualistic ideas on what should and should not be going on in the schools. They are of intrinsic interest, but also raise significant questions for anyone seeking to understand how and why the school curriculum developed as it did in modern Britain. What follows gives a flavour of these files and seeks to interpret them.

Some of these letters were reflections of visions of Englishness which, in retrospect, appear very dated but which still do have their own political resonances. In July 1946, for example, the 'Men of the Trees' wrote to Ellen Wilkinson, pointing out that Britain was an arboreal nation and enquiring 'would it be possible for you to bring the subject of trees and forestry into the curriculum of every school? ... our daily bread is dependent on the fertility of the earth'. They saw it as essential that every child, whether rural or urban, should be able to recognise every type of indigenous tree by its leaf, flower and fruit. At the other end of the political spectrum, only a month later, Lieutenant Nicholson, R. N. R. pressed his case that all children should be able to recognise every kind of maritime vessel: 'it has always been a source of wonderment to me that the vast majority of the population of these islands, whose well-being and existence depends so greatly on seafaring, should be so ignorant of ships and shipping'.

In May 1945, Ellen Winnicroft from Birmingham wrote in arguing that

> facing facts, only a minority of boys and girls will today ever earn their living by doing completely individual and creative work. We must therefore give a broader and not a narrower education ... Let all children learn the basic subjects plus artistic and manual things and plenty of eurythmics and muscular games. Then get them to work on the teachers and give them talent tests ... I

think it would do no harm and a lot of good to have one trained anthroposoph-
ical teacher on the staff of every big school ... simply because they have been
given training in standing back and allowing the child to flow out properly.

The suggestions came in thick and fast: first aid in all schools, 'homecraft and sex
education for all pupils'; industrial visits as work experience; more emphasis on
modern foreign languages as a key to maintaining the peace; typewriters in all
schools as a prerequisite to compulsory typing lessons. H. G. Symes lobbied the
Ministry in May 1945 from Devon to advocate the compulsory learning and study
of chess together with the teaching of ambidexterity 'as a possible provision
against injury'. In September 1946 a suggestion was made that every school
should contain models of notable buildings for 'an awakening of the mind to the
beauty of planning'. Somerset County Council wanted dairying instruction in all
secondary schools in view of their increasing difficulty in finding dairymen. And
so it went on: compulsory swimming lessons, a metric system for all schools (but
one based on the inch, thus preserving the advantages of duodecimalisation!); a
pamphlet on 'Music law and arithmusic' advocating music as the key to successful mathematics; simplified spelling systems in schools; the compulsory teaching
of the history of industrial relations; the compulsory teaching of good manners; a
compulsory weekly lesson on Empire geography with a curriculum centred on
Cecil Rhodes ('let each lesson close with my Empire anthem. I am willing to have
another supply printed to meet your needs').

In November 1947 the British Ballet Organisation asked for 'the new syllabus of
the Royal Academy of Dancing to be introduced in schools as a full part of the curriculum'. To this the Ministry responded frostily 'We do not recommend any
particular syllabus of dancing in state aided schools and no change of policy is
anticipated'. And, rather pointedly, in February 1948 W. D. Thomas, Secretary of the
Welsh Nationalist Undeb Cymru Fydd called for the Welsh language to become
compulsory in all schools in Britain ('a thorough command of Welsh should be at
the command of every cultured British citizen ... a compulsory subject in every
school ... England itself would benefit spiritually'). In July 1950, George Wigg, at
this time a Labour backbencher, pressed the Ministry to consider the introduction of
a national curriculum. This was one representation which did generate a flurry of
backroom activity at Whitehall, although nothing came of it at this time.

Two exchanges are particularly memorable. First, these files contain several
sections of the will of the playwright George Bernard Shaw. In July 1951 his
trustees wrote to the Ministry drawing attention to his posthumous call for a 'proposed British alphabet' which would have forty letters and would be phonic. The
letter called for a full enquiry into the teaching of letters and for the adoption of
Shaw's alphabet in all schools. Helpfully, an offer was made to facilitate this
process by using Shaw's money to have *Androcles and the lion* transcribed into
this new phonic alphabet and printed in sufficient copies for them to be available
in every school. After exhaustive enquiries the Ministry decided to do nothing.
Second, in the same year, there was an exchange of correspondence with Bert
Aza, who was the manager of Gracie Fields, the popular entertainer. He wrote,

We receive dozens of letters from children daily asking for Miss Gracie Fields' photograph, many of which bear only one penny stamp. In this way the child's penny is wasted, added to which is the disappointment at not receiving the photograph.

The obvious conclusion drawn by Mr Aza was that schools could do far more to instruct children in the proper use of stamps and particularly in the use of stamped addressed envelopes. It was the job of the Ministry to see to this and thus add to the happiness of thousands of schoolchildren.

The first point to be made about these wide-ranging suggestions (and it must be emphasised that the examples cited are but a small part of a much more extensive mail bag) is that they help break down any image we may have of a society quietly acquiescing in a curriculum which was shared by all schools. Rather, we gain from this correspondence an image of a society with far more quirkish and idiosyncratic understandings of what went on in the schools, some of whose members at least were ready to put forward ideas and schemes which were at best maverick and at worst outlandish.

A second observation which has to be made about this correspondence is the extent to which the school curriculum (and the whole business of what went on in schools) was becoming, or was seen as becoming, increasingly answerable to the growing marketing industry. Several correspondents wrote unashamedly to advertise their wares or else to propose curricular modifications which would boost their sales. Universal Engineering of Croydon wanted a wind vane in every school; Pitman's of Hastings offered to sell and deliver in bulk specimens of live frogs, newts and snakes; Asbury & Brodie of Birmingham wanted compulsory teaching of shorthand; the Bingham Emergency Tree Planting Service thought every school should be involved in a reforestation policy. Roly Rat, the proprietor of Premier Punch and Judy, asked for compulsory puppetry lessons in all schools. In 1947 another manufacturer suggested helpfully, 'We manufacture a miniature set of traffic lights, electrically controlled, which we think would serve some useful purpose in your demonstrations of road skill'. This correspondent went on to offer to appear in person at the Ministry to demonstrate how useful this apparatus might be in schools. In 1948 the International Wool Secretariat offered to circulate the *Wonder book of wool* to all schoolchildren.

What we have here is no more and no less than the 'commodification' of education. These lobbyists are evidence of the extent to which the education system was seen as an appropriate target for the nascent marketing machine of industry and commerce. The targeting of schools as markets seems to have begun at a much earlier date than many historians have realised. Whether or not these lobbyists succeeded, the fact that they thought it worthwhile to try is in itself significant.

But a closer inspection of these files leads to other observations. First, it becomes clear that there were a number of recurrent themes, not always articulated in the same terms, but reflecting shared concerns about particular elements in the school curriculum. It is possible to identify several. One involved a series of proposals that the curriculum should become far more closely related to the practical needs of the children. Some of these were strangely prophetic. In June 1945 the Plymouth Mercantile Association suggested that schools should allocate: 'every day five minutes from other subjects for arithmetic, writing and spelling ... The general standard of pupils leaving primary schools is remarkably low'. This was one representation which did elicit a Ministerial response. R. A. Butler minuted that this was a proposal 'trim full of wisdom and truth. The modern tendency is to range over a vast curriculum' – a rare insight into governmental thinking on the curriculum and one which suggests that more recent policies may have longer term origins than often realised.

Often the criticisms of the schools which were implicit in the letters presaged what were to become familiar themes by the end of the century. In July 1946, for example, R. C. Dickins wrote in arguing that

> if applicants for jobs had a knowledge of shorthand, typing, modern French and German, they would be in clover ... Why cannot young people be instructed in those things useful to them? ... All should have a working knowledge of the stock exchange, average commercial dealings, first aid, typing, shorthand, modern languages, cooking, darning.

Another called for the compulsory acquisition of typewriters by all schools as a prerequisite to compulsory typing lessons.

One particularly strong representation was submitted in January 1951 by E. A. Mawer of Louth, Lincolnshire. This correspondent accused the Ministry of permitting the schools to produce bad mothers, writing:

> can it be true that these girls have never handled a sewing needle as reported in the *News of the world?* Most girls between the ages of 11 and 14 used to receive instruction and often practical training in cookery, laundrywork, marketing and sometimes mothercraft ... Has the teaching of these useful subjects been abandoned in order to make time for modern teaching in dancing, drama, the art of make-up, sex knowledge and other useless and equally pernicious subjects? And to give more time to games? It is high time there was a searching enquiry into the educational system and a drastic reorganisation.

This correspondent was not alone in her belief that what was needed was a return to a pre-War society which was seen as having been more stable and which involved the education system playing a greater part in the ascription of gender roles.

The theme of the trivialisation of the curriculum, which was to become thirty years later one of the rallying cries of the hard right was in evidence in several of these letters. In January 1952 A. H. Spencer of Cookham submitted a diatribe on all that was wrong with contemporary education, or rather,

> what is accepted as education but which as a matter of fact is either amusement or quite worthless to children who must earn their living ... leaving school unable to read or spell ... a disgrace ... School broadcasts ... music and

movement ... this is a party game ... So called adult education ... I see no reason why rate payers should have to subsidise this ... Nursery schools ... should stop. They are an unnecessary expense ... Apprenticeships ... it seems that if children are not taken out of school earlier and placed in apprenticeships soon the old crafts will be lost entirely ... In reducing expenditure on education Art stands out as being in direct need of investigation. May I point out, first, what is being handed out as 'art'; distortion, degraded and idiotic ideas and mere unintelligible smears. A well-known Communist leads the art world as to picture painting [a reference to Picasso] ... School leaving age should be lowered to 14 ... I see no reason why those who are good learners should not leave at 14 and be apprenticed.

That, in a nutshell, was an extreme but not entirely untypical radical right educational agenda as presented to the Ministry only a few years after the end of the War. It suggests the existence of long-term undercurrents of opinion which were sustained throughout the period and which anticipated by some time the appearance of a more carefully articulated radical right agenda in the Black Papers.

Another theme which featured strongly during the post-War years was the teaching of civics, often linked to new approaches to history, and it is significant that this was particularly strongly stated during Labour's period in power before 1951. Some correspondents wanted world history to be taught in all schools, thinking the curriculum too narrow in view of the increasing significance of world affairs and the dangers of insularity. One correspondent wanted the Potsdam Plan explained to all children: 'I can think of nothing more important than that young people should know all that the Potsdam Plan implies'. Another argued that it was vital to make Russian the first language in schools 'as we must consolidate the prospective friendly relations with Russia anticipated by diplomatic agreement'. Several representations pressed for a greater emphasis on the teaching of modern languages as a key to preserving the peace. Some others saw a greater stress on the role of the trade unions in a democratic society as the key to a surer democracy. In this spirit Ellen Wilkinson was pressed in the Commons on whether she would insist on special lessons on the role and scope of the United Nations and if she might even be persuaded to convert Empire Day into United Nations Day. But, as we will see, this advocacy became muted once Labour lost office in 1951. For many the civics movement was seen as having gone too far under a Labour government. R. Shipman of Market Weighton was one among many who saw the resuscitation of Empire Day in schools as an urgent necessity: 'We must resuscitate Empire Day. Under six years of Socialist government it has become almost a crime to display natural pride in one's nation, Empire and Commonwealth.'

What also emerges from this correspondence is the strength of feeling about rural affairs. It is clear that the experience of evacuation had brought to the fore tensions between urbanites and those living in rural areas and this was reflected repeatedly in the letters the Ministry received. One hangover from evacuation was a particularly prejudiced view of the school curriculum. In 1952, for example, M. Cordelia Leigh reminded the Ministry of the issues: 'Evacuees, many of them schoolchildren from large towns behaved like untrained dogs and cats and ruined some of their hostesses' furniture because they had not been taught better'. Her proposed solution was the teaching of 'social behaviour' to the exclusion of other new subjects which were sweeping the curriculum.

Strangely, this tension between urban and rural expressed itself particularly in a series of representations on the subject of birds' nesting. The Ministry received a succession of letters in the immediate post-War period asking them to control town boys who were wont to go into the countryside on bird's-nesting expeditions. It stemmed from a countryside lobby who clearly thought that town boys did great harm through their ignorance of the countryside. In a nutshell, the farming lobby thought that boys who emptied nests were inadvertently aiding the grubs and insects which were the staple diet of birds, thus affecting crop yields. They wanted schools to be forced to teach proper conduct in the countryside. Whilst this may seem a little maverick, it resonates closely with more recent political issues that have pitted the countryside against the town. One correspondent in particular illustrated precisely the extent to which this issue was politicised during the 1940s: 'do you not think that it is time that kindness and care of all God's creatures should be taught in schools? All children should be taught about kindness to animals'. Shocked by the cruelty of London refugee children who had found themselves in rural locations during the War she went on: 'the LCC was Labour influence. The animals of this country have to thank Conservative pioneers for giving up their lives to the cause'. Unclear and ill-argued as this may be, it illustrates precisely several interrelated themes which run through these files: a hostility and tension between perceived images of urban and rural, the close linkage of this to perceptions of the major political parties and a sense that schools and the education system were now marching to an urban drum and that the needs and interests of country dwellers were being lost sight of by educationalists who were increasingly insensitive to this issue. This does remind us forcibly of one educational consequence of the process by which villages became overspill suburbs in the mass expansion of the towns that took place in post-War England.

A British McCarthyism: the schools and the communist threat

If this correspondence suggests several broad themes which are recurrent, it is also suggestive of lobbying which is uncoordinated, sporadic and often maverick in its nature. It is clear that the content and nature of the school curriculum is contested, but the exact nature and significance of that contest is not immediately clear to a casual reader. However, it is possible to discern a change in both tone and content in these files during the early 1950s, immediately after the return of a Conservative government, which suggests a far more sinister reading of events. This is the moment at which the debate on the curriculum became much more coordinated. As Brian Simon has shown, Britain was not exempt from the McCarthyite backlash which stemmed from the Berlin blockade and the heightening of the Cold War in the late 1940s.[17] It had a major impact on the politics of education at both local and national level. But less well-known is the significance of this issue for the debate on the curriculum. From the early 1950s onwards, clear and politicised demarcation lines are discernible in the debate on the school curriculum, reflecting this changed political context.

An early hint of this comes in the papers relating to a Parliamentary question put by a Labour backbencher, F. A. Cobb, in March 1949. He asked the Ministry to ban the teaching of the concept of profit in arithmetic lessons:

> I don't think we shall ever achieve our objective while we carry on teaching each successive generation all about profit and therefore by inference that profit is a good thing ... If we start altering school books the charge of Communism, totalitarianism and what not will be levelled at us, but is it not possible to do something about it?[18]

There is clear evidence during the late forties that those who were calling for more study of the Empire saw themselves as violently opposed to the currently prevalent view that civics should mean more internationalism in the curriculum.

The first direct tokens of a McCarthyite backlash against what many saw as the malign effects of six years of socialism came in 1950: Maurice H. de L. Coombs wrote to the Ministry spelling out his worst fears: 'Reports of Communist inspired teachers in our schools are causing me much concern ... give me some idea of what your Department is doing to ensure that British schoolchildren are not being crammed with Marxist theory'.[19] He went on to fulminate at length about communist domination of the civil service. But this was only a harbinger of what was to come. From the moment that the Conservative Party found itself back in office in 1951, a succession of right-wing Tory loyalists mounted a campaign to seek to persuade the Ministry to undo what they saw as the damage of six years of socialist propaganda in schools. It was a campaign which was to have enormous ramifications for the school curriculum and how it was managed.

One correspondent asked that the National Anthem (all verses) should be sung regularly in schools. In November 1951 L. N. Relton of Liverpool asked that the Union Jack be put on display in every school 'because I am appalled and worried by the number of teachers, both male and female in Liverpool who support the Communist cause but harbour under the name of Socialists'. Four days later, H. Bessemer Clark of Sevenoaks forwarded copies of two recent letters which had appeared in the *Daily Telegraph*. One read:

> after teaching for ten years in an industrial area, I have definite evidence that many children are converted to Socialism by certain teachers whose methods are ... so clever as to make detection difficult. Subjects used deliberately as vehicles of anti-Conservative propaganda are history, geography and current affairs. The industrial revolution provides a good example of the kind of deception practised. All the more lurid instances of sweated labour and bad housing in fetid industrial areas are quoted with a wealth of gruesome detail.

This lesson is always a winner and has a devastating effect on the wide-eyed youngsters ... I have occasionally found boys, particularly those of moderate intelligence, who firmly believed that within living memory women worked stripped to the waist in coalmines, lashed on, naturally, by top-hatted Tory capitalists.[20]

During the next few years this lobbying became almost remorseless. On Mayday 1952 a letter appeared in the *Daily Telegraph* arguing that

the Communists, in their endeavour to cause economic disaster in Britain, and thus that chaos which will make us easy prey for Soviet domination, rely principally on infiltration into the trade unions and educational and youth organisations ... The teaching profession is infested with Communists and fellow travellers, from professors to elementary schoolteachers. Therefore the Communist peril is great ... all knowledgeable Communists are traitors ... In all educational establishments behind the Iron Curtain hatred of the West and especially GB and the US is part of the instruction that is laid down by the communists and educational authorities ... We must teach the people the truth about Soviet-Communism and its objectives.[21]

The announcement of the death of George VI elicited this exchange between a Conservative supporter from Berkhamsted and the Ministry:

I know you cannot and do not like to give any instructions to local authorities, but could it be suggested that, in every school, Mr Churchill's broadcast of last night about the King's death and the Royal family should be read? I believe that this moment may be a turning point in the history of this country. Communism can never win through if the Royal Family and our traditions are upheld ... the young are taught so little today of what they should know.

Interestingly, this was one of the few letters which received anything more than a cursory response. The Minister, Florence Horsburgh, thought this sufficiently significant to merit a personal reply. She wrote:

I do agree with much of what you say ... There is a long and wise tradition that what is taught in school is left to the teachers, the managers, the governors and the LEAs, and the Minister does not prescribe the curriculum. The State must not encroach or seem to encroach in any way on this freedom of the school authorities and I am afraid I could not issue instructions, even in a case like this.[22]

This remained the official line throughout this period. But we can begin to discern why this may have been the case. Confronted by a backlash against what was seen by those on the right as a decade of state planning and control, it was inevitable that a Conservative government would fall back on a reassertion of the power of the educationalists to sort things out at a local level rather than impose more regulation from the centre.

During the early 1950s a group of backbench Conservative MPs established an action group, the Fighting Fund for Freedom, with the intention of running what was in effect a McCarthyite campaign to pre-empt the spread of communism in schools. It offered visiting lecturers to schools in the south of England to warn pupils of the perils of communism. Among its principal organisers was John Eden, a nephew of the Foreign Secretary, Earl Stanhope, who had held office at the Board of Education, and Lt-General Sir Clifford Martell. What brought their campaign into the spotlight was the naming in the Commons (with, of course, the protection of Parliament) of G. T. C. Giles, Head of Acton County School, as a leading communist. Giles, a well-known trade unionist and author, had been a thorn in the side of the Labour government. As President of the NUT he had chided them for their failure to get class sizes down and his book *The new school tie* was an indictment of the class-based education system which reasserted itself after the War. It was hardly surprising then that he should become the principal target of this group. But their attack on him brought their activities into the open.

On 11 August 1954 *Teachers' World* ran an article on 'Politics in schools'. This highlighted the work of the Fighting Fund for Freedom, but went on to argue, per-haps surprisingly, that although it was important to keep politics out of school it was equally important to support the anti-communist purpose of this group. On the same day the *Daily Telegraph* carried a letter from George Lindsay, writing from the Army and Navy Club. He stressed that 'we must know our enemy, and the only way to do that is to teach the rising generation the truth about commu-nism as General Martell advocates'. All of this evoked a sarcastic response from the *Daily Worker*, which labelled this movement

> the latest example of Tory propaganda in schools ... The Fighting Fund for Freedom is peddling ready-made lectures against communism for delivery in schools ... the propaganda of the capitalist parties has always been taught in schools. We have all had some. But now here it is in the open.[23]

During the summer of 1954 Martell was particularly energetic in his lobbying. In one letter he said:

> If this matter were taken up seriously in all schools, Communism would die out and the plans that are being made by the Communist leaders to ruin our industry could never be carried out. Surely anyone who loves his country must long to see this information spread to all the children.

This letter also went on to outline the success that the organisation was having in schools in Surrey and enclosed a pamphlet for consideration by the Ministry on 'The problem of full agreement between capital and Labour' with a view to its being used in the classroom. When David Eccles became Minister of Education in October, Martell lobbied him vigorously and offered to meet him to report on the success in schools which was being experienced by 'Lord Craigavon's Association'. James Craig, first Prime Minister of Northern Ireland, had been ennobled under this title. Martell's reference is clearly to propagandist work done in schools in Northern Ireland by the Ulster Unionists.[24]

The educational implications of all this were spelt out in simple terms by Vice-Admiral E. J. Hardman-Jones in January 1953. His letter stands as a summary of the curricular implications of this post-War McCarthyism. He wrote:

> I am much concerned, as all thinking people must be, about our people at the present time who seem in large measure a. unable to face up to the facts, b. have not the proper will to work c. seem unable to put the interests of our country above party politics. It appears to me that our best hope is to educate the coming generation as to their responsibilities, commencing at the earliest possible moment ... the curriculum in all schools should include a. the privileges and duties of being a British subject b. what our Empire has meant and must continue to mean to the world at large c. the great importance and responsibility of having a vote at our Parliamentary elections.

He stressed that the central goal of the schools must always be the inculcation of 'responsibilities' and 'discipline'. And the mechanism to do this was to be no less than Winston Churchill himself, at least according to Eleanor Isaac of Haywards Heath, who in June 1955 asked that gramophone recordings of Churchill's speeches be placed in every school that 'we might bequeath to posterity an extensive course in the English language'.[25]

As one reads these files in the Public Record Office one is struck by several points. First, running through them is repeated evidence of the essential docility of the Ministry of Education during this period. A succession of Ministers, of whatever political hue, were quite incapable of conceiving of a world in which the Ministry might initiate or even take a stand on issues, despite the plethora of proposals and ideas flooding in. Rather, a succession of Sir Humphreyesque figures passed minute papers from one to another, devising the most elegant and least committed response to whatever enquiry, however trivial.

The themes and implications of these letters are tantalising and intriguing. They display commitments to an old Britain, with a strong rural element, which was clearly seen as being under threat. For many of these correspondents, the values of the towns and cities were not those of the nation. The authors shared a belief in the power of education to transform society, or equally, since that transformation was one which horrified many of them, to preserve the better elements of Old England. In a post-War world in which established social hierarchies seemed under threat, the education system appeared to be one of the few bulwarks against sweeping social change. The classrooms were to be the battleground on which the shape and nature of the new Britain which was emerging after the War would be settled. Seen through the lens of this analysis, the McCarthyite lobby seems less and less like a group of maverick eccentrics, and increasingly like the spokespersons of an emergent radical right which was to find its full voice only thirty years later. But they were vocal enough, and influential enough, to play a major part in determining the outcomes of the debate on the school curriculum in the post-War years.

Professional responses: the debate becomes polarised

In this context it is hardly surprising that the debate among professionals on the school curriculum became polarised at this time. On one side were those who saw the changes that were under way in classroom practice as evidence of a system adjusting to the new demands and new possibilities of the post-War world. On the other was a group of commentators, several in positions of influence within the education system, who were horrified at what they saw as the gratuitous destruction of all that was best in the schools. These two opposing groups held widely contrasting views of the nature of learning and of society itself.

Thus, at primary level, for the 'progressives' what was needed was a move towards more activity methods in the classroom and there is evidence of widespread support within the profession for this. In 1947 the *Times Educational Supplement* made great play of a report by the Scottish Advisory Council on primary education, reminding readers that classroom conditions were such that much progress still needed to be made towards the goals set out during the inter-War years:

> With the reorganisation of the education system in England and Wales the Consultative Committee's 1931 Report is beginning to come into its own: the process should be given greatly needed impetus by the unqualified endorsement of the Scottish Council of the principles laid down by the English committee sixteen years ago'.[26]

Readers were reminded that this meant that the curriculum was to be thought of in terms of activity and experience rather than facts to be learned and that there was much more to education than the three Rs. But, significantly, the article went on to stress that 'what must be done is to relate education to a stage in biological development'. This oft-repeated mantra was to become the Achilles' heel of the progressives, allowing as it did what went on in the classrooms to be dictated increasingly by the psychologists, many of whom remained obsessed with intellectual hierarchies at this time. In the same year the *TES* reported a NAHT conference on primary education at which the schools 'were condemned in forthright fashion by one speaker after another'. This piece wrote of 'emphatic demands that they be improved without delay'.[27]

Similarly, the Surrey Education Committee sponsored a special report on 'the lower school' which on the one hand stressed that 'the development of the individual pupil is of paramount importance ... the emphasis at the initial stage should be on activities' but, on the other, saw the key to doing this successfully as lying in accurate classification 'according to intelligence and intellectual attainment and such reclassification as was necessary'.[28]

But if there remained tensions at primary level between the drive to broaden the curriculum and modify classroom practice on the one hand and the perceived need to classify on the other, there were far greater and more apparent tensions in the debate on secondary education at this time. Here some saw the future as involving a broadening of the curriculum and a postponement of vocational training. Significantly, one of the strong protagonists of this view was G. T. C. Giles, who used the pages of the *TES* to draw attention to what he believed was happening in secondary classrooms:

> a postponement of specialisation and modification of content and method. Tendencies in the professions, in commerce and in industry point in this same direction – a broadening of the secondary curriculum and a postponement of the more definitely vocational training to a later stage. This tendency is bound to affect and is already affecting the content and method of the secondary school ... already the need for a curriculum common to the first two years of all secondary schools is recognised. Indeed the idea of a common core, embracing the intellectual, practical and aesthetic aspects is gaining ground, even where the tripartite division remains. So too with method. The purely logical and academic approach to abstract ideas traditional in the grammar school is undergoing modification in the light of the experience of the technical and modern schools. Integration of subjects through the project and the local survey is profoundly affecting the grammar school curriculum. At the same time the long-standing demand for modifications to the certificate examinations is about to be modified. What does all this amount to? It means that profound changes are already taking place in the secondary school, reflecting, often unconsciously, the new conception of universal secondary education and the needs of a modern and democratic community.[29]

The promulgation of views such as these, coming as they often did from those identified as being on the left politically, were, to many with conservative views, like a red rag to a bull. Two of the most vocal of them were John Garrett, head of Bristol Grammar School, and G. H. Bantock, a professor of education at Leicester. Immediately after the War Garrett used the columns of the *TES* to warn about the dangers of universal secondary schooling. For him it was not just that the wrong pupils were being admitted to the grammar schools (which was part of his belief system, as it was of many of his colleagues in the selective sector), but that many were unsuited to secondary education of any kind. He argued that the rapid expansion which had taken place in secondary education since 1902 had meant 'large admission into secondary schools of ... children hardly best suited by the curriculum offered them'. For him, in view of the differing abilities and aptitudes of young people, the fault lay not with the grammar schools but with a system which was admitting the wrong children. He quoted Ellen Wilkinson as saying that: 'in general any increase of the present intake into existing grammar schools is likely to hinder rather than help the proper development of secondary education'. Garrett wanted to make clear the function of the grammar school. Purged of those whom wild horses would not drag through an examination for which they are manifestly unsuited ... its duty is to provide a satisfactory education for that section of the population which will provide ... professional men and women ... and then hand them on to university.

Meanwhile those whom he disparagingly called the 'crooked pieces of timber (intellectually speaking)' might be better off in 'small multilateral schools'.[30] Here was the key point, for Garrett and many like him believed the place for classroom experimentation was the non-grammar school sector. In his view these schools should house the majority of pupils who were at best marginally suited to secondary education as he understood it and whose education might be better served by a less demanding course. Thus after the War, and following the introduction of universal secondary schooling, efforts to reform classroom practice in the secondary sector were treated to condescension from the start.

Garrett was one of those who saw secondary schooling as coterminous with the grammar schools and who belittled any prospect of their reform or modification. But Geoffrey Bantock was willing to go much further. In an article in the literary magazine *Scrutiny* in 1948 entitled 'Some cultural implications of freedom in education', Bantock took the opportunity to lambast almost every identifiable aspect of educational innovation. He claimed that 'the emphasis on experiment ... conceals a basic uncertainty, an unconscious attempt to cover insufficiency by surface agitation'. He went on to attack by name Susan Isaacs, M. V. Daniel and in particular H. R. Hamley, a professor at the London Institute who had recently written in *The New Era* on group activity in schools. He quoted Hamley at length as saying that

the glory of the project is its spontaneity, its responsiveness and the evolving situation. No-one knows, not even the teacher, how it will turn out; no-one knows the answer for in many cases there is not one ... there is no prearranged standard either of appreciation or of standard.

'This sort of stuff,' commented Bantock, 'is hardly worth powder and shot ... I am concerned by a deplorable looseness of terminology and a vapidity of expression that are all too typical.' In this spirit he went on to attack the Ministry for its encouragement of innovation in the primary sector and the teaching profession for their increasing readiness to abdicate their proper function. He disputed the view of the famous Harvard Committee that 'all citizens are equally worthy and valuable', adding

no society can exist for long that allows itself to be governed by the values of the mediocre ... with sections of our population limited educational aims are necessary – of course they are. The fact that they are limited must be clearly recognised and explicitly allowed for.[31]

Two years later Bantock used the pages of the *TES* to spell out his own version of educational McCarthyism. It was here that he set out what was to become his famous dictum that 'the expectation that children can somehow recreate from within themselves forms which it has taken many years to evolve seems to me both dangerous and time-wasting'.[32] In a second article he took the opportunity to underline the significance of language in education, seeing this as the great gift of the grammar schools which was currently under threat from new approaches in the classroom:

> sensitivity to language, the capacity to express oneself with precision ... verbal training is perhaps the most valuable way of aiding the enrichment of a child's experience ... the educational world today teems with theoretical statements for new methods. Many of these ... are based on philosophic assumptions about the nature of man which I would regard as highly questionable ... it is the job of modern writers on education to expose some of the ambiguities inherent in many of the modern ideas.[33]

In a context which saw the coexistence of such strongly held and mutually exclusive views of how best to deal with the child in the classroom several outcomes were almost inevitable. First, many became ready to accept the idea of differing paths for different pupils. The continuing influence of educational psychologists helped make this a possibility, although researchers such as Cyril Burt were at this time arguing that intellectual capacity was best seen as hierarchical rather than comprising 'types of mind'.

Soon after the end of the War one contributor to the *TES*, Frank Earle, spelt out the terms on which such a compromise might work. He argued that in the multilateral schools

> the break with tradition which occurs in matters of organisation and classification requires a corresponding revolution in the curriculum ... the development of the child's work may take a different shape and character ... choice might be made from each of the main spheres of human experience. Thus, while the teacher may continue to give the pupil who has literary or linguistic aptitudes a distinct and separate course in 'English', he might find it better, with pupils of other aptitudes, to make their exercises in the use of the mother tongue a component part of some 'composite' activity which has a more direct appeal.[34]

In the weeks that followed the appearance of this article the *TES* ran several articles stressing the need for 'the great majority ... whose intelligence and aptitudes do not fit them for academic studies'[35] to be given something different.

This piece went on to spell out the image of society which underpinned this analysis; it was an image shared to some degree by those on both the left and the right politically. The paper argued that the problems besetting education stemmed from 1760 and the process of industrialisation. That had been the moment, historically, when the common people of England had lost their craft traditions which had flourished in pre-industrial rural Britain. Those absorbed into the towns had lost contact with the custom of apprenticeship. They must be introduced to 'the folk traditions of pre-industrial England. Thus the craftsmanship that built the cathedrals and the mediaeval towns can be rediscovered through a common education'.[36] But this would be one that was necessarily different from what was on offer in the grammar schools.

The same argument was taken on by the left but deployed to different ends. In a conference of the Communist Party in 1952, G. Thompson, Classics Professor at Birmingham University, made clear the extent of communist claims for education. He argued that culture of all sorts had been taken away from the common people by the process of industrialisation and that it was the job of those working within the education system to put it back. But for him the implication of this was a common secondary schooling and a shared curriculum freely available to all.[37] This sense of using the schools and the curriculum to put right the wrongs of history hung over the late forties and 1950s. I well remember my own grammar school English teacher using precisely the same arguments about the need for a resurrection of craft traditions, of a sense of apprenticeship, as he sought to persuade me and thirty other sceptical teenagers of the need to understand the parsing of a sentence.

Conclusions

Thus the picture that emerges of the debate on the school curriculum in Britain in the years immediately following the Second World War is necessarily one that is complex and confusing. On one side there was a strong body of opinion, particularly among leading educators and educationalists, that the time was ripe for a major reworking of classroom practice and of the curriculum generally. For this group the return of peace was an opportunity to rebuild society in a far more collectivist spirit and one of the keys to this was an education system which was more open, more democratised and which catered far more than ever before to the needs of the pupils. For them the establishment of a system of primary schools involved an opportunity to put into practice ideas which had been in circulation for some time, but which meant that day-by-day practice in the classroom would be far more informal and would involve a break with the well-established rote methods and teacher-centred didacticism which had dominated teaching for many years. Meanwhile, the provision of secondary education for all meant an opportunity to rethink the curriculum. At both primary and secondary level the practicalities of the situation imposed an almost impossible set of constraints. But for some the will was there.

But for others, particularly those on the right politically, it was far more important to re-establish what they saw as the best of pre-War practice. This meant a focus on the basic skills of literacy and numeracy at primary level, and for older pupils a reassertion of the primacy of the secondary grammar schools and of a curriculum and teaching methods that owed more to the late nineteenth century than the twentieth. For them the paranoia and McCarthyism provoked by the Cold War had clear educational implications and it enabled the development of what we can view in retrospect as a McCarthyite radical right opposition to fundamental changes in education at this time. In 1955 a major research project on classroom practice conducted by Leslie Kemp was reported on in the *British Journal of Educational Psychology*.[38] Although Kemp conceded that there had been some shift in what went on in schools (particularly since 1931 in the primary sector), the underlying reality was that 'at the same time many teachers have remained belligerently orthodox'. This simply reflected the underlying reality of the 1940s and 1950s: the vast majority of teachers chose to opt for the tried and the known, rather than to respond to the exhortations to experiment in the classroom.

This situation was only compounded by the fact that in their impassioned defence of the elite sector, those on the right looked to schools to deliver the 'right' pupils into the grammar schools to enable them to get on with what they saw as the vital task of educating the future leaders of society. Thus, from the outset, debates on the nature and content of the school curriculum were politicised and were seen to be deeply divisive and deeply controversial. It is a mistake to think that issues around schooling suddenly became politicised during the 1970s and 1980s in response to the emergence of a 'new right' politically. The reality of the matter is that the provision of popular education has always been a sensitive and controversial issue and this was no less true of the 1940s and 1950s than it has been of other historical periods. Rather, the evidence gathered here suggests a deep continuity in the politics of education, and it is only through understanding this continuity that we can begin to understand fully the limited nature of curriculum reform in the years immediately following the Second World War.

3 A golden age? The sixties and early seventies

It seems to be fashionable to choose the success rate in examinations as a criterion for judging the performance of schools. This might be convenient but makes a mockery of education in its widest sense.

The Duke of Edinburgh in his Presidential address to the Association of Technical Institutions, reported in the *Times Educational Supplement*, 21 February 1964, p. 450

By the start of the 1960s a number of social changes were making it inevitable that nothing would ever appear quite the same again. The fifties had brought economic security to unprecedented numbers, and Prime Minister Harold Macmillan was able to make the claim to the electorate at the end of the decade that they had 'never had it so good'. Several things followed from this. Increased affluence meant, for most people, greater disposable income. This enabled a more protracted education and a prolonged adolescence for a youth which had more money in its pocket than any previous generation. As the sixties progressed, it began to seem in a range of areas that society was at last throwing off the austerity and the repressed social attitudes which had marked the whole of the early twentieth century. Changes in fashion, in popular culture and in the mass media might have been the icons of these developments, but it should not be forgotten that this was also to become a decade of social and political movements which appeared in some cases to be worldwide in their scope. The protests against the Vietnam War, a greater realisation of the rights of oppressed minorities and ethnic groups, a liberalisation and secularisation of social values and a worldwide student protest movement can all be seen, in one way or another, as outcomes of this fast-changing situation. It is hardly surprising then that what went on in the schools should be seen to be changing swiftly and to be particularly controversial at this time.

As we approach an analysis of these events, it is perhaps worth remarking at the outset that, even if there were clear limits to the innovations that took place in educational practice immediately after the War, there has been a widespread acceptance, among a wide range of commentators including historians, that, from the late fifties onwards, classroom practice began to change very swiftly. One can even point to the existence of a popular stereotype which has developed during the most recent twenty years. This involves the view that the sixties and early seventies were a time when new ideas on teaching and the organisation of schools were fashionable and widely influential. Right across the country, according to this view, it was possible to discern significant changes in both the ways children were organised in the classroom and in the nature of the teaching process itself. This stereotype also involves the belief that something else changed during the seventies, or, more particularly, in October 1976, when Prime Minister Callaghan went to Oxford to deliver the Ruskin speech. It involves a general acceptance that the 1944 Education Act ushered in a thirty-year period of unprecedented power and influence for the teaching profession, which found itself able to regulate its affairs to a far greater degree than ever before, was treated with widespread respect and took significant steps towards full recognition as a profession, in the process setting about what was little less than a transformation of classroom practice. In these developments the local education authorities played a crucial part at a time when there was seen to be a genuine sharing of power and influence between national government, the LEAs and the teachers themselves.

Equally, this stereotype might suggest that the critical steps towards the re-establishment of central government authority were taken during the 1970s under a Labour government and that the Ruskin speech stands as a useful icon of the moment at which demands for accountability, for economy, and for the establishment of agreed standards in schools, were articulated, leading to the subsequent imposition of firm central government control of the curriculum and, indeed, of pretty well every aspect of the English education system. In the process, much of the ground that had been gained by teachers ready to experiment with new ideas was lost under the influence of those who wanted to set clear limits on the power of the profession to innovate. Whilst never stated quite as crudely or as starkly as this, this stereotype, or something very like it, underpins much that has been written about schooling during the most recent twenty years, some of it by historians.

Certainly, this is the tenor of Brian Simon's influential account of the post-War politics of education. In his book *Education and the social order*, published in 1991, Simon summarises the developments of the sixties in these terms:

> The world of education boomed during the sixties ... these advances had opened the way for a new emphasis on primary education, embodying a decisive shift away from the rigid structures and teaching methods inherited from the past, and ... reflecting the new ... more humanist ideals of the 1960s ... There was advance across the board.[1]

Then, moving on to the Ruskin speech, Simon comments that:

> The intention was clear ... to steal the thunder of the Black Paperites ... but, on a deeper level, to assert new forms of control over the social order – to issue a clear warning that educational developments should not get out of

hand ... in short to slam the lid and screw it securely down. To achieve this a more direct central control by the DES was essential.[2]

Similarly, Clyde Chitty, another well-respected observer of this period, devoted a section of his best-known book to the theme of '1976 as a turning point', concluding that:

> by 1976 the partnership years were coming to an end, or perhaps more accurately, the terms of the partnership were about to change significantly ... It was after 1976 that partnership was replaced by accountability as the dominant metaphor in discussion about the distribution of power in the education system.[3]

A revolution in the primary classroom?

There is much to suggest that Brian Simon and Clyde Chitty captured one undeniable reality of the period. But the evidence on what was actually going on in the classrooms is complex and in parts contradictory, so that it is difficult, if not impossible, to construct a single narrative. However, to those working at the time there was certainly a sense that things were changing quickly, particularly in the primary classroom.

There were good reasons, too, why this might have been so. First, the increased affluence of the fifties meant that unprecedented numbers could afford not only to complete their years of compulsory secondary education, but to stay on beyond the minimum leaving age. This, together with the drive for smaller class numbers, meant more schoolchildren and necessarily an ongoing increased demand for new teachers. The result was a series of recruitment campaigns and a sudden and massive expansion of teacher education. Whatever the intentions, the reality was that many of these new recruits to teaching ended up in the primary sector.

It must be remembered too that the shift to a three-year course of training in 1960 and the publication of the 1963 Robbins Report both had a direct impact on the primary sector. This was felt in several ways. First, a generation of young teachers were sucked away from the classroom within only a few years of the commencement of their careers to become part of this growing army of teacher-educators. (The author was one of them. The college I joined in September 1968 had, like several others, doubled both its student and its staff cohort in only twelve months! Ironically, as was the case with many of those recruited alongside me at that time by the Colleges of Education, although my own experience of teaching had been within the secondary sector, my main brief was the preparation of primary schoolteachers.) It was this group which distilled the new psychology of education and a new educational sociology to intending teachers. One result of the drive towards a graduate teaching profession was that many of these new recruits to the staffrooms of the teacher education colleges were selected precisely because, although relatively inexperienced, they had themselves already undertaken some form of postgraduate educational study. It was widely seen at this time that the key to a reform of the teaching profession lay in the teaching of the four 'disciplines' in these colleges. Whilst it may be difficult to argue the extent to which the history and philosophy of education contributed directly to any kind of classroom revolution, it was undoubtedly the case that the new sociology and, in particular, the new psychology involved both implicit and explicit critiques of much contemporary classroom practice. Suddenly, what was being purveyed to new entrants to the profession involved a heavy dosage of Piaget and a clear discouragement of much of the formality which had marked in particular the post-War primary classroom.

It must not be forgotten, also, that, whatever had been the aspirations of the Robbins Committee, recruitment to the universities continued to favour males throughout the 1960s. This had the knock-on effect that a disproportionate number of very able female students found their way into the teacher training colleges, many of them with high academic aspirations and a willingness and ability to soak up, and themselves practise and disseminate, the new educational ideas which were in vogue. Given that the colleges continued, for several more years at least, to be mainly responsible for training for the primary sector, whilst recruits to secondary teaching either went direct into the classroom on graduation or followed PGCE courses, the effect of all this was felt most directly in the primary schools. Piagetian approaches to the teaching of younger children involved a clear structure to their learning with ample opportunities for practical experimentation. In 1963 a leading article in the *TES* observed succinctly that 'a cynic might suppose that a primary school is judged nowadays not by how far its pupils can read but by how far the place is awash with paint'.[4] This growing army of young teachers found itself deployed in a wide variety of environments, and it is the very complexity of the challenges that they faced which makes it so difficult to offer any simple summary of the development of classroom practice at this time.

Not least, there was the growing contrast between the overcrowded Victorian classrooms which were still widely in use in the inner cities and the new, open plan buildings which were appearing on overspill housing estates and in the suburbs.

But certain trends were felt right across the primary sector. Perhaps the most significant of these was the introduction, in the years following 1961, of the Initial Teaching Alphabet. It was in 1953 that the Conservative Member of Parliament, James Pitman (whose grandfather had devised the widely-used system of shorthand), had first voiced the idea of a novel system of spelling to facilitate early learning. Six years later he came up with an Initial Teaching Alphabet based on ideas currently in vogue in the Simplified Spelling Society. In 1961 this scheme, which involved 44 characters rather than the 26 in the more familiar alphabet, was trialled in twenty selected primary schools in the Midlands under the auspices of the Reading Research Unit at the University of London Institute of Education headed by John Downing. Favourable responses from the teachers involved led to the scheme being extended to seventy-five schools a year later and by 1966 the vast majority of local education authorities were using it in at least some of their primary schools. Through the 1970s this system continued to dominate approaches to early literacy in the primary sector. It was not until research studies began to question the durability of the early gains in reading attainment and to identify some of the difficulties of switching to traditional spelling at age seven or eight that this initiative began to peter out. That, and the residual hostility of many parents to an approach which seemed to be undermining their children's ability to spell in their later school years (always a potent fear in public discussion of education), steadily undermined the popularity of the Initial Teaching Alphabet, as did its mixed reception in primary school staffrooms. But the ITA transformed the character of the acquisition of literacy for a generation of pupils and proved to be extremely influential, becoming widely used in both Australia and the USA.

The second major concern of primary schoolteachers, after the acquisition of literacy, was the approach to numeracy, and in this area too there were major developments. By the early sixties the Stern Apparatus (a system using coloured blocks), the Cuisinaire Method (deploying 241 coloured rods), the Shaw Materials (involving cylindrical rods) and the Dienes Apparatus were all available for deployment in primary schools and it was increasingly likely that children were introduced to number through one or more of these schemes. Zoltan Paul Dienes, who published *Building up mathematics* (1960), followed by *An experimental study of mathematics learning* (1963) and *The power of mathematics* (1964), was quickly to become the best-known and most widely followed of these prophets of a new approach to number work. He lobbied tirelessly throughout a maverick career to polemicise the use of song, games and novel teaching aids as routes into learning mathematics, but is perhaps best known for the Dienes' Rods which became a feature of most primary schools during this period. In September 1964 the Nuffield Foundation commissioned its own primary mathematics project, which was to have a significant impact on practice. All of this meant a major shift away from the recitation of number tables and the rote learning of multiples which had previously characterised much primary school mathematics teaching.

Underlying these innovations in the primary school curriculum was the drive towards de-streaming, which was another notable feature of the primary sector at this time. One of the key agents of this transformation was the journal *Forum*, promoted by two Leicester academics, Brian Simon and Robin Pedley, in 1959 to highlight and support new initiatives in education. From the outset the editors made this aspect of primary education one of their key targets. In 1959 George Freeland, in an article entitled 'The junior school today', complained of the extent to which the primary schools had been imprisoned 'since the War ... within the limits of 11+ requirements'.[5] A year later E. Harvey wrote of the 'overwhelming advantages' of de-streaming a primary school.[6] The summer 1961 edition focused exclusively on the primary schools and P. D. Houghton contributed advice on how to teach an unstreamed class.[7] A year later J. C. Daniels, a well-known supporter of new trends in primary schooling summarised the existing research on primary education and argued that 'the abandonment of streaming should be regarded not so much as a negative act of renunciation, but as a positive affirmation of how junior school education can most effectively be organised'.[8] In the spring of 1963 this journal organised a day conference at the University of London Institute of Education on the theme of 'Non-streaming in the primary school', attracting over 200 delegates and using the opportunity to press the case even more strongly in its pages. In the autumn of 1964 the formal submission made by *Forum* to the Plowden Committee was reported in full. This focused on the need to de-stream and concluded: 'even under the severe handicaps often borne at the present time ... we believe that important advances can be made towards liberating the junior school from ideas and practices which have long outlived their relevance'.[9] In the same year J. W. B. Douglas, in his pioneering study, *The home and the school*, argued strongly that 'an element of rigidity is introduced early into the primary school' by streaming.[10]

During the 1960s several NFER Reports focused on the impact of streaming in the primary sector and the Plowden Report itself had much to say on the subject:

> Streaming is ... by far the most common way of organising junior schools, but there is reason to think that practice is changing ... To judge by the parents in the National Survey professional opinion is swinging more rapidly against streaming than is public opinion generally ... Streaming involves selecting ... We know of no satisfactory method of assigning seven year old children, still less those who are even younger, to classes graded by attainment or ability ... The system of streaming favours girls who are ... more disposed to play 'the good pupil role'... There is also much evidence that streaming serves as a means of social selection ... Selection will inevitably be inaccurate ... Schools which treat children individually will accept unstreaming throughout the whole school. When such an organisation is established with conviction and put into effect with skill, it produces a happy school and an atmosphere conducive to learning. Not all teachers are yet able to go so far ... We welcome unstreaming in the infant or first school and hope that it will continue to spread through the age groups of the junior or middle schools.[11]

As a direct result of this lobbying, by 1970 one survey was able to claim that streaming had disappeared almost completely from the primary sector.[12]

In sum, all of these initiatives and this lobbying represented a major transformation in the underlying objectives of those concerned with primary schooling. For much of the twentieth century the role of the primary schoolteacher had been to fit children into a mould determined by the structure of the education system and the needs of society. Now the drive to enable the child to achieve its full potential became central. In 1962, for example, R. Dottrens, in a publication for UNESCO entitled *The primary school curriculum* stressed that 'the most important thing today is the opening up of the mind, the fostering of intellectual curiosity, the capacity for wonder; for asking questions, and the will and ability to find the answers'.[13] Similarly, Sybil Marshall emphasised in her *An experiment in education* (1963) that 'the real function of the primary school is to create interest, spur curiosity, and open doors through which the children may choose to go in the later stages of their growth'.[14] In this spirit, books such as L. G. W. Sealey's *Communication and learning in the primary school* identified activity methods and the use of project work as the means towards achieving these ends.[15] By the mid-sixties this had become something of a bandwagon. In 1965 the *TES* ran a special edition on 'Self-expression in the primary school'.[16] Here several of the usual suspects used the opportunity to press the progressive case. J. G. Gagg, Sybil Marshall, Dorothy Glynn and Barbara Rapaport of the Froebel Institute all contributed articles, illustrating the extent to which 'the great and the good' of the educational establishment were buying in to this new approach. One of the more extreme expressions of this philosophy appeared in the pages of the *TES* in December 1960. Here K. Laybourn, a chief inspector of schools in Bristol set out his stall in an article on primary education:

> Educative experience for young people lies in real happenings and personal contacts, associated with observation and the development of skills ... By the year 2000 the schools themselves will move closer to the world. The school building will become a base from which children operate, rather than a place in which they are isolated for a fixed number of hours each day. Much of the teachers' work will be to plan and interpret ... The interpenetration of school and neighbourhood will be promoted by buildings in which design will become ever more open ... the classroom 'box' will disappear ... Since the first function of a primary school is to help children to develop as social beings ... the school building will come to be thought of as a social centre ... the main spaces will be very varied so that to pass from one to another will be a pleasing experience in itself.[17]

This was the rationale by which a perceived revolution in primary school practice was vindicated.

It was the 1967 Plowden Report of the Central Advisory Council for England which, during the years that followed, came to be seen as an iconic statement, encapsulating many of the ideas and aspirations of those involved in the primary sector during the sixties. It championed many of the causes of the hour: destreaming, positive discrimination to counter the impact of the social disadvantages which many inner-city children experienced, and a softening of selection at eleven-plus. On the details of curriculum organisation the Report was far less clear, although it did provide ringing phrases which were to be echoed repeatedly during the years that followed. Its famous claims that 'at the heart of the educational process lies the child' and that 'the child is the agent in his own learning' were regularly invoked at educational conferences for years to come. But, as Peter Cunningham has shown, the Plowden Report was in reality opaque on the question of precisely how children's learning should be organised and conducted at primary level. Cunningham observed that 'its wide publicity was perhaps due more to the social recommendations ... though these included tenets characteristic of progressive pedagogy, such as more parental involvement and the abolition of corporal punishment'.[18] This lack of specificity also meant that the annual 'Plowden conference' which was convened for nearly a decade after the Report appeared, became a battleground for supporters of one version or another of progressivism, as rival interpretations vied for the attention of primary teachers.

'Is he in the grammar school stream?': the dilemma before the secondary schools

'Is he in the grammar school stream?' was a question posed repeatedly to those teaching in the few pioneering comprehensive schools during the early 1960s. I know because I was one of them. The question has been posed in gendered terms because that was the way it was usually put: it seemed to matter more to parents that their son was not missing out on what the grammar schools had to offer than their daughter, if they happened to be living in one of the few areas in which all children were allocated to one of the new comprehensive schools at eleven years of age.

Certainly during the late fifties and into the sixties there was an impression that massive changes were taking place in the provision of secondary education, and this sector became a much more central feature of political debates. But it must be remembered that the contest was almost exclusively over the structure of the system, the issue of who should go to which kind of school, rather than over the reform of the curriculum. Ironically, but perhaps not entirely unsurprisingly, the very nature of this political contest militated against, rather than in favour of, sweeping curriculum reform. The fact that politicians were construing the pioneer comprehensive schools as experimental, allied to the trepidation of parents who were concerned that their children should not become educational guinea pigs, meant that these new schools had to be seen to succeed by precisely the criteria by which the grammar schools were judged. It was to be through success in established external examinations, access to elite institutions of higher education and to careers within the professions and through a formal subject-based curriculum that the new comprehensive schools were to be seen as successful. This consideration, from the outset, placed severe constraints on their ability to be truly innovative in terms of the curriculum and teaching method.

The situation was only exacerbated by the fact that almost all of the early comprehensive schools, from the late 1940s until the mid-1960s, were rigidly streamed. This compounded the problems they faced since, following the argument that one of their advantages was that they were readily able to pick up and correct the inevitable errors which occurred in the placement of pupils within streams at the age of eleven, it was necessary to teach the so-called 'academic' subjects right across each year group, meaning that, in the first two or three years at least, all comprehensive pupils were obliged to go through something that looked remarkably like the traditional grammar school curriculum. It was not a situation conducive to significant curricular reforms.

But, at the same time, there was a widespread sense that changes were afoot in the secondary sector and one does not have to look too far to see why this might have been the case. Whilst those teaching in the grammar schools might in the main have viewed their role (particularly in view of the post-War entry of many first-generation working-class pupils to these schools) as fighting to hold onto the best of what the grammar school had to offer, there is no doubt that those working in the new comprehensive sector, as well as teachers in the secondary moderns, saw themselves as breaking new ground at a time when major change was underfoot. To this extent they were to prove far more open to the new ideas which were in circulation on how children should be taught.

Teacher involvement in curriculum reform

This was a moment when the profession itself began to become far more proactive in respect of curriculum reform. This process began within the local authorities. By 1968 the number of advisers employed by the local authorities had more than doubled since the Second World War to 1,260. Some authorities, such as Oxfordshire and Leicestershire, led the way in using them as an advance guard of curriculum reform. The role of these advisors was pioneered and clarified by leading figures such as L. G. W. Sealey in Leicestershire and Edith Moorhouse in Oxfordshire. By the 1960s no teacher, in either the primary or secondary sectors, was unaware of the support and guidance available from local authority advisers. This support had several outcomes. Among the most important was the appearance right across the country of teachers' centres, which served not only as social centres (one popular myth in teaching circles in Birmingham when I moved there in 1968 was that the route towards promotion lay via the bar of the Martineau Teachers' Club run by the local authority!) but also sponsored in-services courses to disseminate new ideas on teaching. By 1972 there were in total 617 such LEA-sponsored teachers' centres.[19]

Another door into what David Eccles in 1960, speaking in the Commons, famously referred to as 'the secret garden of the curriculum', was the appearance, following that Ministerial comment, of the Schools' Council in 1964. The Council took the form it did because the Government's first attempt to impact on what went on inside the schools, the Curriculum Study Group set up in 1962, was seen by both the NUT and the Association of Education Committees as posing a threat to the professional autonomy of the teachers themselves. Accordingly, in October 1964, its duties were taken over by the newly established Schools Council 'whose whole ethos overtly stressed the responsibility of individual schools and teachers in evolving their own curriculum'.[20] Although the Council attracted some criticism in retrospect for its failure to take the lead, particularly during its early years, Brian Simon described the way in which by the late sixties the Council's projects were 'belatedly beginning to reflect developments in the schools themselves ... after the first stuttering and somewhat myopic beginning'.[21] Be that as it may, it remains true that a plethora of Schools Council projects impacted directly on classroom practice by the early 1970s. In a range of subjects, and particularly at secondary level, there was a perceptible shift towards novel methods of delivery, a reconsideration of curriculum content, and, in the numerous cases in which the Council's projects were linked to external examinations, a direct impact on what many saw as the two most vital years in secondary school. Perhaps the most celebrated (or perhaps the most notorious!) of these was the Stenhouse Integrated Humanities Project which advocated both the abandonment of subject boundaries and the promotion of the pupils themselves as the initiators and monitors of their own learning. The Council's Mathematics for the Majority project, its History 13–16 project and its three projects on the teaching of secondary geography, all played a major part in influencing classroom practice. Not least, these projects had the side-effect of involving young and energetic teachers, for whom the experience was, as often as not, a stepping stone towards a career in teacher education, the advisory service or the Inspectorate. The sense of a profession committed to classroom change and offering rewards and encouragement for those most actively involved was thereby heightened at this time.

Much of the work of the Schools Council echoed the style of the Nuffield Foundation, which from the late fifties had been sponsoring research into the reform of examinations at secondary level. This too became an agency which involved teachers and which had a major impact on both the conduct and content of examinations. The subjects which felt the greatest impact of this were mathematics, physics, chemistry and later modern languages. This attempt to reform in particular Advanced level examining through approaches which involved a far greater degree of student enquiry and experimentation was the initiative which had the greatest effect on the grammar schools at this time, although one interesting side-effect appears to have been that the more prestigious the school, the less susceptible it proved to be to 'Nuffield science'.

Examination reform and the curriculum

All of this was taking place at a historical moment when the whole ethos and style of external examining was coming under review. This reconsideration took two forms. First, there was an ongoing debate, reflected in several commissions and enquiries, about the extent of external examining, which children should be examined and whether (at sixteen-plus particularly) the examination should be unitary or should reflect the realities of a divided system. This was largely triggered by the fact that, during the 1950s, the new General Certificate of Education, introduced in 1951 to examine grammar school pupils at sixteen and eighteen years of age, was increasingly being used by the secondary moderns. This early manifestation of the post-War trend (which has continued) to submit growing numbers to the examination process led to calls for a second examination for the less able pupils, and in 1962 the Certificate of Secondary Education was introduced. Although this was introduced as an examination to be largely under the control of teachers rather than examining boards, it posed some real difficulties for those using it in the secondary modern and comprehensive schools, since they had to decide which pupils to enter for which examination at sixteen years of age, and in many cases had to prepare students for both and to make a last-minute decision (often on the basis of performance in the 'mock' examination) about which one each pupil would take in each subject. This was clearly a situation which could not long survive. But this new external examination did offer a precursor of the way in which examinations were to develop generally over the following forty years with its 'Mode III' option, by which teachers could devise their own scheme (much of it involving coursework) and were responsible for their own assessment procedures, subject to external moderation.

Within the comprehensive sector there were many who saw this divisive arrangement of examinations at sixteen-plus as a device to ensure that secondary education remained a two-tier system and the demands for a unified examination which were soon heard were taken up by the Schools Council (part of whose brief was responsibility for the conduct and development of examinations). In 1976 the Council proposed formally to the then Minister, Shirley Williams, that a single system of examining at sixteen-plus be adopted, but, as was the case with several proposals put to the Labour government of the late 1970s, the idea was put out to consultation and effective action was to be delayed for a further decade.

Nonetheless, there remained a sense during the 1960s and 1970s that examinations were one area in which the situation was far from stable and that things were changing fairly rapidly. Several of the examining boards took the opportunity to trial 'joint' GCE and CSE papers in a variety of subjects, and there were a number of pioneers such as Henry Mackintosh, whose particular interest was the development of examinations in history, who were keen to apply the ideas of Bloom and Krathwohl (see below) and to identify more precisely what it was that was being examined. It followed from this that the old-fashioned open essay answer (which was still used in a range of subjects) was insufficiently precise to provide any kind of accurate assessment of a pupil's progress. The result was that several of these trial mergers between GCE and CSE involved not only examining a wider spread of students but also devising new modes of questioning. The sixteen-plus history papers devised by the West Midlands CSE Board in conjunction with the Southern Counties GCE Board were but one forward-looking example of what quickly became a trend, with questions devised to test particular identified skills. In this process it became increasingly common, in part at least, to throw the examination open to performance in coursework, and this was to be a trend with very significant consequences, as will be seen later. Suffice to comment at this point that whilst none of those involved at the time realised it, this was one step towards a situation in which those working in education were more answerable to outside interests than had previously been the case. If novel forms of examining were introduced on the grounds that they enabled much more accurate judgements, they also had the unintended side-effect of making the examining process more susceptible to parental and other external pressures.

Developments in the classroom

If developments in examining are clearly identifiable in retrospect, the precise nature of classroom relations and teaching styles is far harder to pin down. But some trends are clear. There was a general shift away from the use of corporal punishment during these years, and the wearing of academic dress by teachers also became more of a rarity. It is not unreasonable to see these as manifestations of a general 'lightening up' in classroom relations, although this is a ferociously difficult issue on which to generalise. Certainly the author, whose first teaching experience came in the comprehensive sector after a grammar school education (as was the case with many of his contemporaries), was aware of the contrasting nature of staff/student relations in these newer schools, with the style being generally much more informal, although this did not necessarily involve any abdication of the teacher's pedagogic role. It is worth recalling too that the vast majority of the new comprehensives were mixed schools, whilst most of the teaching staff had themselves been educated in single-sex establishments, and this trend (which was to see 80 per cent of the school population in mixed schools by 1980) may go some way to explain this impression.

There were, however, two developments during these years about which it is possible to be much more precise. The first of these was de-streaming. The very first edition of the journal *Forum*, which appeared in the autumn of 1958, asked 'what are these new trends?' and went on to answer its own question in these words:

> the new types of school developing in different parts of the country; the steps taken by modern secondary schools to transcend their earlier limitations; reappraisal of such features of internal school organisation as streaming; new approaches to the content of education.[22]

Streaming continued to be the bête noire of the left throughout the decade. In 1962 one article in *Forum* entitled 'Experiments in an unstreamed secondary school' claimed that the Preston School in Yeovil was one of the very few truly unstreamed schools in the country.[23] In the summer of 1966 the journal organised a conference in London on the theme of 'Destreaming the comprehensive school' which attracted over 400 delegates; and in the following year David Hargreaves' study *Social relations in a secondary school*, argued that streaming was largely responsible for the development of a 'deliquescent subculture' among working-class pupils.[24] This lobbying culminated in 1970 in the publication by Caroline Benn and Brian Simon of *Halfway there*, a progress report on comprehensivisation.[25] Here, one of the main arguments advanced was that no school could consider itself to be truly comprehensive if it retained streaming, which was in reality no more and no less than the old selective system in a new guise. This was to prove extremely influential in the following few years, as almost all of the comprehensive schools set about some form or other of dilution of rigid streaming systems. In some cases this involved the use of 'setting' and in others different versions of 'mixed ability' grouping. whilst a few schools went on to abandon selection on the basis of ability almost entirely. *Thirty years on*, the exhaustive study of comprehensivisation by Caroline Benn and Clyde Chitty, has shown how most comprehensives moved away from streaming during the 1970s, but by the end of the decade were being obliged to revert to more traditional forms of pupil grouping as a result of popular concerns about 'discipline' and 'standards'.[26]

The second significant development at this time was towards the integration of subjects, as part of a general move to bring into question the well-established secondary school curriculum, based on teaching in separately identified and discrete subject areas. Whilst this trend has proved to have less long-lasting impact, it was one which was certainly felt during the 1960s and 1970s. Among the earlier critics of the inflexibility of the traditional secondary school curriculum was William Taylor, who wrote in 1960 of the 'impact of the views of progressive educationalists on the need for a curriculum unhindered by 'external' influences and schools able to develop their educational methods and philosophy along new and individual routes'.[27] The journal *Forum* ran a number of articles advocating curriculum experiments which broke down the established subject-based curriculum. One, in 1964, reported an experiment at Henbury School, Bristol, in which team-teaching had been deployed right across one year group.[28] In the same year a Bow Group pamphlet, *A strategy for schools*, suggested

> a regrouping of existing subjects in the curriculum, a new approach to traditional subjects and, in teaching methods, encouragement for the project idea ... Divide the common core of the curriculum into four groups of topics: communications, human relations, material culture and the arts ... the division between physics, chemistry and biology should disappear'.[29]

Similarly, in 1966, a London headteacher, Peter Mauger, argued that:

> the subject-based curriculum is clearly inadequate in view of the knowledge explosion ... They need a curriculum they can see as an organic whole, related to their present and future needs. The flexible, unstreamed comprehensive school is only a means, but an essential means, to that end.[30]

The element of the secondary school curriculum which felt the greatest impact of these ideas was the social sciences and, during the early 1970s, many comprehensive schools experimented with 'integrated Humanities'. One extreme variant of this trend was the briefly popular 'Man, a course of study', imported from North America, throwing together several subjects and involving the study of such arcane topics as the life cycle of the penguin as a preamble to an engagement with human societies. All this reflects the enormous freedom which the schools had during this period to experiment with whatever curricular variant was thought most appropriate to the needs of the students in that particular school. It was a freedom which stands in stark contrast to more recent impositions on the power of the schools to plough their own furrow.

A new sociology of education?

Much of this reform of the education system was underpinned by reference to 'expert opinion'. The 1938 Spens Report had been one of the most influential public statements leading to the almost universal establishment of a tripartite system of secondary schooling after the Second World War. It had claimed that 'intellectual development during childhood appears to progress as if it were governed by a single central factor, usually known as general intelligence ... Our psychological witnesses assured us that it can be measured ... by use of intelligence tests' before setting out the precise form which such a system might take.[31] Immediately after the War a host of 'expert' advocates of fixed intelligence gave succour to this novel arrangement of schools. As is well-known, the steady erosion of support for this system was also dependent on academic research. Psychologists such as P. E. Vernon and Alice Heim, who authored *The appraisal of intelligence* in 1954, began to question these theories of fixed intelligence at the same time that a growing weight of sociological work came to focus on the social effects of a divided secondary school system. First, in 1953, Brian Simon with his influential book *Intelligence testing and the comprehensive school*, and, within a few years, researchers such as A. H. Halsey, Jean Floud, J. B. Mays, J. W. B. Douglas and, not least, Jackson and Marsden, threw their weight behind this critique of what had emerged in the aftermath of the 1944 Act.

In this context it is important to emphasise that all this involved a focus on the structure of the system, not on the details of what went on in the classroom. England had become a society where much social policy drew upon what might be called 'macro-research' of this kind. The major social surveys of Charles Booth and Seebohm Rowntree had underpinned the shift towards a welfare state, and this tradition, particularly strong at the Universities of Liverpool, London and Oxford, led to a plethora of surveys of the extent of poverty, both before and after the Second World War, which also had a major impact on governmental actions. It became usual to recruit members of this 'expert lobby' on to Royal Commissions and other governmental enquiries as a prompt to the implementation of what was seen as sound policy. Thus this fashionable new sociology of education, heavily focused on the structure of the system, and particularly influential in respect of secondary education and the introduction of comprehensive schools, was securely embedded within a well-established British academic tradition.

Elsewhere, other academic traditions were being established and it was to be these which were to increasingly dominate discourse on education through the 1970s and 1980s. First, two American academics, Dan Flanders and E. J. Amidon, in what they later claimed was no more than a casual conversation which took place in Wellington, New Zealand, in 1957, determined to set out to establish the criteria for a closer analysis of what actually went on in the classroom.[32] Their collaboration with J. B. Hough resulted in a voluminous literature on what became known as 'classroom analysis' or more precisely 'interaction analysis'. In one of their most important works, *Interaction analysis: theory, research and application*, published in 1967, they drew together much of the work being done in this field. In this book

Flanders claimed that part of their task was 'to explain the variability of teacher influence'. Inexorably, the focus of research was shifting away from macro-theory towards an emphasis on what actually went on in the classroom, in terms of both pupil and teacher behaviour and classroom organisation and interaction. This was a development, drawn in part from earlier work done in Russia, which was to prove, indirectly at least, enormously important in Britain. Researchers such as Neville Bennett, Michael Bassey, Maurice Galton and Paul Croll can all be seen as working in the shadow of this pioneering American work. Their influence on the focus of policy was to be very significant during the 1970s and 1980s.

Second, two other American researchers, Bloom and Krathwohl, were setting out at about the same time to construe their own account of the teaching process. Their focus was less on the classroom exchange and more on the identification of the precise objectives of the teacher. In their influential work, *A taxonomy of educational objectives: the classification of educational goals*, first published in 1964, they identified the 'domains' of knowledge (most notably the 'cognitive', to do with thinking skills, the 'affective', to do with attitudes and the 'motor', to do with physical skills). Each of these was subdivided into many sub-categories; and a taxonomy (or list) of possible goals for the teacher was laboriously drawn up. Implicit in their work was the argument that without much closer definition of what it was that the teacher was seeking to impart or convey, the whole process of educating was at best ill-defined. Whilst this may in retrospect appear a little esoteric, it is difficult to overstate how significant its influence was to become in the debate on schooling in Britain, inspiring a generation of researchers and playing its part in bringing about the collapse of 'macro-theory' among British sociologists of education. What, of course, is particularly significant in our context was that it was not many years before 'objectives' were to be reworked as 'outcomes', and a whole new slant of educational policymaking became possible. If the aims of the teacher could be more precisely articulated, what was more natural than the assessment of how effectively these objectives had been met? And what better justification for the distribution of public monies?

All of this was happening at a time when government itself was beginning to raise questions about the nature of the expert help it sought. In a telling admission, A. H. Halsey stated in one review of the development of educational policy during this period that

> Anthony Crosland, the Secretary of State at the DES, surprised me on the day after the publication [of the Plowden Report] in 1967 by the confident assertion that it was the last of the line. His confidence was based on the instinct of an outstanding politician that the amiable reflections of an essentially amateur Establishment of the 'great and good' were too unwieldy and too slow to be of use to modern government. He already had the notion that planning backed by economic and social research could be internalised into DES administration in such a way as to enable an energetic Secretary of State to link social scientific knowledge to political and popular opinion as it expressed itself in Westminster.[33]

It was to be precisely this novel way of seeking expert support for governmental policy making which sounded the death knell of that macro-sociology which had underpinned much of the immediate post-War settlement. It helps explain, if only partially, the loss of control by the professional experts over what was going on within the education system.

Applying the brakes: the meritocratic elitists

Whilst many members of the teaching profession saw this curriculum reform as a pressing need, there is also ample evidence of a groundswell of opinion which was uneasy about the direction and the pace of these developments. Many of the reservations which had been expressed during the late forties and the fifties about child-centred teaching were still being voiced throughout the following twenty years. In May 1960, for example, the *TES* ran an article entitled 'Self-expression', commenting that

> only a little while ago 'self-expression' was a word of power in education ... it was generally understood that those in favour of self-expression were some-how more enlightened, more progressive than the others and hence more worthy of promotion ... Will the expression of a child's ego enable him to drive a car, to read a book, to add up a tradesman's bill? We await the answer.[34]

A week later the same journal argued that

> in the dispute between traditionalism and progressivism, teachers should feel free to take a middle road ... first, a community has a right to expect from the schools that they will produce the scientists, technologists, creative artists and professional people ... they have the right to demand a high standard of literacy in the general population. These are minimum demands and the schools must meet them.[35]

Five months later the *TES* reported on a Conservative Party Local Government conference at which Mrs R. H. Cave from Bristol warned that 'in place of the old fear of privilege and wealth the Socialists had substituted a fear of the power of intellect. There was a real resentment against the child with brains'. On the question of gender she emphasised that 'a girl should be educated as a person although she should be trained as a woman'.[36]

As had been the case immediately after the War, all of the main arguments which were to be deployed by the radical right during the Thatcher years were already in place and being clearly articulated. At the start of 1961, for example, G. H. Bantock returned to the fray with a public pronouncement that

> syllabuses can only be built up as a result of an honest admission of radical differences of ability ... We seem to be committed to the attempt, doomed to failure from the start, to bring all elements of the population to a similar level

of consciousness ... In the school for the average child, the domestic life will concern the girls ... for the boys the interest in the machine would play a major part ... What goes out? Formal history and geography should disappear, though an interest in the past should be stimulated through the history of the domestic life of the machine. Much waste matter could be removed from the mathematics syllabus. No second language should be studied ... What a school CAN accomplish is always sadly limited.[37]

In similar vein the *TES* itself commented on a newly published IAHM report on the grammar schools that 'these headmasters are themselves too interested in education and not enough in scholarship ... grammar schools are ... essentially places of scholarship and sound learning'.[38] At a Conservative Party Teachers' Association conference in June 1961 R. A. Butler spelt out what was to become one of the central themes of the Thatcher years by emphasising the need for technical education at secondary level whilst N. F. H. Butcher, the borough education officer for Hendon, told the same conference that there should be 'less emphasis in infant schools on the play way in view of the slackening of parental discipline'. More time, he argued, should be spent on instilling the rudiments of reading.[39] Others were only too willing to protest at some of the new initiatives during these years. For example, one retired headmaster, Thomas Wilkinson, wrote in to the *TES* condemning the Leicester Plan currently proposed by the Chief Education Officer Stewart Mason. He wrote:

> I am concerned with intangibles like tradition which blooms slowly and is not to be cut down ... Humphrey Perkins School has over 80 students in the sixth form ... the school is rich in amenities ... Are all these to be lost and lavished on junior school pupils who will leave at 14? ... The school foundation deeds, 1717, say it will teach in all sorts of learning; after that they could read in the bible. That was the 11+ of those days ... I plead with the Leicester Education Committee to stop this wanton decapitation.[40]

Fears such as these were summarised at the annual conference of the British Association for the Advancement of Science in the following year, where a chief inspector of schools, Percy Wilson, told delegates that 'this is our last chance to reverse the process of disintegration of knowledge which would bring our culture into decline and most educational processes to a dead stop'.[41] His particular beef was the perceived threat to the teaching of specialist subjects at secondary level.

So, the first Black Paper, which appeared in 1969 and which has attracted much attention from historians, has to be seen as a codification of pre-existing concerns rather than a new rhetoric which dramatically changed the political landscape. Certainly the Black Papers, which continued to appear until 1977, had the effect of ensuring that the question of comprehensivisation remained at the heart of the political agenda. They served as a focus for the concerns of those on the right about de-streaming and new approaches to teaching. But they did not represent a sea-change in the rhetoric around education.

But the Black Papers do stand as the exemplar of a particular critique of schooling which came from an identifiable source. The originators of Black Papers were Brian Cox and Tony Dyson, lifelong friends who met as undergraduates at Pembroke College at the University of Cambridge. Both had been prototypical 'working-class' entrants to the post-War grammar school – Cox via Nunsthorpe Elementary School, Grimsby, to Wintringham Secondary School and Dyson via Essendine Road Elementary School, Paddington, to the Sloane School, Chelsea. Cox reflected on his own elementary schooling with the observation that

> at Nunsthorpe it would not have occurred to the teachers that accurate spelling, punctuation and grammar might inhibit a child's creativity ... Instead of writing disorganised personal prose we learnt the rules of civilised discourse ... We were invited, even compelled, to submit ourselves to the disciplines of study. The rules we learnt were a means of understanding the demands of the outside world, and of controlling them in the service of the community ... the children profited in a rich variety of ways from the traditional teaching.[42]

Both saw the traditional schooling they had received as opening the door to their own careers in academia. Both became university lecturers in English with a deep commitment to the preservation and development of what they saw as the best of English literature. To this end in 1959 they began publishing the literary journal *Critical Quarterly* as, among other things, a launch pad for new poets. It was through their editorial work on this journal that the scheme of a publication offering a critique of trends in education emerged, and some of the contributions to this journal offer a telling counterpoint to the Black Papers themselves. Dyson himself contributed an article entitled 'Culture in decline', railing at the 'levelling down' which he thought characterised post-War British society and in particular its education system. His final peroration sums up one key element in these emergent 'new right' arguments:

> as a result of university expansion, more has meant worse ... students arrive at our universities without the body of knowledge, or the critical intelligence, or the scholarly and moral ideals, or the commitment to learning, or the capacity or the will for self-discipline, which a real university must require. The only sure preparation for real universities ... is an educational system which from the earliest years recognises talent and ability; which inculcates and expects a high code of manners and morals; which recognises and proclaims all levels of success and failure; which matches bright and willing children with bright and willing teachers in appropriate institutions and ... which delights in the fullest development of intelligence and ability, the fullest manifestation of superiority, whenever and however these appear. We need, in fact, the selective, idealistic and astringent educational system which emerged in this country under a high culture, and is currently being destroyed by a low one. Instead what we are getting is an egalitarian levelling ... which functions in a declining culture both as symptom and as further cause.[43]

In similar vein, an article by Bernice Martin was entitled 'Progressive education versus the working classes'. Identifying the grammar schools as 'traditional' and the comprehensives as 'progressive' she argued that

> ritual and rules are crucial elements in the teaching technique of the tradi-
> tional school. Children collectively recite tables, the books of the Bible,
> French irregular verbs, Latin declensions, the chronology of English mon-
> archs, chemistry formulae, geometrical proofs and so on. The rules ... are the
> starting points of a subject. Learning is based on structure and form ... The
> intention is to give the child transferable skills. The teaching methods of the
> progressive school aim at eliminating 'empty' ritual and rules. The child is
> encouraged to explore, to discover for himself, to respond intuitively to the
> idea of number, to sense principles, not rules ... each child is his own Galileo
> and his own Shakespeare. Unfortunately, the effect of the progressive stress
> on immediacy of response is to produce a plethora of non-transferable expe-
> riences, the result of which can all too often be to embed the child
> permanently in a limited context rather than enabling him to be genuinely
> creative.[44]

Thus it becomes clear that the source of this 'new right' attack on educational change may well be some of those very people who had themselves been new entrants to the changed system of the immediate post-War years. Is it possible that the strength of feeling about comprehensivisation and new teaching methods, which can be observed in many contributions to the debate, is attributable to the fact that the experience which many first generation working-class entrants to the grammar schools underwent had the ironic outcome that it made them staunch defenders of the new post-War educational status quo? Are Cox and Dyson the spokespersons for a generation of professionals, schooled in the 1940s and 1950s grammar schools, who became the high priests of a Thatcherite agenda at precisely the moment that the upper echelons of the Conservative Party became accessible to more than a sprinkling of ex-grammar school boys (and to one very famous old girl!)? Is one explanation of the fierce opposition to educational change which became evident the appearance of a new generation of 'meritocratic elitists' who came to dominate educational discourse increasingly during the 1970s and 1980s? Were the writings of Cox and Dyson as much a symptom as a cause?

A complex picture

So, the picture which emerges of educational change during the 1960s and 1970s is one that is very complex and far from straightforward. There was certainly a widespread belief that, as Brian Simon put it, 'there was advance across the board'[45], that things were changing very quickly in the classroom. Giving further credibility to this claim was the establishment of the Association for the Advancement of State Education. This Association, which began life as a

Cambridge-based parents' group in 1960, had grown within two years into a national organisation which Anne Wind, one of the founders, reported on in the pages of *Forum*.[46] It lobbied against reductions in local education budgets and offered advice to parents on aspects of their children's schooling, a counselling service which quickly developed into the Advisory Centre for Education. The appearance of a strong parental lobby actively supporting many of the changes taking place in the classroom certainly helped confirm the impression that this was a moment of significant educational change.

But what must also be borne in mind is the wide range of factors which ensured that, from the outset, these changes were at best partial and were contested at every turn. First, it is worth remembering that, throughout this period, a majority of the teaching profession supported the Conservative Party electorally, and in many cases this would have been linked with a value system which enabled them to see themselves professionally as custodians of good practice, dedicated to the preservation of all that was good in the education system and necessarily sceptical about classroom changes that appeared too radical. Equally important, as I have argued elsewhere,[47] the growing contrasts between suburbs and towns, between north and south, between professional and working-class lifestyles, ensured that there could be no uniformity of educational experience in post-War Britain. The education on offer to children in the newly-built schools on the periphery of the growing conurbations was bound to be in stark contrast to that experienced by inner-city pupils, even though the structure of the curricula they followed may have appeared superficially similar. Further, those teachers most committed to classroom reform were more likely to find themselves in particular kinds of teaching location. I recall the amazement of some of my friends and professional colleagues when, after two spells of teaching in the comprehensive sector, and as a known supporter of comprehensivisation, I chose to move to a teaching post in a single-sex grammar school in the mid-1960s. A profession made up of 'horses for courses' was hardly likely to be one which would uniformly follow the latest trends.

It is hardly surprising, therefore, that many of the research findings of those educationalists involved in examining closely what was actually going on in the classrooms were sceptical about the extent of change taking place. Maurice Galton's work pointed to the widespread use of whole-class teaching through the 1970s in the primary sector,[48] and, in 1976, Neville Bennett suggested that only a small proportion of teachers could be classed as 'informal' or 'progressive'.[49] Whilst children's work had become more individualised, the nature of the teacher–pupil exchange remained heavily didactic. Surveying developments between 1975 and 1980, the Leicester-based 'Oracle' project concluded that, in the primary schools,

> instruction mainly took place between a teacher and individual child ... the
> ᾽nature of the interactions was overwhelmingly managerial and didactic ...
> Little feedback about work was given ... and [there were] large discrepancies
> between the curriculum strategies deployed by schools and the manner in

which the curriculum operated at the tactical level ... Different classroom set-tings appeared to have a minimum effect on teaching style [and] collaborative group work was a totally neglected art. While children were usually sat in groups there were very few cases where children were given the kind of work which required them to collaborate ... It would seem, therefore, that although there had been considerable change in the organisational patterns in the pri-mary schools, within that framework the teaching emphasis had hardly changed. Learning was largely controlled by the teacher. Children were talked 'at' rather than talked 'with' and the focus of the teachers' attention was largely on the traditional areas of reading, writing and computation.[50]

And, as I have argued above, the rhetoric around teaching at this time remained fiercely contested. There were as many educationalists proclaiming the virtues of the existing system as there were calling for radical changes. In the absence of any clear consensus it was inevitable that the shift towards more child-centred teaching methods and towards a reformed curriculum would remain at best partial and, even in those schools most keenly committed, not supported unequivocally by all of the staff. With the benefit of hindsight, it appears that the sixties and sev-enties, as much as the Thatcher years, were the period during which educational reform became unsustainable largely as a result of the context in which it took place. Rather than being the years of 'advance across the board', this was a period of partial and timid reform, which, although it appeared widespread to many commentators, carried with it the seeds of its own undoing. This was the period when educationalists set themselves up for, and made themselves potentially more susceptible to, the Thatcherite onslaught. By the mid-seventies, everything was in place for the next swing of the pendulum.

4   1974–79

The teachers lose control

I know about learning by rote because I was brought up on it. It trains both the memory and the willpower ... It provides a sense of solid achievement and an invaluable and enduring grounding without which much subsequent 'progress' turns out to be ephemeral and insecurely based. It would be nice, if no doubt fanciful, to look forward to a spate of B.Ed. theses with titles like 'an enquiry into the advantages of rote learning in early childhood as the necessary basis for sustained educational growth'. It disciplines the mind and that would be a much better start than most children get.

Tom Howarth, retired Birmingham head teacher, writing in the
Times Educational Supplement, 10 May 1974

This quotation goes a long way towards helping explain why it was that the teaching profession was to prove so susceptible to external influences from the 1970s onwards. Despite the fact that there were a plethora of new initiatives in classroom practice and pedagogy, many teachers (and Tom Howarth was one of them) remained deeply sceptical about the need for classroom reform and the direction it seemed to be taking. They were prepared to argue publicly for whatever version of 'traditional' teaching methods they thought most appropriate. As has been suggested in earlier chapters, these deep and fundamental divisions within the profession about the ways in which children should be taught had existed throughout the post-War period and meant that it was quite impossible for the profession to speak with a single voice. Consequently, at a moment when wider social and economic changes brought what went on in the classrooms under closer public scrutiny, the tried line that the teachers knew best became untenable. The failure to reach any agreed consensus on what constituted best practice meant that the teaching profession was at the mercy of whichever political wind was blowing.

The changing social and economic context

In the swiftly changing circumstances of the mid-1970s, it was inevitable that the schools would come under closer scrutiny than had previously been the case. First, the sudden transformation of the economic context had major implications for schooling in terms of both practice and of how it was perceived. The period of sustained economic growth which had prevailed since the Second World War was clearly coming to an end.[1] Throughout the 1950s and 1960s economic expansion had been a reality, but had been slower than in several rival economies, and this under-performance, which had been masked by a general sense of well-being and unprecedented affluence, was beginning to have severe consequences. The late sixties saw an upturn in industrial unrest and this was matched by a significant decline in productivity and output. Between 1964 and 1973 there was an 11 per cent fall in industrial production and over a ten-year period to 1975 manufacturing lost almost one third of its labour force. If this alone were not bad enough, its impact was worsened by the fact that the balance of payments was tilting sharply against Britain. Throughout the post-War era a surplus in 'invisible' exports had been able to mask the poor export performance of manufacturing industry. The United Kingdom sustained a balance of trade surplus until the late 1960s, but the habit of importing more goods than were exported resulted in a massive and irretrievable trading deficit of over five billion pounds by 1974. As if these were not problems enough, the world oil crisis of the early 1970s culminated in the quadrupling of world oil prices by OPEC in December 1973. One immediate consequence for the United Kingdom was a startling rise in inflation, which had averaged 2.8 per annum through the 1950s and 1960s, then went up for a few years before reaching an alarming 24 per cent in 1974.

This, then, was the economic situation inherited by the incoming Labour government in 1974 and, inevitably, there was widespread discussion in the press and among politicians and educationalists of the extent to which the education system was to blame for these problems as a result of its failure to focus sufficiently on skills, on technology and on employability. These considerations were suddenly to loom much larger in any discussion of curriculum reform.

Secondly, and at a deeper level, a new politics of education was becoming discernible. Whereas just about every commentator since the coming of universal education had taken the benign effects of schooling for granted, during the 1960s and 1970s alternative views of schooling began to come into circulation. The collaboration between Ivan Illich and Everett Reimer which culminated in their both publishing on deschooling during the early 1970s[2] had begun as early as 1958 in Puerto Rico. They attracted around them a group of thinkers, of whom Paulo Friere was probably the most influential. Illich's *Deschooling society*, which appeared in 1971, raised fundamental questions about the nature of learning. It is deeply ironic, and a commentary on the power of formal institutions, that this book quickly became established on student reading lists and so, inadvertently, reinforced the very processes it sought to critique. In Britain, educational sociologists such as Ian Lister took up and disseminated the ideas of Illich and his collaborators. The extent to which popular confidence in schooling was undermined was reflected in 1979 by the bestselling record 'The wall' with its powerful messages that education was little more than a form of thought control and that the classroom was in reality the venue for the 'dark sarcasm' of teachers.

All of this gave a significant twist to the debate on the school curriculum, with both sides now finding grounds to suggest that it was their opponents who were subversive. For the first time, perhaps, since the coming of universal schooling there were many in society at large who no longer remained convinced that popular schooling was a good thing.

This growing suspicion of teachers and of what was going on in the schools was fuelled during the 1970s by the mass media. It is not overstating the case to suggest that the 1970s became a decade of press campaigns focused on education, either major reports, such as that by the Bullock Committee on literacy, or press comment highlighting perceived crises. Fodder was provided by the 1975 Bennett Report on teaching styles, the William Tyndale dispute in the same year and the subsequent Auld Report and the furore over the Risinghill School. The scepticism of some elements of the popular press was summarised on 4 November 1976 by the *Daily Mail* which told its readers bluntly that 'the brutal truth is that standards have fallen'. The impact of all this was brilliantly summarised by the Centre for Contemporary Cultural Studies which concluded that

> central to the reporting were pictures of the current state of British schooling, images of incompetence, slovenly, subversive or just trendy teachers who had failed to teach or control the undisciplined pupils in their charge which became too familiar to need elaboration. Background actors – wild-eyed theorists, out of touch bureaucrats and the complacent self-interested leaders of some unions – were often sketched. Counterpoised to these were some dedicated teachers, particular union leaders and the occasional bureaucrat who had been forced to face up to reality. The lay actors in the drama were seen as those imbued with common sense who were worried about failing standards, industrialists and parents fearful of reprisals about their children.[3]

It was clear that the mood of the general public was changing quickly and that this would make it increasingly difficult for educators and educationalists to sustain their cherished independence. All of this was taking place, of course, at a time when individuals were becoming accustomed to exercising choice to a much greater degree than had previously been the case. If the coming of affluence meant that people became 'consumers', with unprecedented control over their own lives, it was only a matter of time before the consumerist attitudes which applied to the purchase of goods came to prevail in respect of decisions such as the choice of school or the nature of the educational experience on offer.

What made many parents particularly susceptible to these press campaigns was the fact that many of them saw their own children going through a system which had moved well beyond the one they had experienced and about which they felt insecure. This uncertainty made it easier for the press to strike a chord when they focused on educational issues and gave credence to the *Black Papers*, the first of which appeared in 1969. These seemed to legitimate parental anxieties and certainly had the effect of promoting education closer to the heart of the political agenda. If, for much of the twentieth century, it had been possible, even usual, for prime ministers to use the education office as a convenient dumping ground for colleagues they wished to marginalise, by the 1970s this was no longer possible. By the end of the century education was one of the 'tick boxes' which could be of real value for politicians with aspirations to party leadership.

Further, during the late 1960s and early 1970s, the local authorities seemed to have become the most innovative element in educational policymaking, as a growing number of proposals for comprehensive reorganisation came in from all parts of the country. This trend peaked during the four years (1970–1974) that Margaret Thatcher was Secretary of State for Education. So strong was this groundswell that, despite her reservations, she became at this time the Minister who closed the greatest number of grammar schools. The impression was given that it was impossible for Westminster to control the LEAs. One direct result of this was to be that Thatcher returned to office as Prime Minister in 1979 determined to address the problem of the local education authorities, and this goes some way to explain the process by which teachers and educationalists were to become even more marginalised during the 1980s. But, equally important, it gave a general impression during the mid-1970s that the local education authorities were in some way out of control and that the delicate balance between central and local government, which had been such a strong feature of education in Britain since the War, was breaking down. This too placed pressure on the incoming Labour government in 1974.

Further evidence that the tectonic plates around schooling were shifting was provided by the reorganisation of local government during the early 1970s. Following the recommendations of the Redcliffe Maud Commission on local government, the number of local education authorities was halved in 1974. If this was intended to establish a stronger linkage of local government to its growing urban hinterlands, in reality it became the first of a series of initiatives which ultimately destabilised the local control of education. In this new situation, the 1972 Bains Report was widely influential, leading many local authorities to adopt corporate management. This involved closer monitoring of the outcomes of local funding decisions and was to semi-permanently transform the relationship between the local authorities and their schools. In brief, it is clear in retrospect, if it was not at the time, that the established relationships between central government, the local authorities and the schools, which had been such a strong feature of the educational provision in the United Kingdom throughout the twentieth century, were breaking down, and this too was to have enormous significance for the school curriculum.

Finally, it must not be forgotten that the birth rate in Britain, which had remained at around one million live births each year since the post-War upturn, fell dramatically at the start of the 1970s. In the maintained sector in England the primary school population stood at 4,813,000 in 1973, but by 1985 it had fallen to 3,542,000.[4] Teacher supply and the provision of buildings became nightmare issues for planners and administrators, but, most significantly in our context, the position of the teachers themselves became more precarious as their job security, which had been one of the major attractions of the profession throughout the twentieth century, began to look flaky.

Labour back in power and change in the air

Each of these factors goes some way to explain the highly-charged context of the late 1970s. In sum, they generated a situation within which change was inevitable and the one major development which was widely anticipated was that, somehow or other, central government would find ways of exercising closer control over the day-to-day running of the education system. In a review of the challenges facing Reg Prentice, the new Labour Minister of Education, at the moment he took office, Anne Corbett, a *TES* correspondent, reflected that it would be necessary for the DES to assert itself far more:

> the money ... may present less of a challenge for an education minister than does initiating and monitoring a policy which would give the DES more active responsibilities ... Education is a service locally administered. That does not diminish the Secretary of State's responsibility to see that education is provided. There are certain minimum standards which the government should see adhered to.[5]

A sense that change was in the air was confirmed by the setting up of the Layfield Committee to report on the administration and funding of local government. In November 1975 one Conservative backbencher reminded Fred Mulley, who had quickly replaced Prentice as Minister of Education, that the transfer of financial provision for education from local to central government was now widely advocated: he asked whether Mulley foresaw the end of the local education authorities. This question was ducked with the reply that all this would become clearer after the publication of the Layfield Report.[6] Thus, during the autumn of 1975, the question of the central control of educational funding became a key issue, raised time and again in public statements. Roland Freeman, who had for some years controlled the finances of the GLC, told a conference in Brighton that 'education should be paid for out of the Exchequer and not by LEAs, and that 'the transfer of education must be a cardinal feature of proposals to reform local taxation'.[7] The Layfield Committee itself was told by several witnesses that local authority educational expenditure was out of control and that it was overdue for independent auditing. A pamphlet published by the organisation *Aims for freedom and enterprise* received coverage in the educational press when it called for educational expenditure to be taken from local government. Finally, in a gloomy view of the prospects of the LEAs, Dudley Fiske, a widely respected chief education officer, used the Lady Simon of Wythenshawe Memorial Lecture in the autumn of 1975 to lambast the prospects of the local authorities. He described the recently published Bains Report as a

> swingeing attack on LEA performance. In short there are too many people whose main function now appears to be to coordinate, monitor, audit and at times interfere with the activities of others who are perfectly able ... if only they can be freed from the attentions of their colleagues who seek to manage them.

His most radical proposal to counter this was the complete transfer of control of the education service to national level: 'it is unfortunate that, unexpectedly soon after the 1974 reorganisation, it is local government which is once again on trial.' [8] And these concerns were soon picked up by the Prime Minister's office. At the end of November Harold Wilson hinted to the annual local government conference, meeting at Eastbourne, that 'the responsibility for education could ultimately be taken away from the LEAs and given to new regional authorities under devolution proposals', although he did seek to deflect criticism with the aside that 'at the moment no-one could sensibly conceive of the education service being run by anyone other than the LEAs'.[9] Rereading these debates, which marked Labour's return to power, one is left with a distinct sense that, even if they had no clear idea of where they were headed, the protagonists did have a very real sense that this was the end of an era.

When the Layfield Report did appear in May 1976, the whole issue was reignited. Whilst the Report came out against a switch to direct funding of schools by central government, it did point out that education remained by far the biggest financial commitment of the local authorities, both in terms of cost and of numbers employed, and that contrasts in local provision were reflections of the differing priorities and policies of the local authorities. It pointed out, too, that many of their witnesses had argued for greater direct involvement by central government and talked in terms of 'government control of the whole education service'. In particular, it suggested that 'national minimum standards' could be guaranteed only by the involvement of central government and through national rather than local taxation.[10]

If external considerations were bringing the autonomy of the profession into question, so too were some aspects of the debate among teachers. In November 1974, for example, the National Union of Teachers published *Teachers talking* in an effort to impress the Houghton Committee, which was currently discussing teachers' pay, with an account of the difficulties the profession faced. To show how demanding the teacher's job had become in recent years, this pamphlet chronicled a litany of changes which the profession was facing: a shift to new teaching methods, the introduction of new approaches to mathematics, integrated studies, humanities replacing history and geography, team teaching and a move away from whole-class teaching. This allowed the *TES* correspondent, Tim Devlin, to report (whether or not it was the case) that 'chalk and talk lessons have almost gone. So has homework of the old variety'.[11] But in this the union was shooting itself in the foot. By stressing how demanding the teacher's job had become in an attempt to maximise any pay settlement, they left themselves open to the criticism, soon to be widely heard, that only the most able teachers could carry it off and that the majority were being forced to acquiesce in a loss of classroom control and lower pupil achievement.

Allied to this was the increasingly frequent complaint that the changes that were underway in the classroom had the inevitable consequence of disadvantaging the more able pupils. This was the tenor of a lengthy article by Ronald Butt in *The Times* in July 1974. Under the gloomy headline 'A sorry tale of conflicting cultures in the country's classrooms' he described the anarchic consequences of efforts to introduce new methods in the schools of London, where, he claimed, unprecedented numbers of parents were involved in what he called a 'flight to the private sector'. He continued:

> In the present mood of the educational establishment the danger is that the tendency for all schools gradually to conform to an approved type may harden. And it is from this type that many parents are struggling to escape ... So what precisely are people trying to escape from? It is really time that the question was answered and that the politicians involved themselves in looking into it. First, of course, they are trying to escape from schools where the abler children and even the willing children are placed at a disadvantage by their minority position, and by prevalent teaching fashions which make learning harder. Secondly, there is a basic cultural conflict ... a clash between the ethos of the school and the ethos of the home.' [12]

He went on to paint a picture of anarchy in London's comprehensive schools, which he clearly identified particularly with novel approaches to teaching.

Lobbying of this sort during the mid 1970s was to prove very significant. It planted a firm impression in the minds of the public that there was some kind of linkage between comprehensivisation and experimentation in teaching method, on very little hard evidence and whether or not this was the case. And equally it fostered a sense that things were going badly wrong in the education system and that governmental intervention was both necessary and inevitable. In these ways the rhetoric around schooling did much to make the events of the following few years pretty well inevitable.

A challenge turns into a crisis

Through 1975 and into 1976, it is not difficult to discern the making of an educational crisis. On the one hand the Government, under first Reg Prentice and later Fred Mulley at the Education Office, seemed bent on the completion of the programme of the 1960s, pressing ahead with comprehensive reorganisation and presenting Thatcher's period as Minister as some kind of historical aberration or a temporary blip in an ongoing process of change. But events conspired to make this approach appear increasingly dysfunctional. First came the William Tyndale affair, which erupted during the summer of 1975. At this small ILEA primary school the staff set out to introduce their own version of 'child-centred' education, seeking to put into practice much of the philosophy of the Plowden Report. But the manner in which they did this resulted in a growing number of parents withdrawing their children and in a catastrophic inspectors' report in the autumn of 1975 culminating in a teachers' strike. The Auld Committee which was set up by the Inner London Education Authority to investigate what had gone on reported back in July 1976, resulting in the dismissal of several members of the staff and the complete reorganisation of the school.

For supporters of 'child-centred' approaches to teaching this proved to be a pivotal moment. It enabled the press to paint a picture of anarchy in the classroom
and resulted in a clear linkage in the public mind between progressivism and
extreme left-wing politics. This led directly to a questioning of the independence
of the teaching profession. As Brian Simon (1991) summarised it:

> The Tyndale issue raised, in a very dramatic form, a number of issues of key
> importance. One of these was pedagogical – what was meant by 'progressive'
> education? What was the relation between freedom and authority in the class-
> room? Above all what was the relation between learning and the deliberate
> structuring by the teacher of the child's activities? ... A relationship was
> made, in the public eye, between 'progressivism' and the left ... The specific
> recommendations of the Auld Report were perhaps less important than the
> overall political and public impact of the affair as a whole. Teaching had been
> brought into disrepute ... Immense damage had been done to the teaching
> profession as a whole. Teachers' (traditional) control of the curriculum – their
> autonomy – was now very sharply called into question. Teachers, schools,
> even local authorities as a whole, must be made 'accountable'. It was only
> after the Tyndale affair that the whole accountability movement swept the
> schools and their teachers.[13]

Second, 1975 saw a renewed focus on standards of literacy in the schools. James
Britten's *The development of writing abilities*[14] gave a succinct summary of the
approaches to literacy currently employed in the London schools and argued that
there was too great a stress on writing as a test activity and not enough emphasis
on the development of pupils' writing skills. This was to serve only as a preface to
the Bullock Report *A language for life* which highlighted the range of approaches
to classroom literacy currently in vogue and raised fundamental questions about
the effectiveness of what was being done in the schools.[15]

As if this were not enough, the Bennett Report entitled *Teaching styles and
pupil progress*, although based on a relatively small-scale research project, was
used by the press to bring into question the effectiveness of any teaching at primary level which was not heavily teacher-centred and based on what might be
thought of as a traditional 'chalk and talk' approach. This defence of formal
teaching methods enabled the general public to see that educationalists were far
from united on questions of pedagogy. It led to further public questioning as to
whether the teaching profession could any longer be trusted to take responsibility
for what went on in the classroom.

Two further developments worked to make the situation pressing for any administration claiming to be in touch. First, following the appointment of Sheilah
Browne as Chief HMI in 1974, the Schools' Inspectorate had carried out a major
survey of primary schooling and was beginning to canvass the need for a more
clearly defined core curriculum. Secondly, within the Labour Party itself there had
been for a few years growing concerns about children's levels of achievement. In a

policy document published in *Labour Weekly* in May 1974, for example, the Government had been called on to ensure 'minimum standards' in schools.

It is hardly surprising then that, reviewing the prospects for the year ahead, the *TES* reflected, in January 1976, that 'this looks likely to be a year in which the curriculum comes to the fore and, perhaps, a year in which the teachers' grip on the curriculum is challenged'. Pleading for a much stronger input of policy from the DES, this article went on to argue that 'the final decisions will lie with the Secretary of State who must wonder why strategic decisions ... should be prepared only by the professional group ... there is a need to re-establish the public nature of the curricular debate'.[16]

Within a fortnight the attack had been extended to include Mulley himself, who was portrayed as a minister out of touch with the real needs of the education system. His address to the North of England Conference at Lancaster was lambasted by the *TES* as

> a classic example of ministerial hand-wringing in public ... Education institutions would soon respond to the change of atmosphere engendered by a government which really put 'the brutal necessity of earning a living' first, in terms of policy priorities, fiscal policy, government spending, the containment of bureaucracy and so on. Mr. Mulley's cautious foray cannot be said in all conscience to go very far.[17]

In fact, although Mulley had conceded he had 'no magic remedies', he did hint at the changing educational agenda in his speech with the comment that 'we must instil a deeper respect for careers in wealth-generating industries and in commerce'.

There were, then, good reasons why, when Callaghan became Prime Minister in early April, he took it upon himself to take a direct interest in educational policy almost immediately. Not only was the press presenting the image of a department out of touch with the real issues, but several industrialists were weighing in with judgements such as that of Arnold Weinstock, the Chief Executive of the GEC, who described the teaching profession as 'feather bedded and inefficient' in a public pronouncement at the start of the year. He went on to say that 'educationalists should recognise that they do no service to our children if they prepare them for a world which does not exist'.[18]

Further, despite the resort by the Government to the IMF the previous autumn, there was no immediate sign of the economic crisis coming to an end. Education, as the largest item in the budget of the recondite education authorities, needed a tighter rein. This point was brought into sharp focus by the publication of the long-awaited Layfield Report in May, which, as we have seen, reinforced demands for greater central government control and some kind of guarantee of minimum standards in the classrooms.

'A turning point in English educational history'?

The moment he took office, Callaghan's Senior Policy Adviser, Bernard Donoghue, suggested that educational standards might be made a central concern.

In doing so, Donoghue was not only setting in motion a process which led directly to the Ruskin speech but also anticipating a new and lasting power structure which was to hold long after Callaghan left Downing Street. Whilst the office of the Prime Minister was to be brought directly into the policymaking process, the resort to the DES and the Inspectorate as key agents for the delivery and determination of policy appeared, both to contemporaries and subsequent commentators, to ensure that their roles would be pivotal in any new educational settlement. But, in reality, what was happening was that, not only was the power of the teaching profession and the LEAs being placed under threat, but, by using both the Inspectorate and the DES as 'enforcers' in an unprecedented way, the government was subtly changing their role from policymaking to that of administering the new educational settlement.

Mulley was summoned to No. 10 on 21 May, was asked to report on four major questions and 'was surprised' to be told that the Prime Minister's Policy Unit was working on a major speech to be given later that year. Thus it was Callaghan as Prime Minister who identified the primary curriculum, the later years of compulsory education, the reform of examinations and the education of 16-to-19-year-olds as the key battlefields of the summer of 1976. The outcome was a lengthy and confidential briefing paper, which came to be known universally as the Yellow Book, authored within the DES and leaked to the press only a few days before the Ruskin speech, probably in order to soften up the public and test the waters.

There is no doubt that many within the DES as well as Sheilah Browne (the Chief HMI) saw this as the golden opportunity for which they had been waiting. Browne had been encouraged by William Pile, during his period as Permanent Secretary at the DES, to use her survey of primary education to pave the way for more direct DES intervention in what went on in schools. Pile's replacement during the summer of 1976 by James Hamilton, a known centraliser, only strengthened the feeling that something was afoot.

Certainly the press thought all this to be a cue for the strengthening of the role of the Inspectorate. Shortly before the Ruskin speech the *TES* commented that

> large hints have been dropped by Sir William Pile and by his successor James Hamilton to the Association of Education Committees that the privacy of the secret garden should no longer be sacrosanct. The obvious instrument for any such intervention is the Inspectorate – hence the part played by HMIs in preparing a memorandum for the Prime Minister.[19]

During the course of the summer suggestions on the content of the planned speech were invited from numerous sources, although control of it remained firmly within the Prime Minister's Policy Unit. Both Donoghue and his assistant, Elizabeth Arnott are known to have been closely involved in the drafting, and the speech itself was kept away from the DES and the Minister right up to the moment it was given. The precedent set by Callaghan in this way, of side-stepping both Parliament and the DES, was one which was to be copied by both Thatcher and Blair, although in 1976 it was clearly a new departure.

Meanwhile, pressure continued to build for the announcement of some kind of shift in educational policy. At the start of September the *TES* highlighted the newly released birth rate statistics, which showed an ongoing fall. It reflected that the improved staffing ratios which would inevitably follow could only further weaken the position of the teachers themselves.[20] In mid-September Shirley Williams' appointment to the DES as part of a Cabinet reshuffle seemed to presage a new start in education. Within two weeks of her appointment she was telling the Labour Party Conference at Blackpool that she wanted to end the secrecy of the DES and expressed concern about the existing block grant arrangements because, as she put it, the LEAs had 'gone too far'.[21] In this she was echoing the Commons Select Committee which, only a week earlier, had called for greater openness in educational planning, still piqued that the planning documents for Thatcher's *Education: a framework for expansion* (1972) had not been made available, even to them. By mid-October the Select Committee was demanding a separate educational funding body for specific issues: a permanent Standing Education Commission. Within a few years the separate funding flow from the Manpower Services Commission was to enfeeble semi-permanently DES attempts to retain complete control of policymaking.

In his Prime Ministerial address to the Party Conference on 28 September, Callaghan took the opportunity to rehearse what was to be one of the key themes of his Ruskin speech, telling delegates that 'we need to close the gap between education and industry' through far closer cooperation between employers and schools.[22] It certainly seems that one of Callaghan's motives was the expropriation of emergent Conservative education policy. In its document *The Right Approach* and at the Conservative autumn conference, the Tory Party had made it clear that it saw political capital to be made out of education, latching on to public anxieties about both standards in schools and the behaviour of young people. As the *TES* put it:

> Much of the language in which this issue is pursued betrays the small 'c' conservatism which is perennially convinced that things aren't what they were, and that young people are going to the dogs. But underneath it all too there are perfectly respectable arguments about the levels of achievement expected from pupils at different ages and stages, and the methods and styles of teaching appropriate to these expectations.[23]

Against this backdrop, the leaking of the Yellow Book in mid-October set the scene for the Ruskin speech. It is hard to overestimate the significance of this document, since it anticipated several of the key trends which, even if they appeared radical in the autumn of 1976, were soon to be at the heart of policymaking in modern Britain. First, the Yellow Book took the argument advanced earlier in the year by the NUT concerning the increasing difficulty of the teacher's task, and turned it against the profession. Outlining the revolution in teaching method promoted by the Plowden Report, the Yellow Book commented:

in the right hands this approach is capable of producing admirable results ... Unfortunately, these newer and freer methods could prove a trap to the less able and experienced teachers who failed to recognise that they required a careful and systematic monitoring of the progress of individual children ... as well as careful planning ... As a result, while primary teachers in general still recognise the importance of formal skills, some have allowed performance in them to suffer as a result of the uncritical application of informal methods ... the time is almost certainly right for a corrective shift of emphasis'.

Similarly, on secondary education, the Yellow Book highlighted 'the feeling that schools have become too easygoing ... the time has probably come to establish generally accepted principles for the composition of the secondary school curriculum'.[24]

It called too for a greater emphasis on the basics to enhance the job prospects of school leavers, concluding gloomily that 'employers complain that school leavers cannot express themselves clearly'. Finally, it called on the Prime Minister to make 'an authoritative pronouncement' to refute the view that only the teachers should have a say on what went on in the schools.

The signals could hardly have been clearer, and the press wasted no time in underlining the historical significance of the moment. On 13 October the *Guardian* devoted much of its front page to the call that 'The State must step into schools', adding in a leader article that 'just as the clinical independence of doctors is eventually going to have to be reduced ... so too is the far more recent professional independence of teachers'. The author of this article, David Hencke, was under no illusions about the importance of what was going on, calling the Yellow Book 'a plan to introduce a basic national curriculum for Britain's secondary schools', adding that:

> the proposal, which at a stroke would end one hundred years of non-interference in state education, is made in a confidential document specially commissioned by Mr. Callaghan. Its 63 pages constitute a severe indictment of the failure of secondary schools to produce enough scientists and teachers.

His précis of the key points in the Yellow Book put several preconceptions about what was going on in the schools firmly into the public domain. He wrote of the need for teachers no longer to have absolute control of the curriculum, suggesting that many secondary schools were 'too easy going', resulting in many school leavers being deficient in basic communication and mathematical skills. The system as a whole was censured for its over-emphasis on 'preparing boys and girls for their roles in society compared with the need to prepare them for their economic role'. Hencke stressed the argument that, at primary level, informal modern teaching methods might work for the more able teachers but claimed that the Yellow Book gave a warning that 'less able teachers are not able to cope with modern methods and that there may be a need to correct the balance and return to more formal methods'. The route to 'an agreed core curriculum' was to be through 'an authoritative pronouncement by the Prime Minister to refute the view that only the teachers should have a say on what went on in schools'. For him the climate was now favourable for a reassertion of the power of the DES, with the Inspectorate having 'a leading role to play'. The outcome, he claimed, could be a major reform of examinations, a reconstruction of teacher training under a new controlling body and, above all, an agreed 'core curriculum' for the schools. Hencke concluded by quoting Fred Jarvis, the General Secretary of the NUT, who had observed that

> if these proposals are true, all I can say is that the PM is the first person in the country to take Rhodes Boyson seriously. Such proposals are revolutionary and go against the tradition of state education in this country. The proposals for a national curriculum contrast very starkly with the timidity of official statements by Labour ministers, and are against the statements given by the DES to a Parliamentary Select Committee recently.

The paper's editorial line was that, although the time was right for significant change, this did not mean 'Whitehall dictating on what every student does'. Although it might not be the job of the State to dictate which textbooks were used, it was not unreasonable to expect twenty periods in a thirty-five period week to focus on core subjects, and it was the responsibility of government to see that this was the case.[25]

In a similar vein to the *Guardian*, the *TES* argued two days later that

> it now remains to be seen how far Mr. Callaghan is prepared to go in his speech at Ruskin College ... If he acts on the DES advice we have reached a turning point in English educational history – the reversal of the long-term trend which since the early-1920s has steadily diminished the curricular influence of the administrators and the public's representatives. The myth of the teacher-controlled curriculum is strong, so strong perhaps, that the DES have concluded that it needs an initiative from No. 10 Downing Street to begin to dispel it.

This journal went on to spell out the key needs as it perceived them: for HMI to explain the proposals for a core curriculum, for a resolution of the strained relationship between the DES and the Schools Council, and for the development of direct DES funding streams which could put it more firmly and more directly in control:

> Both parties now believe there is a time-bomb ticking away in the schools. The Conservatives think public anxiety must favour them. They strike attitudes in defence of basic standards in the belief that this is the way to exploit the anxiety. Mr. Callaghan and Mrs. Williams may well have reached a not dissimilar political assessment, and believe they must defuse the time-bomb ... This they hope to do by bringing these curricular issues into the open.[26]

Given the extent to which the speech had been advertised in advance its greatest significance probably lay in the fact that it was made at all. But Callaghan did use the opportunity to underline several of the key themes which the press had already brought into public discussion. Perhaps most notably he stressed the extent to which the education system must work within the six billion pounds per annum which it currently claimed. The need to provide an education which fitted children to enter employment and the demands of a core curriculum were restated and a plea was made for a public debate on education involving all parties.

A landscape transformed?

The best and most detailed analysis of the circumstances and significance of the speech so far available is that of Clyde Chitty (1989), who concluded that it marked at the very highest political level the end of the phase of educational expansion which had been largely promoted by the Labour Party and at the same time it signalled a public redefinition of educational objectives.[27] On the right of the political spectrum, as Clyde Chitty has shown, figures such as Rhodes Boyson and Norman St John Stevas were quick to welcome what they presented as the adoption by Labour of long-held Conservative views. There can be no doubt that one major significance of the Ruskin speech was a semi-permanent shift to the right in the grounds of educational debate in modern Britain. The post-War drive for the promotion of a fairer society through education and for the making of citizens gave way to a quest for employability, the inculcation of basic competencies and efficiency and effectiveness in the running of schools. But the problem remained that these things needed to be monitored and measured.

The Great Debate which took place during the months that followed was of less significance than the flurry which the speech caused in educational circles during the immediate aftermath. First, Shirley Williams threw herself into a frenzy of public pronouncements which offered at least the image, if not the reality, of a department which was reining in the LEAs and the schools. At the start of November, clearly trying to appease critics who were worrying that the Government might go too far, she told the Commons she would seek 'basic standards in schools but this would not involve any immediate attempts to control the curriculum'.[28] A week later she announced that she would be consulting LEAs on the school curriculum,[29] and, a week later again, she was threatening greater direct-control of educational expenditure by the DES.[30] In the middle of November she used a *TES* interview to make clear that she intended to push through legislation prepared under Mulley to make comprehensive education mandatory.[31] Then, at the start of December, in a major Commons speech, she depicted a proactive government which was trying to involve parents more closely than in the past by encouraging them to comment on their children's progress through school. She also spoke of the establishment of scholarships to encourage pupils towards careers in industry.[32] Amidst all this she was not averse to a bit of teacher-bashing. She told the North of England Conference in January 1977 that the problem lay with 'poor teachers, weak headmasters and headmistresses and modern teaching methods'.[33] Before the end of January it was the Schools Council which came under attack as she spelt out plans for 'drastic changes' to reduce the influence of the teacher unions and to ensure DES supervision of the Council.[34]

What was to become a constant theme in her rhetoric during her final months in office was the suggestion that the LEAs were failing to meet their obligations, and that many of them, particularly those under Conservative-controlled local councils, failed to spend their agreed allocation for education. In October 1978, for example, Williams castigated the local authorities for failing to support the NFER and the Schools Council, warning them that

> if the future of these national institutions were to be put at risk or their activities drastically curtailed as the result of a reduction in local authority financial support, then I would be bound to consider whether central government should step in to finance them directly with all that would necessarily entail in terms of greater central government influence and control. I cannot believe that is what local government wants.[35]

Amidst all this it is difficult to discern any effective action which emanated from the DES at this time apart from the drawing up of a draft questionnaire for LEAs enquiring as to how they monitored and controlled the curriculum of the schools under their charge. Certainly, by the spring of 1978, Shirley Williams was being lauded by those on the right as the Secretary of State who had put her finger on the issue of falling standards in schools. Noel Annan congratulated her publicly on being 'the first Secretary of State for years to say in public that educational standards were too low'.[36] Brian Simon observed pertinently of this period that: 'procrastination, indecision, delay at all costs – endless consultations became the order of the day ... these marked Shirley Williams' term of office'.[37] Simon argued that the net political effect of all this was to prepare the soil for the 'radical right' initiatives of the 1980s. Equally, her dependence on rhetoric not only anticipated more recent patterns of governance but may well have had the effect of weakening the DES vis-à-vis the Prime Minister's office.

But, even though the approach of the Government at this time was incremental and relied heavily on public statements, the NUT was quick to defend what it rightly saw as a threat to the existing educational settlement and to the teaching profession. In December 1977 the union published *Education in schools* as a riposte to the Government's latest Green Paper on education, arguing that it was mistaken for the imposition of greater external controls and the drift towards a core curriculum to be used to erode 'the day to day responsibility of teachers for the education of children'.[38] The mood of the moment among many members of the teaching profession was captured at the NUT winter conference by one delegate, Don Winters, who reflected that

> with the opening of the Great Debate, the open season for teacher bashing was soundly launched, and the motto of most of those engaged in the debate

seems to have been 'Never Mind if there's no evidence that standards have fallen ... if you say it often enough the public will believe it.'[39]

But, just as the teaching profession had been split on the issue of curriculum reform since the War, so it was now. One commentator who spoke for those members of the profession who shared a concern that things had gone too far was John Rae, a well known public school headmaster. He observed in January 1977 that

> I have been taken to task for describing as hysterical one headmaster's attempt to draw a parallel between the Prime Minister's initiative at Ruskin and Nazi control of education ... senior officials in the DES are already pessimistic about getting agreement on a common core curriculum beyond the age of 14, even beyond 11 ... even if agreement can be obtained they do not know how to persuade teachers to accept it. Such pessimism is hardly surprising in view of the shift of power over the last decade from the Minister and the Department to the teachers' organisations and the Schools Council. It is time not only to restore the right balance of power between teachers and government, but also to call the bluff of the educationalists. What must be taught to whom at what age is not a decision for experts ... As teachers, we know best how the knowledge and skills can be communicated. We are the tacticians. But it is the job of Government to lay down the broad strategy.[40]

Remarks such as these undermined from within the ability of the profession to defend itself at this time.

Also permanently weakened by the Great Debate was the Schools Council. At the start of 1976, Fred Jarvis of the NUT had found it necessary to defend the Council from attacks in the popular press: 'the Daily Mail is giving the impression that the Schools Council has fallen under the influence of the teaching profession who are using it for trade union purposes with the result that it has forfeited all respect'.[41] He went on to point out that whilst the Council had been constituted to require a professional majority, this did not add up to a trade union stranglehold. Papers already open at the PRO show clearly that by the end of 1976 and for some time afterwards, this unease about its functioning had generated a major debate within the Council on its role, the part it might play in pushing through a single examination at sixteen-plus and how it could dovetail with the growing number of educational quangos.[42] At this time the Chief Education Officer for Cheshire wrote to the DES to comment on the extent to which the Schools Council was dominating the debate on examination reform, warning them that, in his view:

> the teachers are being totally naive about teacher control of the coordinating body for examinations. They seem not to realize that it would be quite unacceptable to the thinking public to put the new system completely under teacher control. And the thinking public includes people like you and me, Norman St. John Stevas, Shirley Williams as well as most folk on the

Clapham omnibus ... When I spoke to the Secretary of State ... I recognized this political reality but also (I believe) shifted her from the extreme position of cutting the Schools Council out altogether. That would have been just as unrealistic.[43]

In May 1978, the Council's Secretary, John Mann, drew up a list of 'other agencies at work in the same fields'. It included the Education Policy Unit of the Policy Studies Institute, the NFER, the SSRC, the DES, HMI, the Health Education Council, the CBI and the examination boards. He concluded:

> the Schools Council is a victim of its times. It was called into being in the golden Sixties ... a period of heavy expansion in education. It was acclaimed internationally as an ideal way of promoting educational development on all fronts. In the 1970s the Council has been criticized by both its financial backers, the DES and the local authorities.[44]

Weakened by the events of 1976, the Schools Council struggled on for several years before being wound up under Margaret Thatcher. Its demise stands as a potent symbol of the diminution of the power and influence of the teaching profession at this time.

A profession brought to heel?

How, then, can we summarise the changes in the governance of education in Britain which took place at this time? In essence they are twofold. First, there was a perceptible shift in aspiration, in the ends towards which policymakers were directing the education system. The call for economy and efficiency brought with it a renewed quest for employability, for competence in the core subjects and for the assurance of standards. Out of the window went the explorations of curriculum change, the development of pupil interests and the drive towards a fairer society and a more open democracy through education. These, together with the quest for citizenship, had been the rallying cries of many post-War educators, perhaps of the great majority. Now their voices were overwhelmed by demands for value for money. All of this stopped well short of the target-setting and league tables which came to dominate the educational landscape during the 1990s, but it was, nonetheless, a once-and-for-all tilt to the right.

Linked to all this, and clearly part of the explanation as to why this sea-change occurred, was a shift in the balance of power in policymaking. This, too, was to become semi-permanent. Callaghan's initiative, which was nothing other than predictable to those in touch with contemporary debate, moved 'the education issue' closer to the heart of politics and made it more susceptible to direct Prime Ministerial influence. Earlier commentators, such as Clyde Chitty and Brian Simon, have stressed the significance of Callaghan's personal involvement, and that is not to be understated. But the reading of the contemporary media on which this chapter is based suggests too that much that was said in October 1976 on the subject of educational policymaking was already to some degree foreseeable and even preordained. It was by October 1976, in many ways, inevitable that power would now be exercised more directly by central government.

Many observers have seen this as a strengthening of the role of the DES and the Inspectorate. My own conclusion is that, whether by accident or design, they became far more the enforcers of the policies of others as a result of the developments of the late 1970s. The real losers in this were the local authorities and the teachers. The Association of Education Committees was wound up at this time. It had been one of the major players in the politics of education, particularly since the Second World War. Almost symbolically, in December 1977, its best-known Secretary, Bill Alexander (by now raised to a peerage), resigned from the DES Consultative Committee which was overseeing the work of the Assessment of Performance Unit on the grounds that 'I believe the work now being started by the Unit could be used by a future Secretary of State to control the curriculum.' [45] He was right.

Perhaps the greatest casualty of the late 1970s was the teaching profession itself, which emerged from these events permanently enfeebled. The ill-judged industrial action of the mid-1980s was to be, as we shall see, the nail in the coffin of its ability to dominate the debate on the future of the schools and what went on inside them. Although much of the reality of the late 1970s was one of rhetoric rather than performance, the transition in power structures which was generated has persisted and has shaped the politics of education down to the present time. There can be little doubt that the Labour government which was in office from 1974 to 1979 did much to determine the politics of education down to the end of the century and beyond. The achievements of both the Thatcher and the Blair governments in the field of education are only comprehensible with reference to what went before. They built on the Callaghan legacy, but the edifice was set up during the 1970s.

5   1979–89

A decade of change

No previous government has so successfully aggrandised the power of the State while simultaneously and loudly proclaiming its deepest wish to roll back its frontiers.

Times Higher Education Supplement, Leader article, June 1984

A context for change

By the late 1970s it was becoming clear that, at almost every level, the context within which teachers worked was being transformed, although the longer-term implications of these changes were by no means immediately clear to those involved. First, across the developed world, it was possible to discern the rise of a new politics. One of the starting points for neo-Liberal thinking was Friedrich Hayek's *The road to serfdom*, first published in 1944. He became a leading critic of collectivist approaches to social problems and his book *The constitution of liberty* was brandished in the Commons by Margaret Thatcher towards the Speaker at the time she became leader of the Conservative Party with a cry of 'this is what we believe in'. Equally influential were Milton Friedman's monetarist economic theories, disseminated in books such as his *Essays in positive economics*, and also, like Hayek, impacting on political thinkers on both sides of the Atlantic. Keynesian demand management, which had underpinned the thinking of most post-War governments, found itself challenged by new ideas which raised fundamental questions about the effectiveness and appropriateness of state provision. These ideas came to underpin much policymaking during the 1980s and were particularly significant in respect of education, where it had become generally assumed, even by those on the right politically, that a state-provided education, through the cooperation of central and local government, was the way forward. Thus, since the late 1970s it has been possible to discern a steady drift towards that 'neo-Liberalism' which by the early twenty-first century has come to inform much governmental action in both the UK and America. By 1979 this process was already well under way. Ironically, in Britain in respect of education policy, the implementation of these ideas was to involve much tighter control from central government rather than its diminution.

At a more local level, Margaret Thatcher's assumption of the leadership of the Conservative Party in 1975 meant that the consensus politics which had been such a marked feature of policymaking, particularly in education, were now a thing of the past. A year earlier she and Keith Joseph had founded the Centre for Policy Studies and this Conservative 'think tank' was to herald new approaches to both the management of the economy and to social policy if she ever came to power. The post-War educational settlement which had allowed child-centred education and new approaches in the classroom to flourish found itself increasingly under threat.

Also, the context in which the schools themselves worked continued to change markedly. The ongoing decline in manufacturing industry (1.7 million jobs were lost between 1979 and 1985)[1] meant that employers were, by and large, looking for more highly skilled recruits from the schools than had been needed to enter industry only a few years earlier. The sense that schools were failing to produce suitably trained young adults and that something must be done was deepened. At the same time, sharpening economic competition on a world scale meant that the workplace itself became less secure and there was undoubtedly a hardening of attitudes towards the workforce and, at the same time, less readiness in society at large to go along with an unquestioning acceptance of job security and of professional practice. Teachers were to find themselves a particular target of this new criticality.

As if this were not enough, school rolls continued to fall during the 1980s. The Briault Report, published in April 1980, anticipated a decline in numbers at secondary level of one-third by the end of the decade and reported that the staffing problems generated by a fall in pupil numbers were having a direct effect on curriculum planning. Confronted by the demands of pupil choice at fourteen years of age and the need for groups of differing sizes, many schools were being obliged to cut back on the options available to pupils. It was hardly a situation likely to encourage curriculum experimentation.

Another development which was to have a massive impact on schools was the rise of the school effectiveness movement and, with it, the drive for school improvement. This may be seen as a practical working through of the new approach to the sociology of education outlined in Chapter Three. Two educationalists were to prove particularly influential during these years. First, in North America, John Goodlad published in 1984 his book *A place called school*, reporting the results of in-depth research in over 1,000 classrooms. He began from the assertion that American schools were 'in trouble' arguing that they had lost touch with both the children in them and the parents who needed to be much more closely involved and taken account of.[2] The following year he went on to establish the Centre for Educational Renewal and the Institute for Educational Enquiry, both at the University of Washington, and the existence of these organisations helps explain the wide impact of the school improvement movement worldwide since then. At much the same time in England, Michael Rutter, in collaboration with several colleagues, produced *15,000 hours*, a book which focused on the interactions which took place in the classroom and which had the effect of concentrating the debate on the effectiveness of schooling and on particular aspects of classroom practice.[3] In our context the overall effect was that the call for child-centred education was necessarily reformulated within the confines of a debate focused on school effectiveness. In a nutshell, in the quest for classroom effectiveness, the professionals had less time to consider the longer-term ends of education. This was to prove one key to understanding what I describe later in this chapter as the 'expropriation' of progressivism. As Stuart Maclure (2000) tellingly put it: 'It was time to move away from grand visions of social engineering and concentrate on the practical questions of how to make schools better'.[4]

A new radical right agenda

Both Friedrich Hayek and Milton Friedman were invited to address the Conservative Philosophy Group, another meeting point for Conservative academics and parliamentarians, which had been founded by Roger Scruton in 1974. Its meetings were regularly attended by Margaret Thatcher. Scruton was soon to become one of the leading influences on the evolution of Conservative Party educational policymaking. His book *The meaning of conservatism*, which appeared first in 1980, outlined what were to become two of the central tenets of education policy during the 1980s. First, he argued that the concept of freedom must be subordinated to strong central control:

> the Conservative attitude seeks above all for government ... The concept of freedom cannot occupy a central place ... Freedom is comprehensible as a social goal only when subordinate to something else, to an organisation or arrangement which defines the individual aim.

Secondly, in a passage which seemed to hark back to the famous statements of Bernard de Mandeville in the eighteenth century or of Davies Giddy in the early nineteenth, he argued that

> the attempt to provide equality of opportunity ... is simply a confused stumble in the dark ... It is simply not possible to provide universal education. Nor, indeed, is it desirable ... The appetite for learning points people only in a certain direction; it siphons them away from those places where they might have been contented ... it is important for society that it contain as many 'walks of life' as the satisfaction of its members require ... and that it does not sustain institutions which merely siphon away people to the point where they no longer wish to do what in fact they might otherwise have done willingly and well.[5]

Scruton was only one among a plethora of radical right commentators who came to focus increasingly on education at this time. Well-established organisations such as the Adam Smith Institute, the Economic League and the Freedom Association, as well as the Centre for Policy Studies, attracted well-known public figures who had something to say about schooling. They included Arthur

Seldon, Baroness Cox, John Marks, Antony Flew and Rhodes Boyson. But more directly, these organisations spawned a number of bodies which focused directly on education. These included the National Council for Academic Standards (founded in 1972), the National Grammar Schools Association (1987), the Campaign for Real Education (1987) and the Parental Alliance for Choice in Education (1985).

The outcome of all this was the appearance of a range of publications and public pronouncements which all pressed, in one way or another, for a reworking of the educational settlement which had marked the period since the Second World War. In 1979, for example, Vincent Bogdanor produced *Standards in schools* on behalf of the National Council for Academic Standards and a year later Caroline Cox and John Marks published their *Education and freedom: the roots of diversity*. On behalf of the Grammar Schools Association R. Peach and F. Naylor published *Grammar schools: the pride of Britain* in 1987, and, in the same year, Stuart Sexton's *Our schools: a radical policy*, published under the auspices of the Education Unit of the Institute of Economic Affairs, helped pave the way for legislation on education. The initiative was shifting inexorably away from those involved in the provision of education towards those who were commenting from the outside. It may be seen in some respects as a shift of emphasis which was long overdue, but it certainly had the effect, in the way it took place in Britain, of putting the radical right in the driving seat in terms of educational policymaking.

Four central themes are identifiable in the new Thatcherite educational agenda which emerged from this background during the 1980s. First, to a far greater degree than had been the case previously, there was a direct appeal to market forces, so that schools, colleges and even cost centres within individual institutions became more directly responsible for their own budgeting. This appeal to the profit motive meant that a new and much sharper competitiveness was introduced to the running of schools. Necessarily, the role of the local authorities in ensuring even-handedness and the fair distribution of resources between schools was irreparably eroded. At the same time it opened the schools to much closer external scrutiny and ensured far more extensive use of objective criteria, such as external examination results, to assess the performance of schools. But, at the same time, this meant a narrowing of what society was looking for in the conduct and performance of its schools. Attempts to measure educational performance more closely necessarily meant an attenuation of the definition of what constituted a good education. In this, the debate on curriculum reform fell by the wayside.

Second, although at first glance quite contradictorily, the 1980s saw a renewed effort by central government to exercise much closer control over the day-by-day working of the education system. The mechanisms to achieve this were to be the rationing of funding and the use of a national curriculum. By monitoring the success of individual schools in delivering this curriculum it would become possible to use funding to determine what actually went on within the schools. The use of directives on the detailed working of particular aspects of the system was a further device which guaranteed control to central government. Less directly, inspectors' reports were used (and widely publicised) to provide another determinant of the development of the system and of individual schools. Although the Schools' Inspectorate had been a semi-autonomous quango its redesignation as the Office of Standards in Education gave it a tighter remit, redefined the role of the inspectors and made it far harder for them to criticise government policy. As the nature of the Inspectorate changed it was made possible for people from a wide range of backgrounds, including industrialists and businessmen, to be appointed as schools inspectors, so drawing some of the sharpest critics of what went on in schools into their supervision. All of this was underpinned by demands for increasing efficiency and accountability in the use of public funds.

A third element in Thatcherite thinking was the appeal to a sense of nationhood, which was particularly significant in specific subject areas such as religion, history, geography and modern languages but which underpinned many government edicts on education which were not subject-specific. The fact that schooling was to be used in this way to confirm a sense of common identity served only to marginalise further the growing ethnic minorities. In England at this time, this meant in reality a confirmation of the national religion (a particular version of Protestant Christianity) and a focus on a very narrow and introspective history.

Finally, the new right's interest in education and schooling led directly to the view that education should play a more active role in the regeneration of the economy through the promotion of technology – in this case a new technology. The nation's economic problems were depicted by some commentators as the direct result of the failure of the schools to train a labour force equipped with appropriate skills. Thus information technology, specialist schools and a refocusing on the technological aspects of the curriculum were to be vital contributors towards a national revival.

The rhetoric around these four key elements had several clearly identifiable themes. Perhaps the most frequently heard was the view that those working in the schools and colleges should be far more accountable to their publics. No less powerful was the promotion of education in public statements as one of the keys to national recovery. Thus, these policies were derived from and depended on the belief that the nation was in decline, both economically and spiritually. This involved harking back to some golden age when things had been better. In general terms within Thatcherite thinking this meant an appeal to 'Victorian values', and in respect of teaching it involved a concept of a better past when teaching was focused on the basics and when selective grammar schools transmitted high culture to those who were destined to become the leaders of society. This was not linked formally to any religious revival, although it is worth remarking that the 1980s was a decade which saw a dramatic resurgence of fundamentalism in religion. However, the phenomenon of Thatcherism was marked by strong anti-communist sentiment and many of the pronouncements on education which were made at this time may be thought of as quasi-religious in their invocation of a set of beliefs and attitudes.

The evolution of Thatcherite policy

Initially the policies adopted by the Conservatives in power from 1979 echoed earlier approaches. Tight control of educational expenditure, the defence of the selective schools and of the private sector and the attempt to curb the initiatives of the LEAs were the key elements. Mark Carlisle, the incoming Minister, committed himself from the start to what looked initially like nothing more nor less than a well-established formula of economic cuts linked to a restriction of the power of schools and local authorities to innovate. The Assisted Places Scheme redirected fifty million pounds annually from the state sector to the private as selected pupils were funded directly to attend private schools. This, and the decision to rescind legislation enforcing comprehensivisation, was very predictable. Less so, and more significant in our context, was the announcement that the reports of the Inspectorate would be made public. This had the effect both of submitting schools to more direct press comment and criticism and of modifying significantly the role of the inspectors themselves, who now became far more the arbiters of what went on in schools than the counsellors of teachers seeking to improve their performance. In March 1981, in another echo of earlier Conservative Party education cuts, the funding of the education service by central government was cut, while the 'rate-capping' of the local authorities, introduced a few months later, made it impossible for them to top up any shortfall in educational expenditure from other areas.

But alongside Carlisle, working as a junior minister, was Rhodes Boyson, an ex-headmaster and contributor to the Black Papers who had no hesitation, even at this early stage, in using his public pronouncements to advocate far more radical ideas than Carlisle was ready to implement. Boyson linked what he saw as the increasing anarchy of the classroom to trendy teaching methods and called for greater parental choice of school, as well as the use of vouchers to implement this. Beyond this he supported other proposals which were to become key elements in Thatcherite policy within a few years, including the publication of examination results and the use of 'league tables' of successful schools. Boyson's call to radicalise Conservative education policy gained increasing support from right-wingers such as Stuart Sexton (who later became Special Adviser to Keith Joseph), Alan Howarth of the Conservative Research Department and from his colleague Theresa Gorman, herself an ex-teacher.

In September 1981, probably as a mark of Thatcher's frustration with the rate of progress on educational issues, Mark Carlisle was replaced by Keith Joseph at the Ministry of Education. Thatcher recalls in her memoirs[6] that Joseph expressly asked to be moved to the Education Office so as to be able to implement his view that the anti-enterprise culture, which he believed was crippling British industrial competitiveness, could be challenged directly within the schools. Greater choice and the promotion of technology within the school curriculum were to be the cornerstones of his policy.

This initiated what Richard Johnson has described as a 'crisis of negativity'[7] during which new ideas were floated against a background of deepening cuts. In this context the schools found themselves increasingly under financial pressure and having to look to alternative sources of funding. In 1982 the Manpower Services Commission was used to introduce the Technical and Vocational Initiative, setting up new technological courses and new qualification routes. In practice, because it applied in reality to 'middle ability' pupils rather than the high-fliers, this scheme served only to reinforce the tracking element in the schools, by which students from particular social backgrounds found themselves likely to follow particular routes through school towards particular kinds of employment. This tied in with a government drive to ensure that all schools had microcomputers. Inexorably, the schools were losing control of their own agendas.

But still the stated objectives of the Government remained limited. Education was not highlighted in the 1983 Conservative election manifesto. But, once they were back in office, new initiatives, such as Keith Joseph's proposal for vouchers, were soon floated whilst, at the same time, the cuts programme was maintained. A verbal attack on the profession began in earnest at the 1984 North of England Conference, where Keith Joseph used his speech to attack the professionalism of teachers and to suggest the time had come for a review of their conditions of service. This identified what was to remain the central issue throughout the two-year industrial unrest which followed Joseph's remarks. At the same time teacher education was brought under closer control through the establishment of the Council for the Accreditation of Teacher Education which was set up to monitor the ways in which teacher training courses were following the curriculum laid down for them in Circular 3/84. At this time, too, those involved in teacher education became subject to governmental inspection, although for a few years at least the realities of this new situation were clouded by the fact that inspectors entered college and university premises 'by invitation'.

But, as late as 1985, in the DES Report *Better schools* it was made clear that all this did not add up to an intention to dictate the curriculum:

> It would not in the view of the Government be right for the Secretary of State's policy for the range and pattern of the 5–16 curriculum to amount to the determination of national syllabuses for that period ... The Government does not propose to introduce legislation affecting the powers of the Secretaries of State in relation to the curriculum.[8]

But, equally, there was at this time a preparedness to meddle with the structure of the system. In 1986, for example, the introduction of City Technology Colleges was announced at the Conservative Party conference. These specialist schools, which were to be dependent on private funding, posed a further threat to the autonomy of the LEAs and their power to deliver policy throughout the areas under their control. But looking back at these early years of Thatcher as Prime Minister, it has to be concluded that it was only after the bruising confrontation with the teaching profession during 1985 and 1986 that she was prepared to move towards a truly innovative and novel set of education policies. Perhaps surprisingly, Keith Joseph, who had been in many ways her closest ally in seeking to redirect the Conservative Party, proved in office to be strangely reticent to follow the logic of his own rhetoric.

It was not until Kenneth Baker replaced Keith Joseph in 1986 that Thatcher finally became prepared to move beyond consensual solutions to what those around her saw increasingly as the 'education problem'. In the early eighties, whilst he was at the Department of Trade, Baker had become frustrated at the tardiness of the Education Department in responding to his campaign to provide microcomputers in schools. Now he was prepared to impose policy to a far greater degree than any of his predecessors. He was to recall in his memoirs that:

> As Environment Minister during the rate-capping disputes I had marginalised the local government unions and their leadership by reducing the frequency of meetings ... it had been a successful strategy ... I decided to adopt it at Education. While I would of course meet with the unions ... none of them should feel they could just drop in to the Department and see me at any time.[9]

This new tone in educational politics has been neatly summarised by Stuart Maclure (2000):

> Not only was there an unshakeable conviction that the education system was failing; there was an explanation for this supplied by the New Right in politics. Thatcher and Baker spelled it out in their comments on the DES – the blame was to be laid on socialism and soft-centred liberalism. Schools were failing because teachers were tarred with a socialist brush. Worse than this the whole educational establishment was implicated in a *trahison des clercs* led by the professors and teacher trainers ... The assault on union power and the privatisation of public sector industries were ways of attacking collectivism and socialistic expectations, so too was the attack on professional autonomy in the name of consumers and their rights. Baker's reforms would be rooted in this ideology: he would claim to be the parents' representative, the consumers' friend, taking their part against the self-interested professionals and local politicians.[10]

In this new policy context of the late 1980s, the advocates of child-centred approaches in the classroom faced an uphill struggle.

Empowering the parents

If there had been signs during the 1960s and 1970s that parents were beginning to play a greater part in the politics of schooling it was the 1977 Taylor Report,[11] leading to a White Paper in December 1978 and legislation in 1980, which precipitated them fully into the educational arena. The Report ranged over the whole question of the management and government of schools and whilst it stressed that the LEA should have the ultimate responsibility for individual schools it also argued that strengthened governing bodies should stand in the formal line of responsibility between the LEA and the head of the school. These governing bodies were to represent the local authority, the staff, the community and, most significantly, the parent body. The Report stressed that, although the teachers' unions had made it clear that they thought the staff should have the ultimate responsibility for the curriculum, their view was that it was for the governing bodies to establish the aims of each school, to translate this into more specific goals, to keep the resulting education under continuous review and to take the necessary action to ensure that aims and goals were met. This was to prove a powerful and ultimately unstoppable challenge to the autonomy of the teaching profession. The legislation which followed in 1980 stipulated that, so far as possible, each school should have its own governing body and that there should be at the very least two parent governors appointed, even in the smallest schools. Further legislation in 1986 augmented the powers of these governing bodies and obliged them to spell out the 'desirable curricular aims' of their school (acting as mediators of the broad curricular aims of the local authority) and in particular to specify the content and organisation of sex education. The composition of governing bodies was specified, with local business interests being drawn in. The author recalls one governors' meeting in Birmingham at this time when, in an effort to retain the local vicar on a school governing body, there was a lengthy discussion on whether or not the Church of England could be classified as a business! Not only were the future employers as well as parents being given a direct stake in the running of schools, but the power of these governing bodies to suspend teachers was confirmed. Further, they were given the responsibility of ensuring that there was no political bias in the schools and that sex education was provided 'in a form which projected the values of family life'.[12] This abrupt transformation of the power relations between the teachers on the one hand and the parents and local business interests on the other generated a completely new context for any considerations of curriculum development.

The LEAs under pressure

From the moment that Thatcher came to power the LEAs found themselves under an unprecedented attack. The new Education Minister, Mark Carlisle, used the DES publication *Local authority arrangements for the curriculum* (November 1979) to suggest that 'the LEAs should exercise a formal system of detailed control over the curriculum of individual schools'.[13] It was the unwillingness of many local authorities to respond to this positively, because to have done so would have overturned the conventions of the previous thirty years, which led Thatcher's government towards the next step. Legislation was now used to place strict limits on the expenditure of the local authorities. The 1982 Local Government Finance Act made it impossible for them to seek alternative sources of funding. Rate-capping, which had been introduced in 1981, was now formally built into the system and it became impossible for local authorities to exceed their budgets without severe penalty, and impossible to move funding between categories of expenditure depending on their individual circumstances. The screw was tightened further in 1985 and 1986[14] and a government drive to privatise ancillary services such as cleaning and school meals placed those running the system day-by-day under even more pressure. Although much of this applied to the working of the local authorities as a whole, it proved to be particularly significant in respect of education which was responsible for by far the largest single element in local authority expenditure in most parts of the country.

During this period, too, the Inspectorate was used to report on the performance of individual local authorities, as had been originally suggested by the Raynor Report. In total, thirteen of them came under this scrutiny – in several cases having been selected for reasons peripheral to education. In 1982, for example, Toxteth was selected for this kind of inspection following the riots of the previous year. By extending the remit of HMI in this way to include local administration and finance, the Government was subtly tightening the screw for the local authorities at the same time that it added a significant new component to the role of its Schools' Inspectorate.

The other agency used by Thatcher to weaken further the LEAs was the Manpower Services Commission. Originally set up in 1974, it was the perfect vehicle through which to introduce a new scheme for the creation of ten technical schools for 14- to 16-year-olds, and this was done in November 1982. Lord Young, one of Thatcher's closest advisers at this time, commented that 'if we had gone through the usual educational machinery it would have been the end of the decade before anything happened'.[15] Despite efforts to head them off by Labour stalwarts such as Neil Kinnock, many LEAs and schools joined in this scramble for new money. At a stroke, the established pattern of schools seeing their local authorities as an exclusive source of support was broken and a new competitiveness and entrepreneurialism was introduced into educational planning. Within a few years several initiatives in the area of further education had taken this process further and had made deeper inroads on the autonomy of the LEAs.

For most of the post-War period the local education authorities had been an important source of support and resources for teachers seeking to develop new approaches in the classroom. Now, thrown into what felt increasingly like a struggle for survival, the LEAs had far less scope to encourage old-style curriculum innovation, and to have been seen to be doing so would have risked the judgement that they were antagonistic to the changes taking place. Thus, these tighter financial controls allied to a new set of power relations between central and local government had an immediate impact on what went on in the classrooms.

The empowerment of the DES

One early token of the determination of the DES to keep a closer eye on the performance of schools had been the setting up of the Assessment of Performance Unit in August 1974. It was not long before it became clear that those within the DES were increasingly determined to control what was going on within the education system far more effectively – at first through advocacy, then through the reform of examinations, and later more directly. But initially this was to be done through persuasion. The publication in 1980 of *A framework for the school curriculum* (with its stress on the importance of emphasising the core subjects in the school curriculum) and a year later of *The school curriculum* both stopped short of compulsion, although they made it clear to the LEAs what was expected of them.[16]

Through the early 1980s the DES pursued its efforts to exercise greater influence on what went on in the schools through the reform of examinations. It is impossible to overestimate the impact for those at work in the classrooms of the introduction over a very brief period of time of the CPVE, of A/S examinations and of the new GCSE. Some contemporary commentators saw this as part of a concerted attempt by the DES to establish greater central control of the education system. It certainly had the effect of focusing the attention of the teachers on the questions of how to administer and how to manage these new examinations and away from other issues. The fact that they all demanded a significant element of coursework which was to be assessed had two immediate implications. On the one hand the professionals were obliged to devote a significant part of their time to coordinating and assessing this element of their students' work and, on the other, at the same time, their ability to become involved in any other aspect of curricular innovation was necessarily restricted.

In 1984 the setting up of the Council for the Accreditation of Teacher Education brought the training of teachers under more direct governmental influence and gave a further fillip to the powers of the DES. A year later the Department published *Better schools*, a document which, among other things, gave it control of the in-service education of teachers through specific grants targeted at particular courses. However, in the same publication, reassurance was given that the ambitions of the DES remained limited:

> It would not be right, in the view of the Government, for the Secretary of State's policy for the range ... of the 5 to 16 curriculum to amount to the determination of national syllabus. The Government does not propose to introduce legislation affecting the powers of the Secretaries of State in relation to the curriculum.[17]

At the same time the practical difficulties confronting anyone wishing to influence what went on in the schools was recognised. Schools were known to be hamstrung by staffing problems which resulted in many cases in separate subjects being taught together, in staff teaching those parts of the curriculum for which they were not properly trained and, in some cases, the complete abandonment of parts of the curriculum. But despite this, in 1985, those within the DES did not think it appropriate to go beyond indirect means of control.

One key to the empowerment of the DES was the demolition of the Schools Council, which was widely seen as giving voice to the teachers themselves in matters of curriculum reform. As we have seen, it had come under attack from several sources quite soon after its inception. The Yellow Book drawn up as a preamble to the Ruskin speech in 1976 had commented that 'the Schools Council has performed moderately in commissioning development work in particular curricular areas ... It has scarcely begun to tackle the problems of the curriculum as a whole. Its overall performance on both curriculum and examinations has been mediocre'.[18] In 1981 the Trenamen Report claimed that 'the Schools Council has not had a wide effect in the classroom'[19] but concluded that it still had a part to play. But the Council was by this time seen by many observers as standing for piecemeal reform of the curriculum and as being in the way of any more comprehensive reforms coordinated from the centre. It was seen, too, as a bastion of teacher influence. Accordingly, following the Trenamen Report, Keith Joseph announced that it would be wound up in January 1984. It was to be replaced by two bodies: the Secondary Examinations Council and the School Development Curriculum Committee. The fact that the first of these quickly came to play a significant role while the second was allowed to wither on the vine, having little discernible impact on policy, speaks volumes about governmental approaches to curriculum change during these years.

It must be emphasised though that, in the new order that was developing, the DES was only to be given power so long as it conformed to the aspirations and views of the Government itself. This became particularly evident when Kenneth Baker took over as Secretary of State for Education in May 1986. Baker's own account of his tenure of the education office emphasised that when he took over: 'Ministerial morale was low; due in no small part to an inability to push distinctly Conservative policies past powerful civil servants' opposition'. In his view,

> of all Whitehall Departments the DES was among those with the strongest in-house ideology. There was a clear 1960s ethos and a very clear agenda which permeated virtually all the civil servants. It was rooted in 'progressive' orthodoxies ... It was devoutly anti-excellence, anti-selection and anti-market ... Not only was the Department in league with the teacher unions, university Departments of Education, teacher training theories and local authorities, it also acted as their protector against any threats which Ministers might pose. If the civil servants were the guardians of this culture, then Her Majesty's Inspectors ... were its priesthood.[20]

Against this background, the 1988 Education Reform Act was to confirm this growing power of the DES. The Act's significance has been neatly summarised by Richard Johnson who claimed that

> it introduced an unparalleled degree of central direction into curriculum matters. It continued the erosion of LEA powers in relation to schools, colleges and polytechnics. It abolished the major rival to the central state, ILEA. It completed the long-standing moves away from consultative and representative bodies and towards managing agencies like the new Schools and Examinations Assessment Council and the National Curriculum Council. It was accompanied by Baker's assumption of power over salaries and conditions. In short, the 1988 Act and its associated policies destroyed the conventions about 'partnership', subordinated LEAs to the DES and restructured professional relationships.[21]

It was a step-change which transformed permanently the way in which curriculum reform was approached in modern Britain.

A new role for the Inspectorate

The 1980s saw a transformation of the role of the Schools' Inspectorate, but this was at the expense of what many involved saw as a complete reorganisation of their duties and their mode of working. Whilst the decision to publish their reports on individual schools gave them unprecedented influence, it also led to the swift realisation that the criteria upon which their judgements were based must be agreed and must be more transparent. The consequence was that this became a decade in which the day-by-day procedures of the Inspectorate were repeatedly sharpened up and became increasingly specified. The accepted wisdom that inspectors could form their subjective judgements of the effectiveness of learning and confine themselves to relatively brief written reports was replaced by the insistence that clearly identified criteria must all be worked through and assessed.

Many experienced inspectors complained that this meant that much more of their time was devoted to paperwork, reducing the number of schools they had time to visit. One inspector commented at the time that

> at the beginning of the 1980s HMI saw their task as being to judge the quality of work. Examination results were peripheral ... partly because they reflected pupils' ability at least as much as teaching, still more because they told nothing of the educational experience ... It was quite a shock when in the later 1980s word came down that what concerned Ministers was 'standards', 'performance' or even 'output', not quality ... In 1990–91 all HMI subject committees were required to draft criteria for justifying the quality of work seen, as part of the drive to achieve greater precision and objectivity in reporting ... The years 1980 to 1992 were characterised by a continual sharpening of the focus of inspection and systematising of procedures.

In an even more crucial tone, one of his colleagues commented that by the mid-1980s for the inspectorate

> the situation had drastically changed. In the misguided belief that, if sufficient detail were committed to print on every aspect of every visit, then someone, some day, would have the means, time and inclination to 'retrieve' it, we were gradually driven to spend more and more time writing longer and longer notes on ever fewer visits ... All that happened was that, as the trees proliferated, the 'wood' became more opaque.

Beyond this, he added,

> there were two other; and even more pernicious developments: the demand for published 'inspection criteria' and the heavy reliance on 'performance

indicators' ... The ready availability and apparent objectivity of 'performance indicators' ensured that, quite regardless of their validity, they would erode and finally eliminate the scope for professional judgement.[22]

These observations reflect the difficulty which many experienced professionals had in coming to terms with the changes taking place during the 1980s. They reflect a deep sense of contest which pervaded the education system at this time. It was a clash between those who saw established and tried practice, in which they saw value, being undermined and eroded, and those who welcomed the application of new ideas and new practices to a profession which some saw as being in need of new challenges and greater accountability. But, in this contested situation, the redefinition of the role of the Inspectorate meant that it became one of the mid-wives of a new educational settlement. It also meant that, during the early years of the implementation of the national curriculum at least, HMI became one of the voices which, through their published reports, had the capacity to comment, if only obliquely, on government policy itself. In this way the Inspectorate was to become one of the key reasons why it proved necessary to rework the national curriculum introduced by the 1988 Act within a few years of its inception.

The reform of examinations

By the early 1980s the reform of examinations was beginning to appear long overdue. The GCE examination, which had replaced the old school certificate in 1951, had been supplemented in 1965 by the CSE, which catered for 'middle abil-ity' pupils. The CSE, like GCE, was a subject-based examination and in most subjects there was a significant element of assessed coursework. The teachers themselves came to play a central role in both the administration and conduct of these courses. As early as 1960 the Beloe Report had advocated a single examina-tion which could serve a far wider spectrum of ability. During the late sixties and early seventies one of the outcomes of the work of the Schools Council was the appearance of a significant number of limited experiments in which one or other of the GCE examining boards would cooperate with a sister CSE board to devise a shared examination which was applicable to a much wider range of students than either of the individual examinations. These GCE–CSE projects fostered a widespread anticipation that some kind of merger of the two systems was only a matter of time. In the event both Shirley Williams and Mark Carlisle procrasti-nated over this move, leaving it to Keith Joseph in June 1984 to announce the introduction of a new GCSE examination to replace the two pre-existing systems, to be implemented in 1988. Three things followed from this: the assessment of coursework became a permanent element in almost all examining procedures; the influence of the teachers was necessarily diminished; and by preserving many of the features of the GCE the new GCSE was established as, at heart, an elite exam-ination, serving above all the most able pupils. The teachers themselves were left protesting that they were short of resources and time to trial and introduce the new examination in the announced timescale.

Whilst on the one hand the greater emphasis on continuous assessment and coursework seemed to militate against the worst evils of the unseen written examination, it was also, in reality, a gift to those members of the middle classes who had more resources to provide a supportive home environment and might have more chance, for a variety of reasons, of giving practical help. It also helped inexorably change the practical realities of examining by enabling the introduction of an element of negotiation between student and school assessor which had not existed previously and which also worked to subtly undermine and transform the role of the teacher.

Equally significant for the development of the curriculum as a whole at this time was the Government's introduction of the Certificate of Pre-Vocational Education for those 16-to-17-year-olds thought unsuited to Advanced level. Morris and Griggs (1988) have neatly summarised this as typifying 'the government's educational approach: general education on more traditional lines for a minority of young people; vocationally directed education for most'.[23] Alongside this the reinforcement of vocationalism continued apace with the introduction of the Technical and Vocational Initiative, funded through the MSC. This introduction of alternative sources of funding for schools further weakened the LEAs and the scheme itself gave power to the government's intention to reinforce distinct and different routes through school for pupils from differing backgrounds and with differing aspirations.

Finally, under the legislation introduced in 1988, Standard Attainment Targets were established for pupils at each of the four key stages identified by the Act. They were to be administered by the School Examinations and Assessment Council, and, like the other reforms made to the examining regime, they were to involve the teachers in lengthy procedures to ensure compliance and necessarily involved an incremental increase in record-keeping. By the end of the decade much of the day-by-day functioning of the teaching profession had been transformed into a series of chores to meet externally specified criteria. The records of achievement which also became universal at this time meant, on the one hand, a further increase in paperwork and, on the other, that what went on in the classrooms was increasingly susceptible to external moderation and influence. The 'golden age' of teacher autonomy was well and truly over!

The expropriation of progressivism

The politics of educational change during these years developed in such a way, and had such a profound impact on classroom practice, that it became possible for the most enthusiastic advocates of this new regime to lay claim to being the inheritors and interpreters of a well-established tradition of child-centred approaches to teaching. So, for example, the educational aims which were laid out in the DES publication *Better schools* (1985) at one level appeared to be uncontroversial and in line with much progressive thinking. According to this policy pronouncement the aims were to help pupils develop lively enquiring minds, to acquire understanding, knowledge and skills relevant to adult life, to develop effective use of language and number, to develop tolerance and moral values and to help towards an understanding of human interdependence:

> It is vital that schools should always remember that preparation for working life is one of their principal functions. The economic stresses of our time and the pressures of international competition make it more necessary than ever before that Britain's work-force should possess the skills and attitudes, the understanding, enterprise and adaptability ... that the pervasive impact of technological advance will increasingly demand ... The balance within the curriculum, and the emphasis in teaching it, now need to alter accordingly.[24]

One contemporary commentator, James Avis, put his finger on the ways in which the new examination routes being pioneered at this time were able to appeal to, and at the same time distort, some of the key themes of progressivism. He argues that

> many of the themes raised in the CPVE are an appropriation of progressive education. This is reflected in the concern with a student-centred, activity-based education that relates to the interests and needs of the learner. This progressivism, which presents itself as radical, is in fact deeply conservative. The focus on relevance, needs and interests is the bulwark of progressivism, and in radical versions these are used to transcend the present, to consider possibilities and to develop critical insights into the nature of society. Yet the curriculum framework of the CPVE limits this possibility.

He went on to argue that this new examination route effectively reinforced the distinction between mental and manual labour by establishing vocational education as an alternative to academic for those pupils following the CPVE programme. His view was that both the new YTS courses and those set up by the new Further Education Unit involved precisely this expropriation of progressivism, attaching it to and using it to justify a far narrower set of educational and social goals than those sought by earlier supporters of progressive education.[25] He concluded glumly that 'the strange fate of progressive education has been its transformation into a form of conservative education'.[26]

The teachers brought to heel

The structural changes which took place in the teaching profession itself at this time become a key part of any explanation of how the curriculum came to develop as it did. As the schools and colleges became larger and more bureaucratised (a process accelerated by the Thatcher reforms) new power structures emerged and clear career structures for teachers through carefully graded jobs and roles began to develop. This made schools more managerial in several senses and resulted in the appearance of a new kind of career professional who was attuned in performing not only his or her (more usually his!) immediate professional role but also a set of defined tasks and chores which were seen to be leading towards the next rung of the career ladder. And this in turn helped to generate a 'can do' approach in some teachers which helps explain internal divisions within the profession and a dilution of staffroom collegiality during these years. The appeal to a new kind of professionalism made it easier for Thatcher to steamroller the teaching profession during the mid-1980s.

These changes were also underpinned by a transformation of in-service education for teachers which had a devastating impact on curriculum reform. During the 1960s and early 70s, almost all of the work of the teacher centres set up by the LEAs (as well as the evening courses offered by the university education departments) had been focused on the curricular reforms of bodies such as the Schools Council or the Nuffield Foundation. The process of teaching was at the heart of in-service work. Inexorably, during the 1980s the nature of the courses offered by the universities and colleges shifted from teaching to management and administration (two of the buzz-words of the decade). 'Section Eleven' money (the funding used to resource in-service work) was deployed to direct teachers increasingly towards work which focused on management issues. This became a significant element in the career progression of teachers and involved the semi-permanent marginalisation of curriculum reform. Those in-service courses which did deal directly with curricular issues were, as often as not, preoccupied with questions about how best to implement and administer the new forms of examination which were being introduced. The preoccupation with continuous assessment came to dominate much of the discourse around the curriculum at this time.

One example of this new managerialism within the teaching profession itself was the relatively warm reception given to Keith Joseph's speech at the North of England Educational Conference at Sheffield in January 1985. This was described as winning 'remarkable bipartisan support' by one contemporary.[27] The managers (a term which was becoming increasingly applicable to those running the education service and which would never have been used twenty years earlier) were becoming increasingly ready to acquiesce in the emerging Thatcherite educational settlement.

During this decade also, there were shifts in the balance of power which meant a diminution in the influence of the profession. One of the most significant increments in this process was the imposition of the Teachers' Pay and Conditions Act in 1987, following the arbitrary termination of their industrial action by Kenneth Baker. It had been little short of folly for the teachers' unions to think they had a real chance of successful industrial action after the brutal suppression of the miners' strike only months before. Inter-union rivalries served only to weaken their position. The extent to which all this had been counterproductive was made clear when the 1987 Act imposed the humiliating condition that teachers must work 1,265 hours each year and that this was to involve their being available for no fewer than 195 days. At the same time the teachers' negotiating rights on both pay and conditions of service were summarily taken away from them, in the first instance for three years. It would have been difficult to devise a more potent demonstration of governmental lack of faith in the professionalism of teachers.

What all this amounted to was the de-professionalisation of teaching. Writing at the time, Richard Johnson reflected that perhaps the most significant strategy of the Government was, as a calculated act,

> de-professionalisation. Plans to transform teacher education, to introduce untrained teachers, to break up national rates, already point in this direction. These measures will increase direct control of the curriculum; they amount to the proletarianisation of teaching ... There is a world of difference between professionals who can take pride in what they teach because they have some control and expertise in it, and 'staff' who 'deliver' a curriculum which actually controls *them*.[28]

The 1988 legislation: a new settlement confirmed

Emboldened by her success in quelling the teachers' long-running industrial dispute, Margaret Thatcher announced at the time of her third electoral victory in 1987 that

> we are going much further in education than we ever thought of doing before ... there is still so much wrong, so we are going to do something determined about it ... There is going to be a revolution in the running of schools.[29]

Within a year her government had rushed through the Education Reform Act, which many saw as an attack on most of the assumptions which had underpinned educational policymaking in twentieth-century Britain. This legislation certainly laid down the main lines of policy and practice for the whole period since then.

The Bill was published in November 1987 following a brief two-month period of consultation, which had coincided with the summer vacation and which, despite this, saw three van-loads of protest letters arrive at the DES. In respect of the curriculum the Bill made clear from the outset the key components of what was to become a new educational settlement. A national curriculum was to be established through three interlinked initiatives. First, the knowledge, skills and understanding expected of pupils at four key stages of their schooling were specified by means of 'attainment targets'. What was required to be taught was specified through 'programmes of study' and, no less important, assessment arrangements were spelt out to provide for the monitoring of student progress towards the end of each key stage. At a stroke, the questions of both what should be taught and how it might be taught were taken away from the teachers and put under the care and control of a supervisory state mechanism. What made this particularly powerful was the determination to place it all in the public domain. The publication of results facilitated (as it was meant to do) the drawing up of 'league tables' of schools. A further blow to the autonomy of the educational establishment was the provision to bring to an end the Inner London Education Authority, which was seen by many within government circles as the embodiment of all that Thatcher's government was opposed to in education. This was a development which, by demonstrating their vulnerability, undermined further the viability of all local authorities. Perhaps most significantly, the Act set school against school by making their funding in large part dependent on their ability to attract students. If vouchers had proved unacceptable during the early eighties, now making the students themselves the vouchers became politically feasible. This is what the Act did and, in the process, it ensured that there would now be a new element of managerialism in the running of schools in England and Wales. Above all, as one of the key authors of the legislation, Nick Stuart, a Deputy Secretary at the DES, stated at the time in a training video for teachers, the central intention was to make the system accountable in ways it had never been before. The outcome was that each school, and to a lesser extent each teacher, was obliged to keep their public and their market constantly in mind. Never again would the profession be able to dictate what went on in the schools.

Duncan Graham, the new head of the National Curriculum Council set up by the legislation, was in no doubt about the longer-term significance of all this. In his memoirs (1993) he commented that at this time

> I became acutely aware that in its implementation and substance this was a Civil Service driven curriculum and not the property of HMI. This was the first evidence of a huge de facto power shift in the way education was controlled in England and Wales. The HMI were adjuncts and the inspectors on the working group were extremely helpful but they were not the driving force: that was the civil servants. The national curriculum was their baby, the first major educational reform in Britain that had not been created by the education professionals.[30]

Classroom realities

Meanwhile, it is far from clear that the 'classroom revolution' which had set alarm bells ringing amongst those on the right politically, in reality added up to very much at all. Jane Woodhouse, who researched classroom practice at this time, pointed out that extensive inspectors' reports during the late 1970s

> revealed that public anxieties about teaching methods were misplaced and many government criticisms unsubstantiated ... Standards had not fallen. Children were generally quiet and well-behaved, and were being taught in a largely didactic manner under the teachers' firm control. In particular ... far from having abandoned the basics, children were spending most of their time in the repetition of isolated tasks in literacy and numeracy. This picture of the primary classroom hardly conformed to the Black Paper image, or the government's impression of schools where modern methods had got out of hand ... The primary revolution had hardly fired its first shot, let alone progressed to threatening the social order. The child-centred approach, though it had become the established theoretical orthodoxy, had clearly failed to percolate down to the grassroots level of education.[31]

In a similar vein, Don Jones, writing about developments at this time has commented that 'the research findings of the ORACLE project at Leicester University have cast doubt upon whether, from a pedagogical point of view at least, any revolution at all has taken place in the primary school'.[32]

But even though the new right were playing on fears which may have been largely unfounded, or at best only partially justifiable, there can be no doubt that the working through of government policy at this time, in response to these fears, had a dramatic impact both on what went on in the classrooms and in the attitudes of the profession as a whole. First, the involvement of teachers in wide-scale curriculum reform became far more difficult to sustain. In-service education and out-of-school activity became largely concentrated either on aspects of management and administration or on the issues and problems raised by the new examinations. Meanwhile, within the school, teachers were confronted by a set of chores involving far more paperwork than had previously been the case. The loss of negotiating rights, as well as the whole tenor of governmental rhetoric about the teaching profession, involved a massive loss of self-esteem and a sense that teaching was being de-professionalised. This became the decade during which there was a collapse in much out-of-school activity (previously provided on a voluntary basis and reflecting the enthusiasm of many teachers for what they were about). In this respect school sport suffered particularly badly. But perhaps most debilitating was the widespread sense within the school staffrooms that teachers were becoming the deliverers of other people's messages rather than (as had been the case previously) the arbiters of what went on in the schools. Alongside this, the new situation, in which both the local authorities and the Schools' Inspectorate found themselves, meant that they could no longer provide the kinds of practical support for teachers which had been a hallmark of their work since the Second World War. The professional partnerships which for many years had been such a strong element in the state provision of schooling in Britain were being eroded under the impact of these new Thatcherite educational policies.

Against this background, the profession found itself split into those who were prepared to work through and implement the new regime (and in the process confirm new routes towards promotion) and those who remained unsympathetic, at best acquiescent and at worst uncooperative. These new tensions within the school staffrooms were exacerbated by the strong feeling aroused by the protracted industrial dispute of the mid-1980s. The establishment of the new Professional Association of Teachers, which was opposed to any form of industrial action, served only to confirm that there were deep-rooted divisions within the profession. Its very existence had the side-effect of eroding further any residual sense of collegiality within the school staffrooms. This was indeed the decade during which a new order was established, but it was one which had the effect of permanently drawing teachers away from issues such as the establishment of child-centred education towards meeting the demands of the new target-setting regime and of new routes towards career advancement. For many within the profession, there was a sense that things might never be quite the same again.

6 'Forging a new consensus in education'[1]

The implementation of the Education Reform Act, 1989–97

Once you have put out an approved curriculum, if you have got it wrong the situation is worse afterwards than it was before ... I do not think I ever thought they would do the curriculum in such detail.

Margaret Thatcher, quoted in the *TES*, 17 April 1990, p. 18

Underlying this chapter is the question of why things turned out as they did in the years following the passage of the Education Reform Act in 1988. Whilst it may appear that once the Act was in force the die was cast, in reality the nature of the new educational settlement which emerged was the result of a series of messy compromises and power struggles between a range of interest groups which determined the nature of both what was to be taught and classroom practice into the twenty-first century. What follows is my attempt to describe and explain this process.

There can be no doubt though that Kenneth Baker cast a long shadow. His bruising style and his determination to push through a reform package was evident both in the run-up to legislation and in the immediate aftermath. His determination to hurry through the setting up of subject working groups which would hammer out the details of the new national curriculum, his imposition of deadlines which had to be met (shortly after the Third Reading, the national curriculum was announced as coming into effect in September 1989) and the introduction of new procedures to test the effectiveness of the new curriculum arrangements meant that his reputation as Cabinet hard man, which he had won in the run-up to legislation, was merely underlined. This all meant that the few years following the passage of the legislation were, for those involved in any way in teaching or education, among the most tumultuous in living memory, in terms of both their massive long-term impact on classroom practice and their consequences for the politics of education at the start of the twenty-first century.

A profession under stress

The first direct result was that there was soon clear evidence of the teaching profession undergoing considerable stress. This worked itself out in several ways, but had enormous implications for the curriculum. At the start of 1989 the *TES* was reporting that across the country training programmes were being set up to help teachers cope with the new demands. In many counties, such as Hertfordshire, cascade methods of training were used in a situation where there were simply not enough resources to release all teachers from school to attend in-service classes. The educational press was quick to point out the massive increase in paperwork and record-keeping for teachers which was implicit in the new regime and there were soon predictions that many of the demands of the national curriculum would be beyond individual teachers working in isolation, particularly in the primary sector. Some commentators saw the need for unprecedented cooperation and collaboration between individual teachers, suggesting that the whole nature of the primary school experience would need to be transformed. Presciently, a growing need for supply teachers to cover the inevitable gaps caused by the introduction of the national curriculum was also foreseen. The *TES* reflected gloomily at the start of 1989 that 'some heads see themselves as being like First World War generals, sending their troops over the top without question on the orders of Field Marshal Baker. They warned that there would be casualties and desertions'. One head said: 'I can see some of my staff saying this is not worth the bother, and I will lose teachers'. The *TES* added pointedly: 'without non-contact time and cover, it will not work. There would be less time for teaching and a danger of lessons becoming "stylised" which would lead to curriculum atrophy'.[2]

The educational press continued to take a dim view of the prospects for those working in the schools. Another lead article in the *TES* in January 1989 reflected that 'taken at face value the flood of orders and ukases threatens to overwhelm the education service'. It foresaw demands for in-service education which could not possibly be met and pointed out that to introduce at the same time the new funding arrangements involved in the Government's new Local Management of Schools programme would necessarily result in 'severe professional overload ... To meet the financial targets set out in the public expenditure White Paper there will have to be staff reductions in many schools ... Local school management automatically ends the LEA's executive power to relocate its staff'.[3] By the summer the head teachers of every secondary school in Luton had banded together to call for a postponement of the introduction of LMS since no allowances had been made for the age profiles of teachers in individual schools or the state of the buildings.

Six months later the publication in *Junior Education* of the findings of a research project conducted by Ted Wragg, Neville Bennett and Clive Carre into stress levels among primary schoolteachers resulted in another *TES* leader article reflecting lack of confidence in the prospects for the national curriculum:

> The small confidence scores in regard to design technology, music and especially science are serious because Mr. Baker cannot afford the national curriculum to go off half-cock. But it is profoundly unsurprising. Until now the primary schools have had few specialists in science, music or design technology ... How can they be confident of teaching these subjects in the

national curriculum if they have only a hazy grasp of these matters? Perhaps it is more worrying that one in five primary teachers don't feel competent to teach the prescribed syllabus in English, and one in three lack confidence in maths – subjects which have always been the primary core.

This article foresaw the need for 'in-service training on a grand scale' if there was to be any hope of the primary schools coping with the demands being placed on them by the government.[4]

Some hint of the increased tensions between the teachers and their masters which were generated by this situation became clear when, in March 1990, sources at the DES suggested that it was the teachers who had brought this stress upon themselves. A press release was used to suggest that the vast increase in workload which had accrued since the Act was passed was the result of teachers 'jumping the gun' and undertaking tasks not yet required of them.[5] Certainly, there were some members of the profession who had set to with a will once the legislation was in place, but there can be no doubt that the situation provoked significant foreboding about what was going to be entailed for the teaching profession if the legislation was going to be made to work. Many responded by seeking to get ahead of the game if modifications to their day-by-day practice were going to be required anyway. One result was that, as a survey by the NASUWT showed, by early 1990 most women teachers were working twice as long as the minimum imposed by the Government in their 1987 conditions of employment, more than half of this time being spent on the new 'non-teaching' activities which were accruing from the legislation.

During the months that followed these pressures resulted in new and unprecedented levels of absenteeism among schoolteachers. By April 1990, according to one estimate, absenteeism was costing the education service an extra £230 million each year, with one-third of all teachers actively seeking jobs outside the teaching profession and two-thirds considering such a move. Professor Gary Cooper of UMIST, who had researched this issue, claimed that dissatisfaction rates in teaching were currently five times those for the industrial sector. Teaching was no longer being seen as an attractive career and this fact alone was to be of major significance for teacher recruitment during the following twenty years.[6] Three months later a report by Professor Jim Campbell of the University of Warwick on teacher stress resulted in major lobbying campaigns being mounted by AMMA, the NUT and the NAHT on behalf of their members. It seemed, if only on this issue, that the Government was succeeding in doing what had proved impossible for over a century, and that was to unite the teaching unions.[7]

Increasingly, it was the teachers of older pupils in the primary sector who were seen as being under greatest pressure. The chief HMI, Eric Bolton, singled out 'the upper years of primary school as showing cause for concern' in his 1991 annual report. In his view the reasons for this were clear. The new curriculum demanded a wide range of expertise. The tradition of class teaching rather than subject teaching persisted at this level. There was little time for in-service work or even to prepare lessons for most classroom teachers. The result, according to

Bolton, was that 'in about two-thirds of schools the curriculum is not demanding enough for the older and abler pupils: in effect many pupils are capable of higher achievements than those expected of them or made possible'.[8] Two years later this view was confirmed by Bolton's successor as Chief HMI, Stewart Sutherland, who, on the basis of three HMI reports on the difficulties of introducing the national curriculum in the primary sector concluded that 'almost a third of lessons in the top end of the primary schools are unsatisfactory and some are downright poor'.[9] This new and rather dismissive rhetoric to which teachers became subject during these years, as outside authorities pontificated on their ability and performance, only added to the sense of stress within the profession. Thus, one first casualty of the national curriculum was, almost necessarily, the self-esteem of the teaching profession and this was to have an enduring impact on the preparedness and ability of teachers to set about classroom innovation. The key reason that the profession felt an acute sense of stress was that the initiative had been taken away from it in matters of classroom practice. As Ted Wragg pointed out at this time, there were 11,789 responses from within the profession to the first proposals for a national curriculum. All were ignored. This semi-permanent marginalisation of the classroom teacher was to have long-term consequences for curriculum development.

Finding the 'gold star' teachers: meeting the staffing challenges

Set against this gloomy account of the impact of the 1988 legislation on many teachers was the Government's drive to promote and reward those who could make the new settlement work. No sooner was John MacGregor appointed as Education Minister in September 1989 than he announced a new pay package which would involve bonuses for what he called the 'gold star' teachers who provided a role model for their staffroom colleagues.[10] At much the same time the licensed teacher scheme was unveiled, as an attempt to head off a foreseeable and growing teacher shortage. It offered a fast-track route into teaching on half pay for those wishing to enter but lacking the normal qualifications.[11] The first entrants were to begin work in the autumn of 1990 through twelve pilot schemes intended to generate 500 extra teachers. By the late autumn, Tim Eggar, Secretary of State for Education was able to claim that this school-based approach was to be the model for all future teacher training. Beyond this, before the end of the 1980s, the *TES* was reporting the first steps towards a privatised teacher-training system which was starting to appear alongside the established routes into teaching. Chris King, an Islington Labour Party councillor, was reported as setting up 'Time Plan Educational Services' to offer licensed teachers to local authorities. The object was to recruit teachers from untried routes and from overseas to meet the growing staffing crisis, particularly in shortage subjects. Within a few years there were several such agencies providing what were in essence privatised staff recruitment services. These developments were all tokens of deep-seated transformations in the profession which did not augur well for the preparedness of teachers to initiate curriculum change in the ways they had done previously. Teaching was coming to be seen as a contractual job rather than a profession by many new entrants.[12]

As well as this restructuring of initial teacher education, the government set about an even more significant project during the early nineties, the introduction of performance-related pay for teachers. By 1991 the *TES* was able to report that one head in Stockport was to become the highest paid in the country with a pay rise of over £12,000. Although one delegate at an SHA conference warned of 'the dangers of reaching for the greed button' and another spoke of 'heads topping up their salaries with flexible payments to the detriment of colleagues', this did not stop many head teachers from moving at this time onto performance-related pay deals. Andy Dixon of the NUT commented that 'this is very divisive when most teachers are facing pay rises well below inflation to see individual heads trying to cream off school funds'. On the one hand this has to be seen as one aspect of the new managerialism, which was impacting on many parts of the economy at this time, and on the other it is evidence of a growing rift in the profession between those who were being more highly rewarded for managing the implementation of the new settlement and those classroom teachers who did not aspire to headship or were antagonistic to the changes taking place. It was a set of tensions which the profession could have done without and which did little for the cause of curriculum reform.[13] It was during the following few years that the Government moved towards introducing performance-related pay and annual appraisals for all teachers.[14] Also, the nature of in-service work was transformed at this time, with a plethora of courses appearing on educational management (and within a few years on leadership too) as a growing number of tutors were recruited to the university education departments as much for what they had to offer in terms of administrative expertise as classroom excellence. In 1990 the *TES* announced the appearance of the first government centre for training potential head teachers at Oxford Polytechnic, sponsored by British Telecom. Its functions were to identify and train potential head teachers and to offer support to those already in post. Within a few years formal qualifications were being introduced for those intending to become head teachers.[15] So a further consequence of the 1988 legislation was that the routes into and through a teaching career were permanently transformed. The key developments took place in the years immediately following the passage of the Act and they meant that perceptions of teachers and a teaching career were never quite the same again. In the immediate post-War period teachers had played a central role in curriculum reform. These changes meant that it was extremely unlikely that this would continue to be the case.

The bureaucratisation of the system

A second consequence of the introduction of the national curriculum, also pregnant with significance for what went on in the classroom, was the bureaucratisation of the system. The new arrangements were implemented through a flood of circulars and directives and, beyond this, far more extensive documentation of classroom practice became necessary as records of achievement became pretty well universal.

Two letters published by the *TES* captured neatly the response of some teachers to these demands. First, on 20 July 1990, T. W. Hall, head of Newnham Middle School, Bedfordshire, summarised the frustrations felt by many teachers:

> I have just received another package of bureaucracy from the DES. This time it's ten copies of the Annual Curriculum Return, three copies of the new statutory regulations concerning it and three copies of a letter explaining the revised form of the return. This lot, with the plethora of information/advice/requirements arriving on my desk from other bodies such as the National Curriculum Council, the School Examinations and Assessment Council and the local authority must account for at least three Amazonian rain forest trees sent to the school this year.
>
> Some fairly senior bureaucrat at the DES came up with the idea last year, or was it the year before, of requiring schools to produce an annual CPD (curriculum development plan) for their governing bodies. Many head teachers argued that they had been involved in curriculum planning for the whole of their professional lives at one level or another, but these arguments were ignored. They were told this would be a useful exercise as the document, or at least the processes leading to its production, could be regarded as a useful planning tool. This became a statutory requirement for all schools. All it turned out to be ... is a great deal of extra work to produce a formal document encapsulating what had previously consisted of a number of informal processes – with precisely the same end result. And, beyond this, Bedfordshire wants written school development plans![16]

The tone may have been cynical, but the message was of a new imposition on the teaching profession. This bleak picture was confirmed by a Leverhulme Report in January 1990 in which 'headmasters painted a graphic picture of mounds of documents and paperwork sitting on their desks ... the time they could spend with their children was decreasing as the amount of administration increased.' [17]

Beyond this the new wave of paperwork meant not simply, as many teachers saw it, a distraction from class teaching, but it also had a direct impact on the process of teaching itself. A recognition of this development was implicit in another letter sent to the *TES*, this time from Neil Leathers of Watford. He wrote in December 1992:

> When the core subject folders were thrown at teachers three years ago I leafed through the pages and skimmed what was, basically, a new language. Astonished that anybody could really believe that this neat, new system of ticking boxes, compartmentalising and dehumanising education would actually work, I sat back and waited [for the reaction]. Now, six other folders and numerous changes later ... we're in the biggest pickle ever. The national curriculum is too weighty, wordy and jargonistic ... Still, it's a no-loss situation for the government: if the national curriculum appears to be trundling along well it will slap itself on the back: and if it's the huge messy failure I know it really will be, it'll be the teachers' fault.[18]

What is significant about this letter is not so much its assumption that the national curriculum would in some way fail, but the realisation that its implementation involved the imposition of a new discourse on teachers and an approach to the classroom which was focused on meeting specified objectives. This 'tick-list' approach to teaching meant that the teachers were becoming, whether they liked it or not, the deliverers of other people's messages in ways that they had never been before.

The financial implications of the new order

The introduction of the national curriculum also confirmed the new financial context within which schools would now have to work. This, too, was to be an important determinant of what was possible in the classroom. It became clear immediately that problems of underfunding were bound to impact on the introduction of the national curriculum. In January 1989 a *TES* leader warned that 'in order to meet the financial targets in the public expenditure White Paper there will have to be staff reductions in many secondary schools', adding that the problem was only exacerbated by the introduction of LMS at the same time, since this curtailed the ability of local authorities to relocate staff between schools.[19] In July David Hart of the NAHT wrote formally to Baker to warn of the dangers posed to government plans by the underfunding of schools, a problem which his union felt could only be made worse by the introduction of LMS.[20] At the end of the year John Dunford, a Durham head teacher, pleaded publicly that the implementation of the national curriculum might be delayed for a year because of staffing shortages.[21]

By the spring of 1990 news was beginning to come in of schools in deep trouble. The April conference of the Secondary Heads' Association highlighted several local authorities, and one school in particular: Royston Comprehensive in Barnsley. Here, in an area which already had one of the highest pupil/teacher ratios in the country, as well as one of the lowest staying-on rates at sixteen years of age, the local authority was seeking to cut ten million pounds annually from its budget and the school faced complete financial destabilisation.[22] A month later the first sackings of teachers under LMS were announced in Oldham and Surrey.[23]

The implications of all this were succinctly summarised in a letter to *The Times* from a Berkhamsted teacher. He wrote:

> the government's national curriculum looks towards the best practice ... In his recent party political broadcast Baker was advocating throwing away logarithmic tables and slide rules in favour of calculators and computers in schools. Sadly the 400 pupils in the school where I work have only two old computers which work intermittently and nine calculators. With the minimum amount of finance available for implementing the national curriculum I shall soon be having maths lessons where pupils make their own slide rules. Quite simply, there is no way in which our children have adequate access even to low level technology ... This is because the government has the ability to make laws but the inability to cure its own myopia and realise that to move forward requires a massive investment.

He went on to predict that it was inevitable that there would be

> an unprecedented resignation of head teachers and questioning the logic of becoming a head teacher in the future ... our children are not going to get the education they really deserve if all politicians do is make statements and fail to invest in full and proper resources.[24]

'The road back to the 1930s': the drive for magnet schools

In 1986 at the Conservative Party conference the introduction of City Technology Colleges had been announced. For over a century there had been people who were prepared to advocate differing curricula in different schools. During the final third of the nineteenth century the call was for modern secondary schools to complement those offering a Classical curriculum. At the end of the century higher grade elementary schools were advocated to raise standards in technological subjects. For much of the twentieth century 'tripartism' involved the setting up of three different kinds of secondary school and many had seen this as the preferred route to universal secondary schooling. If the calls for comprehensivisation had seen a muting of this lobby, it had never entirely disappeared. In one way or another, those who believed that there were significant contrasts in interest and academic performance between individuals which were largely inherent and which no education system should militate against had continued to influence public policy. Many onlookers saw these arguments as being in reality no more and no less than grounds on which those already advantaged (the middling classes) were seeking to ensure that their own children did not run the risk of being squeezed out of preferred career routes through an open education system which offered the same experience to all pupils. At the start of the 1990s, the government drive to establish 'magnet' schools has to be seen as the most recent increment in this long-running saga.

The City Technology Trust had been set up in 1987 with a target of organising twenty pilot schemes in the first instance. Kent was one county to be keenly attracted by this initiative and by the summer of 1989 the *TES* was identifying Geoffrey Chaucer School as its first county technology college. It was to receive £500,000 from the local authority with 'verbal promises of support from industry and commerce'. The *TES* saw this as evidence of 'a push within Conservative controlled LEAs towards specialist schools', which were increasingly becoming known as 'magnet schools'.[25] The significance of this development was neatly summarised in an editorial:

> Kent, if anywhere, is the natural home of such an initiative since it was a pathfinder in the post-War technical school movement which assumed that technical aptitude could be measured in pupils at 11 as much as academic ability ... Admission would be by parental preference and, if over subscribed, by interview, aptitude tests and primary school recommendations.

The *TES* went on to explain that 'Wandsworth plans to turn every comprehensive into a magnet school and is looking to experiments such as "tracking" and streaming children according to their ability in different subjects'. The old dogmas were coming back with a vengeance!

But so too were old antagonisms. In Wandsworth the heads and governors of all twelve secondary schools sent an open letter to the council threatening legal action if the Borough went ahead with its plans for magnet schools, which, they pointed out, were modelled on current practice in New York after a brief visit by some councillors.

> The Conservative controlled council ... announced last week that it would offer £10 million to encourage schools to specialise in areas such as languages, law, sport and the performing arts ... The real priorities are the recruitment of shortage subject teachers, the updating of science and technology facilities and the maintenance of school buildings.[26]

The Director of Education for Wandsworth, Donald Naismith, was identified by the *TES* as an enthusiast for magnet schools. Defending this initiative he argued that the existence of the national curriculum legitimated what his council was attempting, since it guaranteed a minimum curricular coverage for all pupils: 'Comprehensive schools can now allow themselves far greater specialisation without violating the principle of equal opportunities because we are safeguarded by the national curriculum which guarantees a broad, balanced curriculum to all'. The *TES* commented pertinently that there remained a risk that magnet schools would threaten a comprehensive system by creating two classes of school: high-status academic ones and the more vocational.[27]

The significance of these developments was seen immediately by some commentators. The new President of the NAHT, Walter Ivers, warned his members in 1989 that

> these government reforms will put schools on the road back to the 1930s ... and give advantages to mobile and articulate parents ... Children whose parents are apathetic, poor or inadequate would be sent to the nearest school prepared to take them. Such schools would increasingly be poorly resourced.

He predicted that they would struggle to attract staff and quickly become sink schools.[28]

Undeterred by these criticisms, the government pressed ahead with its plans for schools to opt out of local authority control and to take on more specialised roles. Soon after taking office, Secretary of State John MacGregor declared himself 'a great enthusiast for grant-maintained schools: I described them recently as the jewel in the crown for parent power. I have been struck by improvements in motivation and morale that they bring about'. Some parents, he added, were even to be seen wearing Grant-Maintained School stickers![29] This stance was maintained into the 1992 general election. The Conservative Party manifesto stressed continuing support from the Government for magnet schools and promised to make opting out from LEA control even easier.[30]

In July the Government published its White Paper *Choice and diversity: a new framework for schools.* This promised 'the formation of different types of schools and schools specialising in particular subjects, sometimes in partnership with industry'. It promised also to remove existing barriers to the creation of new schools.[31] These proposals generated something of a furore in educational circles. Desmond Nuttall of the Institute of Education observed that 'there is no evidence that selection testing for aptitude is viable' citing the experience of the immediate post-War years as evidence.[32] The *TES* was also sceptical, arguing that 'the strongest caveat comes from the evidence that, far from raising achievement in deprived areas, some magnet schools are creating white middle-class elite schools in the heart of black ghettos'.[33] Nonetheless, the Government pressed ahead with legislation in 1992 to encourage opt outs and, at much the same time, the first publication of 'league tables' of schools to facilitate parental choice and decision-making.[34] The idea of differing secondary schools for different pupils was well and truly back on the political agenda.

Progressivism and the national curriculum

In this context it is hardly surprising that the impact of the 1988 legislation on what went on in the classrooms quickly came to be seen as at best controversial. Working parties were set up to recommend the details of the national curriculum subject by subject. Thus, from the outset, the assumption that class teaching would be subject-based was central to the planning process. No sooner were these working parties up and running than it became apparent that there were significant tensions, both within the working groups and between them and the Government, on the extent to which these new curricula should be enquiry-based. For example, as early as the summer of 1989, the *TES* had intercepted a leaked research report from the Assessment of Performance Unit which dealt with the science curriculum. The editor commented:

> when the interim report of the national curriculum science group was published, the Education Secretary criticised it for promoting investigation, communication and science in action over facts. However, the APU report on *Science at 15* argues that 'evidence supports the view that there is greater scope for producing a rewarding science curriculum based on investigating science rather than one which is based on the transmission of concepts from the major science disciplines'. The APU's work raises questions about how far available testing techniques will be up to measuring the improvements in overall standards the national curriculum is meant to bring about.

These two key questions, of how far the curriculum should involve independent enquiry by pupils and what the implications of this might be for any testing or examining regime, became central ones which were to hang over the deliberations of all the working groups.[35]

For many educationalists, the outcome of these events was predictable from the start. For example, in November 1990, Patricia Broadfoot and Marilyn Osborne reported on an ESRC comparative study of primary schools in England and France. They concluded that the French national curriculum had stultified child-centred approaches to teaching and they predicted that this might become inevitable in Britain:

> Although at present many English primary teachers express a strong determination not to sacrifice child-centred methods to the demands of the national curriculum and assessment, the lessons from France suggest such a shift may be inevitable as time pressure to cover attainment targets and to deal with more formalised record-keeping and assessment begins to bite. Associated with this there may be a move towards a more didactic approach and an increasing use of whole-class teaching ... In England a decentralised teaching system gives much greater autonomy for teachers in matters of curriculum and teaching methods ... In England the approach is usually active, emphasizing discovery-based learning. The teacher often seems to be encouraging children to think creatively: in France, the effort is more likely to be directed towards leading children to the right answer.[36]

Within a year it was becoming clear that on this issue there were deep and growing differences between the government and many members of the teaching profession. Towards the end of 1991 the *TES* reported a spat between David Hart General Secretary of the NAHT on the one side, and Schools Minister Michael Fallon on the other. Hart was warning of the danger that 'the national curriculum may oblige schools to stream children as young as nine'. He was immediately challenged, at the same union conference, by Michael Fallon who called for

> more whole-class teaching ... Does so much topic work deliver appropriate, differentiated and challenging learning for children? ... While topic work could stimulate, and through exploration, lead to better subject application, exploration was no substitute for instruction ... he found it disturbing to come across so little whole-class teaching, particularly in junior classes ... At worst this kind of practice makes primary schools like pre-school playgroups, with much happiness and painting but very little learning.[37]

Both sides seized on Robin Alexander's recent report on primary education in Leeds, which had argued that the primary curriculum as it had been delivered in the past had resulted in low expectations of the pupils. Kenneth Clarke, the new Minister for Education, was not above speculating publicly on the need for the Government to insist on setting and streaming at primary level. Hart responded angrily that 'he rejected the idea of a return to the pattern of ability-based classes common some forty years ago ... An arrangement that was supportive of the few while depressing the achievement of many'.[38]

The arguments over these conflicting views of the implications of a national curriculum rumbled on and became inextricably entwined with the clash between radical right polemicists and those who took a different view of the nature and needs of the child. In the autumn of 1992, for example, the *TES* concluded that John Patten's support for the new review of English teaching which had been demanded by some right-wingers was 'more than mere fodder for the flog 'em and hang 'em brigade. It is ... a new consensus in education'. This suggestion, that a new order was emerging from the controversies over the implementation of the 1988 Act was backed by a lengthy quotation from Martin Turner, head of the Dyslexia Institute, who had gone on record as saying

> It is not true that a right-wing clique is now running the education system ... What is true is that notions of egalitarianism and child-centred education cannot go on because they do not work ... The Left has not taken any account of standards and has allowed the Right to make it an issue ... The Socialist programme, born in the post-War creation of the Welfare State is now history. The events of the late-1980s showed that.[39]

This increasing politicisation of the debate on the curriculum was recognised as such and pointed out at the time by the *TES*. It quoted one statement by Sheila Lawlor, one of the darlings of the radical right, to the effect that 'there is a cultural canon of knowledge that forms our educational heritage ... a distinct body of knowledge that children should be taught ... only once this is taught can you have pluralism'. The *TES* identified Lord Griffiths of Forestfach, David Pascall, John Marenbon, John Marks and Arthur Pollard as the leading figures in this escalation of radical right rhetoric on education, commenting that

> ironically, it has been under John Major that the Right has had most success in increasing its sphere of influence ... The Prime Minister's speeches on education have often read as straight lifts from Centre for Policy Studies tracts. The CPS populist message slides neatly into the rhetoric of the *Daily Mail*, calling for good old-fashioned values and the 'proper' education we all think we can remember in the halcyon days when children could spell, knew the date of the battle of Trafalgar and did long division.[40]

By the mid-nineties it was becoming clear that this 'new consensus' in education, heavily influenced by this radical right rhetoric, was resulting in a stultified experience for many pupils in the classroom. The OFSTED annual report for 1996 claimed that the national curriculum was driving primary schools towards a curriculum focused on the basics. The new testing regime was resulting in the core subjects, English, science and mathematics, receiving disproportionate attention. 'Primary teachers have a tendency to expect too little of their pupils ... They rely too much on one teaching method. Pupils need to be taught how to work independently'. There was a similar impact on the secondary sector the report claimed: 'Setting, as advocated by David Blunkett last week, is becoming common in Key Stages 3 and 4'.⁴¹ Indeed, one teacher blamed the national curriculum for increased levels of aggression among younger schoolchildren, complaining in a letter to the *TES* that

> the way in which the national curriculum has been implemented in many infant schools has meant that young children have been sitting down doing formal work for a much greater proportion of the day than hitherto ... the result ... increasing levels of aggressive behaviour in the playgrounds.⁴²

Similar disquiet was voiced in a report from the National Curriculum Council to the Education Secretary at the start of 1993. It claimed that teacher overload was leading to superficial teaching in the primary schools: 'depth of learning is being sacrificed in pursuit of breadth ... there is insufficient time for the basics of reading, writing and spelling'. Although the NCC had already emerged as one of the more liberal influences during this period, it was now ready by this time to call for more subject teaching, setting by ability, and 'a more focused approach to topic work'. Across the field there was increasing acceptance that the new national curriculum could only work within a context of teaching which was more rigidly structured and which allowed less time for the pupils to pursue their own interests.⁴³

An evolving politics of education

Hardly surprisingly, during this decade, the politics of education were tumultuous and fiercely contested. On the one hand was a government determined to ensure that what emerged was a settlement in which classroom practice and the whole organisation of the education system reflected its wish to reaffirm 'traditional' values. On the other, the teaching profession found itself riven by the enormity of the changes taking place: many saw what was going on as a juggernaut which had to be deflected at more or less any cost. For others, these transformations represented a challenge and opened up the possibility of new approaches to management and leadership in schools. It was clear to all involved that the education issue had moved to the heart of political debate and was widely seen to have a political significance which had not previously been fully recognised. For all participants there was a sense of being in uncharted waters.

On the government side, a succession of Conservative Ministers for Education each brought their own style to the attempt to impose a settlement on the teaching profession. Initially, it was the bruising and dismissive style of Kenneth Baker which coloured early negotiations. His successor, John MacGregor, appointed in the autumn of 1989, began by seeking to follow Baker's uncompromising line. Before the end of the year, for example, the final report of the History Working Party was being held back because of MacGregor's insistence that 'leaving the content historical knowledge out of the attainment targets would result in "too little emphasis on the facts"' in the teaching of history. The *TES* observed ruefully that 'some see Mr. MacGregor's insistence on statutorily defined facts as purely political in motivation; not just to emphasize his Party's commitment to rigour but also to secure a version of history favourable to Conservative values'.[44]

But it was not long before MacGregor was obliged to listen and respond to the growing crescendo of complaints from within the teaching profession that the national curriculum, in its undiluted form, simply would not work. By March 1990, the *TES* was reporting that MacGregor was under pressure from all sides to reduce the burden of testing imposed by the new curriculum, although the journal reflected that the pressure to reduce testing to three core subjects might be seized on by the Prime Minister to insist on a return to more formal examining methods than had been foreseen when subject attainment targets had been announced. 'Mr. MacGregor must slow up the juggernaut before it goes too far', the *TES* warned.[45] A month later, in a gesture which was widely seen at the time as MacGregor's attempt to sort out the impasse left behind by Baker, the Minister attended the AMMA annual conference and announced that testing for seven-year-olds would be reduced to the core subjects to give what he called 'valuable flexibility in planning your statutory assessment programme'.[46] In August of the same year MacGregor used a conference of the Professional Association of Teachers to announce further concessions. Art, music and physical education were now removed from the list of compulsory subjects at age fourteen. The extent of the governmental retreat was pointed out by the *TES* with the observation that 'only 18 months ago Mr. Baker (in DES Circular 5/89) said that the statutory duties in regard to the curriculum applied to all pupils regardless of age and that he had no plans at present to make revisions'. Equally, the journal foresaw dangers in this concession, pointing out that many education professionals were calling for fewer lessons a week in the core subjects so that the curriculum as a whole did not become attenuated. This new announcement ran the risk of much greater emphasis being placed on testing in the core subjects, a development which would be largely counter-productive.[47]

What did become clear as these events unfolded was that Margaret Thatcher herself was beginning to get cold feet about the way in which the national curriculum was being implemented. A *Times* leader on 17 April 1990 commented that 'the full implications of the Education Reform Act have taken her aback. She says she thinks the imposition of a national curriculum is too rigid'. She was quoted as saying publicly that

> once you have put out a national curriculum, if you have got it wrong, the situation is worse afterwards than it was before ... I do not think I ever thought they would do the syllabus in such detail. I believe there are thousands of teachers who are teaching extremely well ... I always felt there must be scope for each teacher to use her own methods, her own experience, the things which she has learned and which she really knows how to teach ... Otherwise we'll lose the enthusiasm and the devotion and all the extras that a really good teacher can give out of her own experience.

The Times was quoting from a lengthy interview given by Thatcher to the *Sunday Telegraph* and went on to comment, tellingly:

she now recognises that teachers discover in the classroom for themselves what works and what does not. Too rigid an imposed curriculum could undermine their enthusiasm and devotion. Here is the voice of the teacher pitting professional independence against high-flown academic 'expertise', the practitioner against the theoretician ... The Government originally sold the idea of a national curriculum to parents as a conservative reform, a switch in emphasis towards traditional teaching techniques, which would squeeze out the wilder notions to which teachers – left-wing ones of course – were said to be tempted. Nobody in government appears to have asked what would happen if the curriculum itself moved that way, and caused teachers, many of them staunch traditionalists already, to abandon their well-tried methods for imposed educational novelties. That may be what Mrs. Thatcher described succinctly as 'getting it wrong'.[48]

In November the *TES* observed wryly that

over on the Radical Right, polemicists, junior ministers and Mrs. Thatcher herself profess shock and horror on discovering that an egalitarian and prescriptive national curriculum is allowing the educationists to regain control of education. Certainly the replacement of MacGregor by Kenneth Clarke as part of the reshuffle when John Major became Prime Minister signalled a new style, in which the teaching profession itself was increasingly blamed for difficulties in implementing the national curriculum as well as for what was going on in the classrooms.[49]

One letter to the *TES* from Michael Duffy, the head of King Edward VI School, Morpeth, in January 1991 neatly summarised the situation. The letter was written to plead for a suspension of the national curriculum beyond the age of fourteen, but went on to comment that

Clarke is simply blaming teachers and LEAs for failings after 14 ... Suddenly it is not what is to be taught that is the national educational issue, nor even how it is to be tested, but the alleged weaknesses of those who do the teaching. So sharply has the focus of debate been shifted away from the quick-fix prescription of the Baker Act and towards the deficiencies of the schools themselves that one is tempted to conclude that, in political terms, the national curriculum is getting too hot to hold. Hence the need, with a new Secretary of State installed ... for diversionary tactics such as appraisal, or the attacks on teacher training and the wicked local education authorities ... This barrage of politically inspired and destabilising criticism – from even the *Independent* and the *Guardian* – is beginning to damage our children's education ... At Key Stage 4 chaos reigns. A combination of over-prescriptive legislation, a well-meaning but disastrously complicated assessment system and an indefensible decision to use GCSE for the statutory end-of-stage assessment, produce a conundrum even more difficult than the Schleswig-Holstein question ... The Secretary of State should be persuaded, in the interests of achieving the better schools that all of us want, to suspend the national curriculum at the end of Key Stage Three.[50]

On similar lines the final annual report of Eric Bolton as Chief HMI derided Clarke with the observation that 'indiscriminate fault finding was hindering otherwise good progress'.[51]

But this did not prevent Clarke from continuing to target the shortcomings of the teachers. In October 1992 he commissioned what was to become known as the 'three wise men' report, asking Robin Alexander (a Professor of Education at the University of Leeds), Jim Rose (the Chief Inspector for primary education), and Chris Woodhead (chief executive of the National Curriculum Council) to comment on the progress of the primary sector. Although they were far from unanimous, some sections of their report were to provide valuable ammunition to the Secretary of State. One section commented that 'over the last few decades, the progress of primary schools has been hampered by the influence of highly questionable dogmas which have led to excessively complex classroom practices and devalued the place of subjects in the curriculum'.[52] Clarke used this to call publicly for 'fundamental changes in the bulk of schools' which he claimed were necessary if the national curriculum was to be delivered effectively: 'the report will give teachers the self-confidence to do the things which common sense tells them are required. There will be no sense of guilt about correcting mistakes, grouping by abilities or teaching the whole class at a time'.[53] For several years this report was seen as iconic, being cited frequently in educational debates, but at the moment of its publication it was certainly used by Kenneth Clarke as a whip with which to continue his public lashing of the teaching profession.

After the 1992 election, Clarke was succeeded by John Patten as Secretary of State for Education, an appointment which coincided with the Government's announcement that successful schools were now to be allowed to expand, to the detriment of neighbouring schools. Within a year the *TES* was complaining that Patten had followed the example of his predecessor and had snubbed eight parent organisations, including the National Confederation of Parent Teacher Associations, claiming on Radio 4 that

they did not speak for real parents ... They were protesting against things which I thought were common things of agreement between everyone now; that we should have a national curriculum; we should have testing that should be published. They are arguing against that. It's Neanderthal!

The journal did gently remind its readers of Patten's own recent introduction to the White Paper, *Choice and diversity*, in which he had argued that 'parents know best the needs of their children – certainly better than educational theorists or administrators'.[54] But, despite the internal inconsistencies in some ministerial rhetoric, the Government's stance remained one of being firmly committed to imposing its own interpretation of the legislation.

In September 1994, Gillian Shepherd took over as Secretary of State. Her personable style and avoidance of direct confrontation with the teaching profession did not go unremarked. Ted Wragg, an acerbic commentator on the contemporary educational scene offered his own witty summation of her period in office in the *TES* in June 1995:

> I've gone off Gillian Shepherd a bit. She seems to me to be a very nice person and to have one big selling point – she isn't called 'Baker', 'Clarke' or 'Patten', which is an enormous plus in my view. On the other hand she is frequently described as having launched a 'charm offensive'. Fine! But a big smile and a warm handshake are poor substitutes for the loss of thousands of teaching jobs.[55]

It is clear in retrospect that this succession of Ministers, however varied their personal styles and tactical approaches, shared an unswerving governmental commitment to the imposition of a national curriculum, and a new educational settlement, which incorporated as much as possible of the radical right rhetoric which was increasingly dominating educational debate. In sum, they played a not inconsiderable part in generating the 'new educational consensus' which became such a marked characteristic of this period.

Another element in this evolving politics of education was the steady ongoing erosion of the power of the teaching profession to control its own destiny. The *TES* reported in July 1992 that there was growing evidence of governors taking over the running of schools:

> heads of more than half of the 250 grant maintained schools have privately told ministers that over-powerful governors are jeopardising their attempts to raise standards ... and have sought to apply a degree of day-to-day control which ignores the head's leadership role and which prevents efficient management.[56]

For many observers the fact that the developing politics of education seemed to be becoming increasingly a power struggle between the Government and the teachers could only be seen as a source of regret. One letter to the *TES* at the start of 1994 summed up this frustration neatly:

> Teacher workload is not the heart of the problem. The provision of a good quality education for all our children is at the heart of the problem and teachers are fed up with seeing children's needs pushed to the back of the political agenda. When do we see a return to a balanced view of coursework? What about an end to the desire to label children? Could not all schools be properly resourced instead of a select few? Why not a programme of support for teachers recognising the best of 'traditional' and 'progressive' teaching styles? Since last year, however, the workload issue has threatened to take over.

In the view of this correspondent, the unions were as guilty as the Government of making the power struggle between them paramount, with pedagogic issues marginalised.[57]

In February 1994 the establishment of the funding agency for schools was announced. This was to have 200 employees, an annual budget of two million pounds and would be used to fund schools in the areas of non-compliant local education authorities. Even more significantly, in December 1996, the Government unveiled its new National Literacy Project, which was designed to set out what primary teachers should cover, term by term, and introducing 'at the heart of the scheme ... an hour a day of direct and exclusive teaching of either reading and writing or number skills, with a combination of group work and whole-class teaching'.[58] So, a further outcome of this ongoing political struggle was the firm establishment of the basics at the heart of the primary school curriculum. In one sense it had been a long journey from the 'reading, writing and arithmetic' of the late Victorian era. In another it had been no journey at all.

'Burning the tick-lists': rethinking the national curriculum

It became clear early on to those working within the system that the demands of the national curriculum would have, sooner or later, to be reconsidered if it was to have any real chance of working in the long run. The letter from G. R. Walker, head of the Cavendish School, Hemel Hempstead, to the *TES* in December 1989 neatly summed up this perception:

> for those of us actually trying to implement a whole curriculum, the situation is becoming reminiscent of the Emperor's clothes ... the current education of many pupils is suffering on account of the staff training associated with the Reform Act ... State schools are now massively engaged in piecemeal curriculum development in a mode that runs counter to all the best practice of the past decade.[59]

One agency which played a key role in placing question marks under the whole governmental conception of a national curriculum was the National Curriculum Council led by Duncan Graham. From the outset this Council sought to widen the debate to include consideration of the ways in which cross-curricular themes could be incorporated under the terms of the new legislation. As the *TES* reported in the autumn of 1989,

> one particular issue was whether the schools should be given the NCC's advice on how the foundation subjects should be combined into a whole curriculum, enriched with nourishing cross-curricular, personal, economic and social themes. DES officials ... wanted advice on the national curriculum limited at this stage to the bare subject necessities, as those who fear the dead hand of rigid, narrow prescription always thought they would.[60]

Two months later the *TES* was reporting his talk to the Girls' School Association in which he argued that it was impossible to teach the ten GCSE subjects properly within the confines of a forty-period week. In Graham's words: 'either pupils must work harder and learn more in the time available ... or they must do rather less in some foundation subjects than expected at the moment for a GCSE'.[61] A year later the NCC, under Duncan Graham, proposed formally to Kenneth Clarke that all ten national curriculum subjects should be retained at GCSE level but that modifications should be made to both teaching and content to make this a coherent process.[62]

Graham's arguments attracted the attention of those on the right politically. Katie Ivens, a well-known radical right campaigner, produced a pamphlet at this time attacking the NCC with the observation that 'government advisers who control lessons in 25,000 state schools should be dismissed as they are deliberately undermining education reforms, allowing control to pass to left-wingers'. She went on to accuse the NCC of turning the government's reforms into 'a zealots charter' by adding on lessons in subjects such as multi-cultural studies, anti-racism and anti-sexism to an already overloaded curriculum.[63]

During the spring of 1990 Tim Brighouse, the Chief Education Officer of the Birmingham LEA, was another to throw his weight behind the questioning of the whole direction of government policy on education. In a co-authored article on the national curriculum, which was dubbed 'too clever by half', he commented that

> at the time it seemed too good to be true. Now it is looming nightmarish over the nation's schools. The TGAT prescription seemed to us all a miracle. It offered the traditionalists on the one hand the certainty that they had always craved about what children would be taught and that at last they (the traditionalists) would have the means of knowing whether the children were actually learning; and, to the progressives on the other, the flexibility which would enable the child to benefit from the best formative, diagnostic and criterion referenced assessment ... It was, of course, an illusion and historians will one day wonder that we could ever have deluded ourselves otherwise.[64]

For Geoffrey Samuel, head of the Heathland School, Hounslow, the central problem was that, confronted by these reservations, the Government was conniving in making the coursework elements in GCSE examinations less demanding. He wrote to the *TES* complaining that

> pupils' grades on the coursework component were higher than in the examination. Schools which have adopted 100% coursework may have achieved better results – but the standard has been sadly debased. Is a deception of this kind really to the benefit of pupils?[65]

Pressure for some kind of postponement of the implementation of the legislation continued to grow. In December 1990 a delegation from the NAHT pleaded with Clarke to delay for at least one year the introduction of the Key Stage 4 reforms involving 14- to 16-year-olds. The *TES* reported that 'the Association has also told Mr. Clarke that by requiring students to study more subjects with less class time, the present proposals from the NCC will lead to a lowering of standards and a drop in numbers staying on after 16'.[66]

By the end of 1992 there was clear evidence that the teaching profession was unwilling to meekly acquiesce in what was widely seen as the Government's heavy-handed imposition of the national curriculum. The NASUWT was warning that there would be a widespread teacher boycott of national curriculum testing unless there were some signs of government flexibility, while Michael Barber of the NUT highlighted the English Key Stage 3 tests as a particular cause for concern. Doug McEvoy, of the NUT, went on record as saying that 'teachers are angry and insulted by the attack the government has made on their professionalism and judgement'.[67] Fearing that it might prove impossible to administer the new tests in the existing political climate, Walter Ulrich, of the National Association of Governors and Managers said:

> It is our job to ensure that the law of the national curriculum is enforced and we would not want to flout it. However, we are sympathetic to the criticisms ... and we would impress upon ministers that it makes our job very difficult if we are expected to implement measures that the bulk of education professionals are opposed to.[68]

Even the Headmasters' Conference came out in support of a boycott at this time, its chairman, Robin Wilson, commenting that 'this goes far wider than union action'.[69]

Another ploy to help re-establish governmental control of a process which appeared to be running out of control was the reorganisation of the quangos. The NCC in particular had proved to be an independent-minded organisation, by no means quietly acquiescing in government policy. In the summer of 1992 it was announced that both the NCC and SEAC would be wound up and their duties incorporated into the single School Curriculum and Assessment Authority, an organisation which it was believed would be more answerable to the DES. But, before the NCC had finished its work, Graham was dismissed and Chris Woodhead was briefly made chief executive. He was quite prepared to put a completely different gloss on the work and impact of the NCC. Claiming that many heads were strongly supportive of NCC attempts to interpret the national curriculum, he used a public pronouncement to pave the way for a reworking of the national curriculum, pointing out that

> it is becoming too complex and over-prescriptive ... the collective weight of content is leading to curriculum overload and superficial teaching ... Depth of learning is being sacrificed in pursuit of breadth and teachers are finding it impossible to provide the rigour and challenge which are essential ... As teachers' subject knowledge increases ... some at least of the difficulties will diminish.[70]

By the spring of 1993 it was becoming clear that this was bluster which did not fully capture the realities of the situation. The English curriculum was now the key battleground, and, ironically, it was Brian Cox, the originator of the Black Papers, whose 'road to Damascus' conversion neatly crystallised the issues. Cox, as a known radical right polemicist, had been invited by Baker to sit on the Kingman Committee established in 1987 to make recommendations on the teaching of English. He went on to chair the NCC working group whose job was to draw up the basis for implementation of the newly announced orders on the teaching of English. As the *TES* succinctly summarised it: 'Professor Cox listened to the views of teachers, academics and advisers, went "native" and is now a fierce critic of government policy'. Cox was warning that the new orders on English teaching would cause chaos and claimed publicly that Baker, and later Clarke, repeatedly interfered with the working party to ensure that a traditional English curriculum emerged.[71]

At the same time, Joan Clanchy, the head of North London Collegiate School, resigned from the NCC, placing a lengthy article in the *TES* to protest about the way it was being run: 'the dominant aim has become a curriculum designed for tests and the result is a model of English teaching which is barren and anti-intellectual'. Although she was described by the *TES* as a traditionalist who favoured standard English and the teaching of grammar, she was quite ready to lambast the NCC for ignoring the advice of experts and favouring right-wing views.

> It is well-known that some members of the Council belong to Right Wing think-tanks. I have never objected to that because ... such organisations are going to produce activists who have ideas to contribute. But I did object as a Council member only being given Centre for Policy Study pamphlets to read by way of homework.[72]

By this time the *TES* was in no doubt that the Government was using every device available to it to ensure that its view of the national curriculum, and not that implicit in many professional responses, was the one which prevailed. In an angry leader article in March 1993 the journal complained that

> ever since the heads of the NCC and SEAC were peremptorily removed by Kenneth Clarke as Education Secretary, to be replaced by two former members of the No. 10 Policy Unit, both councils and committees have been progressively packed with people of similar political persuasion. The effect of this – and the antithesis between the prevailing business jargon and the subtleties of English language teaching – have been lucidly described this week in Brian Cox's *Channel 4/Times* lecture, and in Joan Clanchy's explanation of why she has resigned from the NCC. Curriculum debate illuminated only by Centre for Policy Studies pamphlets and a demand for 'back to basics' terseness were a far cry from the original concept of a national curriculum.

This, the journal thought, was the key reason why John Patten was now being forced to backtrack and to make concessions to the teaching lobby which a few months earlier would have been unthinkable.[73]

During the summer of 1993 this all came to a head when the national campaign against SATs, which had been going on for two years, resulted in a considerable number of parents picketing the tests by keeping their children away from school. The Advisory Centre for Education stated in one circular at this time that 'there is already evidence that quiet sabotage, a gentle non-compliance with daft and damaging policies, is working its way into the system'.[74] It fell to the newly-established School Curriculum and Assessment Authority, which began work in October 1993 under Ron Dearing, to provide a formula which could sort out the mess. Chris Woodhead commented at the time that 'the task now is to restore public and professional commitment to the national curriculum after the damage caused by the teachers' boycott'.[75]

Dearing wasted no time in compiling his report, which, when it appeared at the start of 1994, was warmly received. A letter to the *TES* from Louise Kidd, Principal of Rutland Sixth Form College, serves as a fair summary of much professional opinion:

> Dearing's final report fully justified the trust placed in him by teachers ... He has steadfastly worked towards his goal of placing a high-quality education service in the hands of the profession. He has continually stated his firm belief that people in high places cannot decide what should happen in the classrooms. The government has accepted his advice on the 1994 tests. They will be limited to the core subjects and the testing time will be halved ... He has produced proposals which satisfy the wishes of the profession for a slimmed-down curriculum with flexibility for decisions to be made locally. He has promised that the administration and marking of external tests will be simplified and there will be a cut in the number of attainment targets resulting in a slimming-down of recording ... He has opened the doors to a constructive partnership which will produce a high-quality national curriculum in a realistic time ... He says, and I agree, that teachers must accept the need for accountability, the need for external moderation of standards.[76]

What Dearing had done was to recommend the dropping of history and geography at Key Stage 4 and the use of the existing GCSE rather than tests specifically designed to match the new key stages of the national curriculum. The NASUWT called off its boycott of the tests immediately, although the NUT dispute dragged on for a few months more. In a major interview which he gave to the *TES* Dearing underlined the centrality and importance of tests in English, Maths and Science but stressed that his central aim was 'burning the ticklists'; He pointed out that since nearly 2,000 teachers had been involved in preparing and trialling the tests they could hardly complain about lack of consultation.[77] The way was at last open for the implementation of a version of the national curriculum and the testing that went with it which both sides, government and the teaching profession, could accept.

The persistence of the radical right

An important element in the public debate on education, as it developed during the decade following the 1988 Education Act, was the intensification of radical right rhetoric. It soon became clear that the Black Paper movement of the late sixties and early seventies had not been some kind of aberration, but was in reality a portent of a new popular discourse which sold newspapers and offered sound-bites to ambitious politicians. At one level, there were fears, as the *TES* put it, that 'government control of the curriculum could lead to the indoctrination of children'. Fred Smithies, the NASUWT General Secretary, saw history as one subject particularly susceptible to this threat and warned that, although 'parents trust teachers to be impartial ... very few believe politicians are capable of that objectivity and impartiality'.[78]

But, beyond this, the media remained willing to offer stereotypical views of what was going on in the schools as a basis for support of teaching approaches centred on the basics. For example in the spring of 1991, an east London primary school, Culloden, became the subject of a BBC 'fly on the wall' documentary. As the *TES* summarised it:

> despite the approval of the TV critics, Culloden became the unwitting vehicle for an attack on 'modern methods' when the *Mail on Sunday* ran an article claiming that its pupils were not being taught how to read and write. Culloden's caring approach and play school atmosphere were castigated.

Kenneth Clarke used this as an opportunity to order the Inspectorate into Culloden in response to what one DES official called 'much publicised concern about reading standards'. The *TES* concluded gloomily that 'there is a clear feeling that the school has been "fitted up" by right-wing critics of modern teachers'. Although the governors wrote formally to Clarke pointing out that articles in the *Mail on Sunday* and the *Daily Telegraph* hardly added up to 'public concern', the real damage was done by the follow-up by the *Mail on Sunday* which arranged for a private reading test of thirty-nine Culloden pupils, claiming subsequently to have 'discovered the real truth ... that these children, many of them very bright indeed, cannot read or write properly'.[79]

This was matched by much of the rhetoric which came from the government on education. John Major, in particular, was all too ready to draw on radical right thinking in his public statements. In July 1991, for example, in a much publicised speech to the Centre for Policy Studies he went on record as saying that there was

> a national prejudice against brain power ... this ancient prejudice was reinforced by the Left, with its mania for equality. Equality not of opportunity, but of outcome. This was a mania that condemned children to fall short of their potential; that treated them as if they were identical – or must be made so. A mania that undermined common sense values in schools, rejected proven teaching methods, debased standards – or disposed of them altogether.

A canker in our education system that spread from the 1960s on, and deprived great cohorts of our children of the opportunities they deserved. I for one, cannot find it easy to forgive the Left for that.[80]

This radical right rhetoric, which played a major part in colouring the debate on the curriculum during these years, was to be heard right across the media. In 1993, for example, the *Spectator* got involved, with an editorial arguing that

the state sector includes the worst schools in the land. The private sector includes the best ... The reason? Teacher-training colleges ... are staffed by Marxists who peddle an irrelevant, damaging, outdated ideology of anti-elitism ... those who can't, teach ... those who can't teach, teach teachers.[81]

In June 1996, educationalist David Reynolds was used by the BBC for a Panorama programme in which the teacher educators became the target. This broadcast was used to argue that the key to raising standards in the primary schools was sitting children in rows facing the teacher. It suggested that student teachers were being given the impression that whole-class teaching was 'politically incorrect'. Ian Kane, the chair of the Universities Council for the Education of Teachers, responded fiercely that 'none of OFSTED's reports on primary teacher training support the myth that training institutions are locked into the 'Sixties. They show that the vast majority introduce their students to a variety of methods'.[82]

Another voice raised against this ongoing chorus of radical right views was that of Philip Gammage, Professor of Education at the University of Nottingham, who, in the autumn of 1996, used the columns of the *TES* to pen a stout defence of child-centred education. He wrote:

The position at statutory school age is now more bleak than I can recall ... Teachers now talk as though children fall logically into key stages. How such Black Paper language has been accepted so uncritically by the teaching profession utterly defeats me. These silly terms mask individual differences ... Nowadays it seems popular to deride the 1967 Plowden report, to misrepresent its attempts to put the child at the centre of the curriculum, to accuse it of having caused a series of societal ills. But the tenets of Plowden were surely right ... Have the Black Papers of the late 1960s, with their crude simplistic arguments, been accepted? ... it seems to me that child-centredness contains much to commend ... It is simply about matching the learning to the child, building on their motivation and curiosity. Have we forgotten the slow march forward, the research which showed how damaging streaming was?

Hardly surprisingly, this elicited a scathing riposte from Chris Woodhead, whose reply focused on the clear need, as he saw it, for didactic, teacher-centred methods.[83] Thus, although many within the teaching profession saw these as unfair and unprovoked assaults, and some were prepared to go on record opposing them, the reality of this period was that events unfolded against a backcloth of ongoing radical right invective which had an impact on all aspects of public discourse. Equally important, it fuelled the thinking of many parents and observers, so that public discussion of educational issues took place in an environment which was far less sympathetic to the teaching profession than had been the case thirty or forty years earlier.

'Lazy and incompetent': the teachers under attack

One central element in this radical right rhetoric was a series of direct attacks on the competence and commitment of the teachers themselves. This was to prove a decade in which, if anything, attacks of this kind intensified rather than diminished. One early example was the major coverage in the *Sunday Times* given to the views of Mary Hill, a teacher educator, who was reported as claiming that there was a 'critical shortage' of acceptable teachers. For the *Sunday Times* this was clear evidence of the 1950s 'baby boomers' going into a quickly expanding teaching profession, with no proper controls over their entry

> in the middle of a world-wide turmoil of campus revolutions, flower power children and questioning of traditional values. Teacher training did not escape. Many persuasive voices preached the virtues of rejecting the establishment, refusing to teach "the conventional wisdom", and breaking the bourgeois pattern of achievement. More than a handful of those convinced by such arguments found their way into the classroom. The nation was short of teachers. It was not difficult to find reasons why even the lazy and incompetent should be allowed to pass ... Those who thus entered the profession have not only brought lower standards to their own classes: they have stayed on to influence the next generation.[84]

Even Duncan Graham, who was prepared to stand up to the government as head of the NCC, but who was also known to be something of a polemicist, was not above disparaging the work of teachers when he addressed the BERA annual conference in 1991. He was reported in the *TES* as having 'misjudged the mood of his audience when he criticised the more child-centred approach which preceded the national curriculum. It had been implied, he said, that children could learn by osmosis and that so long as they were enjoying themselves they would be adequately educated', a comment which drew cries of 'Shame!' from his audience.[85]

But Graham's comments were only the preamble to much more vigorous condemnation of the ability of teachers to implement the national curriculum. His replacement as chief executive of the NCC was Chris Woodhead, already a recognised public figure as one of the 'three wise men' who had co-authored the 1992 discussion paper 'Curriculum organisation and classroom practice in primary schools'. In January 1993, Woodhead used his new position at the NCC to produce a very upbeat report on the introduction of the national curriculum at primary level, suggesting that the glitches which had become apparent were largely attributable to teacher inadequacy. For Woodhead, a new approach to management was helping to sweep away the obstacles to improved classroom performance:

> it is a period of profound change in primary education ... the curriculum is now broader and more balanced. Many schools are reviewing their approaches to curriculum organisation and classroom management. Local management has brought a new flexibility to resource allocation, and, more important ... a new sense of ... professional responsibility ... Those who are threatened, ideologically or territorially, will do their best to undermine the progress being made.[86]

The central thrust of these ideas was clear. A teaching profession which contained far too many who were undercommitted, incompetent or obstructive could only be restored through firm leadership and a new approach to educational management in which the profession was made far more answerable to its public. It was a set of perceptions in which the government of the day was only too happy to acquiesce, and which was soon to inform governments of whatever colour. Radical right rhetoric had become a semi-permanent feature of the educational landscape.

A restructured Inspectorate

One key element in Kenneth Clarke's legacy was the restructuring of the Schools' Inspectorate, which now became OFSTED, with, for the first time, registered inspectors being recruited from non-educational backgrounds. The 1988 Act had, from the outset, threatened to make massive new demands of the inspection service, and initially many within the system foresaw a massive expansion as the only way to cope with these new demands. But Clarke was anxious to impose a solution which would bring the Inspectorate under closer governmental control, whilst enhancing its power to arbitrate on what was going on in the schools themselves. The answer lay in the privatisation of the service.

One direct result of these changes was the divorce of the Inspectorate from the DES, which the outgoing Chief Inspector, Eric Bolton, saw as potentially very significant: 'I fear ... that HMI is being shunted into a siding ... its work will in future be directed away from the government and towards the schools ... downgrading, almost to vanishing point, inspection intended to inform policy-making'.[87] The strength of feeling within the Inspectorate at these developments can be judged from the fact that HMI staged an unprecedented 'day of action' in January 1992 to protest against the privatisation of their service.

Initially OFSTED was headed up by Stewart Sutherland, but on his return to a vice-chancellorship, in September 1994, Chris Woodhead became the new chief HMI, a position which was to give him the opportunity, during the next few years, to become an outspoken and widely reported commentator on the educational scene, criticising, first, progressive teaching methods and six months later mounting a widely-publicised campaign on class size, suggesting that teacher competence was a bigger issue than the number of pupils in a class. Woodhead used his first annual lecture as chief HMI, which was given at the Royal Society of Arts, to lambast progressive teaching methods. He identified those teachers who were wedded to sixties child-centred education as the major obstacle to raising standards ('the unhelpful influence of progressive teaching methods whereby children are expected to learn by discovery and are never told anything'). In particular he castigated primary classes where children were allowed to work on different activities in groups with teachers as facilitators. 'Despite much evidence which suggests that it is easier for teachers to explain new material and challenge their pupils when the class is taught as a whole, there remains hostility to such an approach', he claimed. He cited one experienced LEA officer as asking

> Why is it that I rarely, if ever, see a primary school teacher teach anyone anything? ... But the problem is not merely a resistance to change. It is, as I say, a commitment to particular beliefs about the purposes and conduct of education: beliefs which constitute the real impediment to the development of a better educational system and which lie, of course, far beyond the legislative ambition of even the most interventionist of governments.

The *TES* did not let this pass without comment. The journal saw this as an echo of the 'three wise men' report (of which Woodhead had been a co-author), adding that

> the culture which prevails in schools, according to Mr. Woodhead, is characterised by the belief that education must be relevant to the immediate needs and interests of the children, and that the teaching of knowledge is less important than the development of core skills ... Chris Woodhead's lecture this week is the ideological equivalent to the polemical rant with which Kenneth Clarke launched the 'three wise men' enquiry on primary schools ... It is likely to prove just as counter-productive. Woodhead lays into the primary schools for their dogma but without any evidence to substantiate his assertions. His lecture is an entirely fact-free zone. It is clearly designed to give a pre-emptive news spin to whatever the Report [the forthcoming OFSTED annual report] might subsequently say.[88]

In a subsequent edition, the journal went on to stress the extent to which Woodhead's remarks had goaded his audience:

> It is not clear what reaction HMI Chief Inspector Chris Woodhead expected to his lecture at the Royal Society of Arts ... But the Great and the Good and even the teachers gathered in the bemuralled lecture hall were duly provoked.

Peter Smith, the General Secretary of the Association of Teachers and Lecturers, had responded that

> I find it astonishing, almost beyond belief, that at the very moment that a fragile consensus is emerging that the reforms which are in place could be

made to work for the benefit of children, you have chosen to raise a debate
which is based on polemic and which actually leads to further distraction.

David Hart, on behalf of the NAHT, commented that 'I very much fear that teachers will feel they have been attacked again. This could drive people back into their
burrows'. Fellow-panellist Keith Anderson, the Chief Education Officer for
Gloucestershire, also had reservations: 'the scenario drawn by Chris Woodhead of
teachers acting solely as "facilitators" and unwilling to impart knowledge is one I
do not recognise ... It's not a picture I would endorse'. More directly, Eric Bolton,
a predecessor of Woodhead, added succinctly: 'It's ridiculous to believe that the
process could grind away like a coffee-grinder without a bean. People do select
content'. But, despite this savaging from fellow professionals, the *Daily Express*
still felt able to report the lecture and the subsequent discussion under the headline 'Trendies in class who harm pupils'. Woodhead's rhetoric was finely
calculated to irritate education professionals and to provide copy for rightist-
inclined newspapers at one and the same time.[89]

It is important to recognise the extent to which this marked a change in the conduct of the Inspectorate. Whilst historically HMI had played a key role in quietly
advising governments of whatever hue, this new willingness to get involved in public debate was in reality a sign of the extent of the Inspectorate's divorce from
government. It was a development which left a gap which successive governments
were to prove all too ready to fill through the deployment of 'special advisers'.
Unelected 'experts' were to become increasingly those who determined the detail
of educational policy. The think-tank was, like it or not, becoming an ancillary of
government itself. This privatised civil service was left to adjudicate publicly on
the performance of schools and colleges and to involve itself more directly than
ever before in the public discussion of education. The implications of these
changes may not, even now, be fully clear, but they certainly marked a significant
shift in the government of education and in the context within which teachers work.

The repositioning of New Labour

It became clear immediately after the enactment of the 1988 legislation that the
Labour Party was undergoing its own transformations in respect of education policy. Before the end of 1989 the *TES* drew attention to the way in which Jack Straw,
as education spokesman was

> carefully positioning his party in the moderate centre, attacking the
> Government where it is vulnerable on issues such as City Technology
> Colleges and opting out, while quietly dropping some of the 'progressive'
> policies which have given comprehensives (and therefore Labour) such a bad
> press. Under Straw Labour is now in favour of testing, firm management,
> monitoring schools' performance and teacher appraisal ... Straw insists that
> US style specialist or 'magnet' schools will be 'out' under a Labour adminis-
> tration but does not rule out individual schools developing a specialism. In
> other words ... magnets in all but name.[90]

In April 1992 David Milliband, then a researcher at the Institute of Public Policy Research, publicly warned his party to learn from the recent General Election. He argued that:

> Labour must look forward and see what the education service will be like in five years' time. Selectivity will have been introduced to significant parts of the service by then and nine out of ten schools will effectively be secondary moderns.[91]

In 1995 the *TES* drew attention to the way in which, unlike Gillian Shepherd, his opposite number, David Blunkett, the then shadow Education Secretary, was quick to welcome Chris Woodhead's vitriolic attack on the teaching profession at the start of the year. Blunkett welcomed Chris Woodhead's support for a debate on standards, adding that 'Labour has been urging such a debate for some time'.[92] During the spring of 1996 Blunkett went further, outlining Labour's educational programme to an NAHT conference at Torquay and, in the process, demonstrating the extent to which his party was now ready to sign up to a new right programme. He planned

> a back to basics drive in the classroom ... more emphasis on basic skills ... whole-class teaching will become part of a drastic overhaul of teacher training ... Teachers must be taught more about how to mange a class, including how to teach a whole class, as teachers in other countries are taught.[93]

During the summer of 1996 Tony Blair announced his commitment to setting and streaming in comprehensive schools, a policy initiative which drew this comment from one observer:

> Tony Blair's decision to announce his views about setting in comprehensive schools is a bad step ... It tells us a great deal about the way the Labour Party is thinking about controlling education ... Blair's announcement suggests that he believes that the evidence is clear, but that he does not trust teachers to work it out for themselves ... We are more used to seeing the Conservatives behave in this way – it is alarming to see 'New Labour' adopting the same approach.[94]

It was becoming clear that once in power Labour would look far more like its Conservative predecessor than many of its supporters would have cared to admit.

Conclusion

This period proved to be an extremely significant one for the development of schooling in England. The evidence gathered here makes it possible to offer a few provisional judgements on these events. First, the education system was irrevocably transformed. The contest over the implementation of the 1988 Act generated a situation in which the schools were answerable to their publics as never before. Schools were not exempt from the consumerism which impacted on many aspects of modern life. In the process, heads found themselves in a competitive struggle for students and placed in the public spotlight by inspectorial reports and press comment in ways they had never been before. The new financial regime which saw much of the security of LEA support stripped away from them served only to heighten this tension. The elements of privatisation which also became semi-permanently incorporated into educational provision at this time led directly to more entrepreneurial styles of headship. The introduction of specialised schools also forced heads and managers to think very carefully about their positioning in their localities and their funding sources. For the classroom teacher the challenges were no less. Whilst the profession was able, in the event, to play some part in determining the final shape of the national curriculum, the teachers had become the deliverers of other people's messages to a far greater extent than ever before. One clear outcome of the popular rhetoric around education was that, given the demands of the national curriculum, much more classroom work became teacher-focused. The freedom to initiate in the classroom, which had been such a marked feature of the 1960s and 1970s, was gone forever. By 1997 it was clear that the 1988 Reform Act, and the power struggle which it generated, had transformed the context within which educators worked in Britain. How much of the previous settlement would a Labour government be prepared to restore? For many observers of education in England, that was the big question in 1997.

7 New Labour and the curriculum since 1997

> You enjoy some lessons, particularly those which are challenging and allow you to use a range of skills and to work collaboratively. However, you drew our attention to some lessons which were uninteresting and failed to capture your imagination. We have drawn these concerns to the attention of the teachers and over the coming months they will be working hard to bring about improvements which will make many more lessons interesting and enjoyable. We have asked the school to improve the quality of your lessons as quickly as possible.
>
> An open letter to the pupils of a secondary school in the north of England from the inspection team at the conclusion of an OFSTED inspection, February 2006

Labour returned to power in May 1997 with the mantra 'education, education, education', identifying as of one of its central targets further reform and improvement of the education system. The new government quickly proved adept at managing the economy, and the outcome was that through a combination of low interest rates, the reliance on private finance for many major public projects and the enabling of massive and unprecedented levels of individual debt, as well as a growing balance of trade deficit, economic growth was sustained uninterrupted for over a decade. But this growth was achieved only at the cost of a widening gap between rich and poor, despite several government programmes, including 'sure start', which were intended to take large numbers of people out of poverty. The educational outcome was, hardly surprisingly, that the significant changes which were made impacted differently on differing elements of society, often being calculated to ensure no erosion of middle-class support for the Blair project, so that, after a decade of Labour in power, it is difficult to identify ways in which the disparities in schooling in modern Britain have been eliminated and all too easy to point to glaring social contrasts in the educational provision. It follows, therefore, that any account of the developing politics of the curriculum during these years is necessarily complex and riddled with contradictions.

This is particularly so in view of the fact that childhood itself seems to have changed radically during the most recent decade. One correspondent in the *TES* observed in an article in 2005 that various factors meant that the experiences of childhood bore little relationship to those of earlier times. In her view, exposure to graphic images of violence, explicit depictions of sex, the remorseless marketing of consumer goods, the increased consumption of junk food, changing play and sleep habits and, in many cases, a poor parental work/life balance, meant that 'children no longer have a childhood as we know it'.[1] Globalisation and the coming of the internet were further factors. In September 2006, 110 experts with interests in childhood wrote in a letter to the *Daily Telegraph* that 'we are deeply concerned about the escalating incidence of childhood depression and children's behavioural and developmental conditions'. Citing junk food, changed patterns of play and changing relationships with close adults as key factors, they added: 'in a fast-moving, hypercompetitive culture, today's children are expected to cope with an ever-earlier start to formal schoolwork and an overly academic and test-driven primary curriculum'. Claiming that eleven-year-olds were 'on average between two and three years behind where they were fifteen years ago', one of the authors, Sue Palmer, a retired head teacher, emphasised that children were 'put in an academic straitjacket from a very early age which restricts creativity and the enrichment of childhood'.[2] One inevitable outcome of all this was that both parents and children had changed expectations of schooling. Consumerist attitudes were now more deeply entrenched than ever before and this goes some way to explain the increasing commodification of education, as well as the conciliatory approach to pupils implicit in the letter cited at the beginning of this chapter. Further, there is some evidence that children themselves were coming to be seen as a commodity: one teacher who contributed to a BBC Radio 4 programme debating this letter asked 'are we enriching children or producing a product?' Another outcome of this was that many teachers undoubtedly believed, rightly or wrongly, that children were becoming harder to cope with in the classroom; also that they faced growing difficulties in attempting to meet their professional goals, not least because this proved to be a period which saw unprecedented levels of pupil absenteeism, particularly in the secondary sector.

'An epidemic of policymaking'[3]

During the 1997 election campaign the Labour Party emphasised the need for LEAs to exercise close control of their schools through development plans, with literacy and numeracy, the raising of standards and the reskilling of the teaching profession being key targets. Ironically, the education manifesto of the outgoing Conservative government proposed to make all state schools semi-independent, forcing them to compete for students and placing a heavy reliance on tests and league tables. The Conservatives proposed to transfer even more of the powers of the LEAs to the schools themselves. All of these were to become key elements in Labour Party policy within a few years! A list of twenty-one steps necessary to rescue the education service was presented to the electorate by Labour and, once they were in office, the Queen's Speech identified education as 'the first priority', with standards and class sizes highlighted.

All this was a preface to a period of almost unprecedented government action, with a plethora of directives, statements, press releases and twelve Acts of Parliament in ten years, ensuring that education was never far from the public gaze. David Blunkett, the new Minister of Education, sought to reassure head teachers with an open letter promising 'an open door policy ... partnership is essential if schools are to succeed. We are not interested in dogma. We are interested in what works'.[4]

Perhaps more indicative of the way the new government would operate was the announcement of the appointment of Michael Barber as head of the new Standards and Effectiveness Unit. The device of placing unelected and newly appointed civil servants in charge of policy was one which was to rankle increasingly with the teaching profession, and, across a broader spectrum of policy, with back-benchers. Its significance was realised immediately by the TES, which, pointing out that Barber would be in charge of a department of forty staff, commented that

> this signals the scale of direct intervention in schools being planned by the new administration ... Professor Barber will have more leverage than the senior civil servant he has now become ... It may be the first time that a political appointee has been given a specific civil servant role ... The appointment was met with some resistance from the Civil Service and was confirmed after the personal intervention of Tony Blair ... The political fortunes of OFSTED and, in particular, of Mr. Woodhead, will no longer be promoted by an alliance with advisers in the No. 10 Policy Unit, who have lost their jobs in the wake of Labour's election victory.[5]

In 2001 *The Times* offered a succinct and not unfair appraisal of Blunkett's impact at the Department:

> within three weeks of coming to power Blunkett had 'named and shamed' failing schools ... had created a standards unit headed by an outsider and designed to ensure that his more controversial reforms were driven through regardless of civil service misgivings ... Initiatives have poured out at more than one a month, and press releases at nearly two every working day.

This article pointed out too that this plethora of activity necessarily contained its own internal contradictions, citing Blunkett's much publicised mantra, 'Watch my lips: no selection', but pointing out that the party's election manifesto had promised parents the final say![6]

Another portent of what was to come was the announcement that the 281 schools identified by OFSTED as failing were to be put into special measures. Stephen Byers, the new Educational Standards Minister, promised that 'for those schools which are unable to improve we will close them and order a fresh start. Good schools which co-exist with the bad will be brought in to support them ... We will not shrink back from tough decisions'.[7] All this was quickly followed by a White Paper and legislation. A new literacy strategy was quickly put in place, the Assisted Places scheme was scrapped and a General Teachers Council was announced. Within six months the *TES* was commenting on 'an announcement every day and a leak every other', adding that 'the pace of change over the last six months has been remarkable'.⁸ This new, frenzied style of government was to persist under New Labour and was to become a growing thorn in the side of the teaching profession.

Some of the key initiatives which impacted on the classroom during the years that followed were the introduction of Education Action Zones announced in the spring of 1998; of a new, honed-down national curriculum which was to be far more detailed in respect of primary schooling than had any earlier version, announced in September 1999; a further overhaul of the 14–16 curriculum and examinations, announced by David Blunkett at the January 2000 north of England education conference; and, in a dramatic loosening of the purse strings, in March 2000 the announcement of an extra billion pounds to be disbursed directly to schools. The *TES* commented tartly that 'Gordon Brown is having a more positive effect on education than David Blunkett and Tony Blair put together'.⁹ Later in 2000, in a sudden reversal of policy, the Government announced the introduction of salaries for teachers in training and before the end of the year Blunkett had announced a further cash windfall for the schools. In the following year 'golden handcuffs' of up to £15,000 were announced for teachers who stayed in the same post over a given period in an attempt to control the staffing instability which many schools were experiencing.¹⁰ In February 2002 the Government announced it was planning to drop science subjects from the core curriculum at 14–16 in an attempt to enable schools to offer more vocational courses and to extend work experience for older pupils.

As this frenzy of new policy initiatives was sustained during Labour's second term in office there were signs that the press was becoming increasingly cynical and wearied, ever more ready to criticise whatever was the most recent development. When, in August 2002, another education Act was outlined which would give successful schools the power to opt out of the national curriculum, the *TES* ran a leader article pointing out that 'critics warn of a two-tier system'.¹¹ A month later, when the Government unveiled its 'Innovation Unit', described by Estelle Morris, the then Secretary of State, as a 'powerhouse and incubator' the journal warned of its likely expense.¹² When, in July 2004, the *TES* reviewed Labour's education manifesto for the forthcoming general election, it highlighted the expansion of the Government's academy programme, with a new target of 200 academies by 2010, as well as the aspiration that all secondaries would become specialist schools in the near future. 'Will every school be independent?' asked the *TES*. 'The future looks bleak for the local authorities.'¹³

But there seemed to be no end to the Government's readiness to innovate in education. In July 2004 a new five-year plan was unveiled, involving choice for parents and pupils, more specialist schools, the expansion of the foundation schools programme, the right for parents to set up new schools and a policy of encouraging all schools to adopt uniforms for their pupils.¹⁴ For the 2005 general election Labour unveiled ten education pledges, including three-year budgets for schools; a renewal of the drive towards specialist schools; allowing popular schools to expand; the establishment of 200 privately sponsored academies by 2010; and the expansion of pupil referral units as more unruly students were removed from the classroom. It was at this time that Blair said: 'we will put parent power at the heart of the education system, giving all parents, not just a minority as in the past, the choices and opportunities needed'.[15] Later in 2005, announcing yet another White Paper which would prepare the ground for a 'post-comprehensive era', Tony Blair reflected that 'if anything we have not pushed hard and fast enough.'[16] Yet at the same time the *TES* was commenting that the one billion pounds put into the 'Excellence in Cities' programme five years earlier had produced no tangible results and no evidence of improvements in GCSE scores by the students concerned.[17] Thus, one reality of this decade for those in schools was a constant sense of flux, and of changes with uncertain outcomes, which seemed more kaleidoscopic than anything which had gone before.

'A basics and little else curriculum': the drive for literacy and numeracy

But, amongst this welter of activity, it is possible to discern an evolving pattern of key governmental initiatives, as particular aspects of educational policy moved into and out of close political focus. There can be little doubt that, during the Labour Party's early years in power, it was numeracy and literacy which dominated the headlines and this was to have a major impact on what went on, particularly in the primary schools. Within a month of coming into office Blunkett had announced pass rate targets (targets were to be one of the key devices used repeatedly by this government) of 80 per cent for literacy and 75 per cent for numeracy in the key stage tests, to be achieved by the end of the Government's first term.[18] It was not long before educationalists and the educational press were pointing out that this emphasis necessarily involved an attenuation of the primary school curriculum, with far more time being devoted to the core curriculum than had been the case even in recent years. At one conference towards the end of 1997, Professor Robin Alexander commented that 'it would be wrong to focus on basics and downgrade the rest of the curriculum', adding that the whole-class teaching which the government was advocating as a way of raising standards in literacy and numeracy 'is not a guarantor of educational success ... The dominant values underlying Britain's current obsession with literacy and numeracy targets were the same as they were in the 1870s – economic instrumentalism, cultural reproduction and social control'.[19]

But this did not stop the Government from pressing ahead. In January 1998 it was announced that in order to allow more time for effective teaching in literacy and numeracy, the detailed requirements of the national curriculum would be suspended for two years for primary schools, and then reviewed. In what was little less than an about turn, it was made clear that only English, mathematics, science, IT and RE were now to be compulsory. John O'Leary, education editor of *The Times*, observed that the decision represents a victory for Chris Woodhead, the chief inspector, over the government's curriculum advisers. In a rare alliance with the teaching unions, Mr. Woodhead argues that the targets could be met only if more primary schooling was devoted to the basics.[20]

The extent of disarray among government advisers on this issue was illustrated by the fact that Nick Tate, the Chief Executive of the QCA and a known sympathiser with government aspirations, was reported in the same edition of *The Times* as arguing that

> the schools with the best results in English and mathematics are those which give a lot of attention to other subjects as well. A 'basics and little else' curriculum in primary schools may have been acceptable when the main purpose of state education was to service a low-skill economy. It cannot be acceptable today.[21]

Despite the Government's determination to put this issue at the heart of its educational reforms, within a few years there were those ready to put major question marks alongside its effectiveness. In August 2001 the *Observer* reported newly published research which suggested that in respect of literacy, society was steadily regressing: 'despite the government's efforts to improve literacy skills, the study found that 15% of people aged 15 to 21 are functionally illiterate. In 1912 inspectors reported that only 2% of the young were unable to read or write.' [22]

There was certainly some evidence that this initiative was having a direct impact on classroom organisation as evidence began to come in of an increased readiness among primary school heads to introduce setting and streaming in order to facilitate the teaching of literacy and numeracy. One OFSTED report, *Setting in primary schools*, published in January 1999 and based on a survey of over 900 schools, encouraged this trend, claiming that children of all ages benefited from setting and streaming: 'very few schools avoid setting because of ideological objections ... About a quarter of those schools not setting at the moment expressed their intention to do so in the near future'.[23] This reported that the number of pupils working in sets had doubled during the previous year, so that four per cent of all lessons in the primary sector were now setted. One important finding was that setting was most commonly used in deprived urban areas. The *TES* cautioned: 'OFSTED found that setting polarised the quality of teaching'.[24] And it was a trend that became even more evident. In the summer of 1999 the *TES* reported that 'nearly two-thirds of English and Welsh primary schools appear to be adopting ability grouping in response to government pressure for higher educational standards ... 62% of all primaries have altered their grouping methods since 1997'.[25]

'Towards a post-comprehensive era': the drive for specialism and independence at secondary level

A second major thread in Labour's educational policies was the drive towards more specialised and less rigidly controlled secondary schooling. This became an increasingly central theme during their second and third terms in office and, whether consciously or not, drew on major elements in the Conservative Party's educational policies which had been vociferously opposed at the time Labour came to power.

But the intention was clear from the start. In May 1997, the new government anticipated its own White Paper with the publication of *Diversity and excellence* proposing 'three kinds of school': aided, foundation and community. The grant-maintained sector was to be integrated into the system and the Funding Agency for Schools dismantled. The *TES* pointed out that this would cause major problems for counties like Kent (most of whose schools were grant-maintained), Essex and Gloucestershire. All of these were already 'only skeleton LEAs' and this proposal could only deepen their difficulties.[26] By the autumn beleaguered chief education officers were warning that these new categories of school could only 'foment division, distrust and widespread disruption', adding that this was a proposal which had not appeared in the Labour Party's election manifesto. It was a complaint which came to be heard repeatedly during the years that followed.[27]

During the next few years the Government's reservations about the secondary sector grew and were increasingly reflected in policy. In the summer of 2000 the *Sunday Times* reported seeing a leaked copy of Labour's draft policy for a second term which admitted serious failings in state schools: 'the comprehensive system developed in the 1970s and 1980s has not delivered what its advocates hoped for, never mind what we require for the twenty-first century'.[28]

At the end of 1999 Blair attacked 'standardised, monolithic comprehensives that failed to cope with pupils of widely differing abilities'.[29] By this time 'Labour's big idea', as *The Times* put it, was

> to adopt the Tory idea of the specialist school and expand it massively. Comprehensives will now be allowed to develop specialisms in areas such as language, maths and music and in return be free to select a tenth of their pupils. Half of secondaries will be encouraged down this route by 2006, fuelling claims that Labour is simply creating another hierarchy.[30]

A few weeks later Blair's press officer, Alastair Campbell, backed this shift in policy with his widely publicised reference to 'bog standard comprehensives', a remark so far ahead of most contemporary educational rhetoric that it immediately drew rebukes from both Blunkett and Prescott.[31] *The Times* commented succinctly in a lead article that 'it will require radicalism to prove that, on education, this is more than a bog-standard government'.[32]

All of this was posited on the understanding that it was only through the exercise of choice that parents could work to drive up standards in schools. This variegated secondary system was to be opened up increasingly to market forces. The ensuing heightened competition between schools would be the guarantor of what went on inside them. But this choice was far from unproblematic. In a vitriolic piece in the *Observer* in 2001, Kate Kellaway pointed out that there were still 164 grammar schools setting selective examinations and that, in the previous year, her son's primary school had sent sixty children to twenty-eight different secondary schools in the London area:

> What we are seeing is a return to the old days of the 11+ ... But now we have a new 11+ experience ... Even those of us who have no grander aim for our children than the best of the local comprehensive schools may be disappointed. It, too, is over-subscribed ... We are told this is a good thing ... that we can enjoy a marvellous choice. That choice is a mirage ... So who does the choosing? The schools themselves of course![33]

Another aspect of this drive towards distinct contrasts between schools was the determination to encourage the establishment of faith schools, even though they were widely unpopular with Labour Party backbenchers and many members of the general public. In October 2001 the *Observer* reported the publication of *Faith in education*, published the previous month by Civitas, which called into question the unthinking policy of expanding faith schools, 'laying bare the myth that church schools are centres of excellence'. The *Observer* commented that

> dissent was growing among back bench MPs, Ministers and educationalists concerned that an increase in faith schools would create 'educational apartheid' in a Britain already shocked by a summer of race riots and scenes of sectarian violence outside schools in Northern Ireland.[34]

A month later a You/Gov *Observer* poll showed that over 80 per cent of the population was opposed to any further expansion of the faith schools programme.[35] The facts that, on the one hand, Blair chose to send his own son to a faith school and that, on the other, Ruth Kelly was fast-tracked into the education office in December 2004 (an appointment which immediately came under attack because of her links to Opus Dei), both did nothing to assuage those who feared that the Government had as part of its agenda a particular view of the linkages between schooling and religious faith.[36] In January 2006 the TES revealed that one-third of all city academies were sponsored by Christian groups, with the United Learning Trust, a non-denominational Christian charity and the evangelical Emmanuel Schools Foundation being leading players.[37] The potential impact of these policies on students going through the schools is illustrated by a *Guardian* report in August 2006 that over 30 per cent of students in Britain believed in creationism.[38]

But, despite widespread reservations about the direction of policy, Tony Blair pressed ahead, telling his October 2002 party conference that they could look forward to 'a post-comprehensive era' with more specialist schools and 'advanced specialists' to be unveiled in a series of ministerial roadshows during the autumn.[39]

The continuing influence of government advisers was demonstrated in January 2004 when the *TES* reported that Andrew Adonis, Blair's personal education adviser, was pressing for 'US style privately run secondary schools' to be a part of the Labour Party manifesto for the next general election and to be introduced in the near future.[40] This resulted in legislation during the spring of 2006 which enabled all schools to become trust schools, owning their own assets, employing their own staff and setting their own admission arrangements. The legislation could only be got through with support from the Conservative Party and after major concessions to Labour backbenchers on the use of interviews for selecting pupils. Simon Jenkins, one of the most vocal opponents in the press of this development, pointed out in the *Guardian* that this was no more and no less than 'a straight copy of Kenneth Baker's 1988 Education Act as amended by John Patten in 1992'.[41] Even more pointedly, in the *Sunday Times* he described this legislation as

> originally the love child of Tony Blair and Lord Adonis, with Ruth Kelly as the surrogate mother. Its one substantive power – allowing local schools to opt out to become independent trusts – is a classic of structure over substance ... It is what happens when you put an unelected Lord in charge of sensitive social policy.[42]

But this drive for greater autonomy for secondary schools was one which contained its own internal contradictions, neatly encapsulated in a letter to the *TES* from Kevin O'Regan, a teacher at Wolverley High School in Warwickshire, who pointed out that

> since 1997 we have suffered an onslaught of initiatives that have heaped responsibilities on local authorities and schools and established control of education by central government. We have battalions of consultants employed to promote national strategies, taking good teachers out of classrooms: we have armies of administrators to manage the empire; and of course we have OFSTED to ensure that we all conform to the crushing orthodoxy imposed by No. 10. We cannot be anything but cynical about Blair's claim that he wishes to promote independence when the evidence of his past leadership so emphatically contradicts it.[43]

'A mixture of exhortation and blame'[44]: government attempts to galvanise teachers

Closely linked to this attempt to restructure the system was a governmental attempt to ensure that the teaching profession was kept onside and was galvanised into supporting its policies. As we will see later in this chapter, this was to prove difficult given the stress that many teachers felt themselves to be under at this time, but one constant in Labour policy was its determination to find ways of rewarding those teachers who were more successful, more sought after or simply more ready to go along with its proposals.

In October 1999, a leak to the press was used to trail the fact that 'Tony Blair will today hit out at the "culture of excuses" in schools as he appeals for £70,000 super heads to help him change the education system'.[45] A few months later the National College for School Leadership was described in the press as 'his pet project'. Blair told the *TES* that he wanted 'outstanding headteachers to bring on a new generation of dynamic, charismatic school leaders'.[46] It was at this time that the 'golden handcuffs' for teachers prepared to stay in the same post were announced.[47] In March 2003 an additional sixty million pounds was announced to reward high-achieving staff, most of whom, the *TES* commented, would have rather seen the money devoted to pre-empting job cuts that enhancing their own incomes.[48] In May of the same year, a similar strategy was employed in an attempt to stem the haemorrhaging of teaching staff from London schools, with plans to support 'high quality teachers' in the capital through monetary inducements.[49] A year later the same strategy was proposed by a governmental enquiry into the shortage of teachers of mathematics.[50] Thus, a policy of rewarding selected teaching staff (and in the process compounding the sense of alienation felt by those staff not included in these schemes) was one which was deployed repeatedly by Labour in office, as threshold payments and enhanced head teachers' salaries became a permanent feature.

Mortgaging the future of curriculum planning: the PFI initiative

Perhaps the most notable evidence of a determination to privatise the educational provision, and certainly the one with potentially the greatest long-term impact on schools and the curriculum, was the private finance initiative which was used extensively by the Labour government and was urged on local authorities when it came to the provision of new buildings. Originally introduced under John Major in 1992, PFI was a device which became central to the plans of the Labour government. It meant that rather than having new schools financed directly by central or local government, private consortia were encouraged to invest in the public sector through extremely appealing long-term contracts, usually twenty-five years in duration. Under the terms of PFI these private companies won the contract to design and build new schools and to operate those services, such as cleaning and school meals, which were not directly educational. The provision of the curriculum within these schools remained the responsibility of the governors and the local authority, which usually retained the ownership of the site and building. By the start of 2003 there were twenty-five PFI schools at work and a further 500 planned during the following three years at a cost of over two billion pounds. It was frequently suggested that this was the only realistic way to raise the funding necessary to embark on a building programme of the scale that was needed to compensate for earlier underinvestment.

In February 2001 an *Observer Business Supplement* survey showed that PFI was a natural development from the practice of 'outsourcing', by which outsourcing specialists organise everything from recruiting teachers to organising payrolls, ordering stationery and IT supplies and maintaining classrooms ... Companies are beginning to flex their muscles ... For the City 'education support' is a growth sector ... Capital Strategies believes this sector will grow from 1.6 billion today to 5 billion within five years ... Nearly 20% of the more than nine billion committed by the government since 1997 to rebuild schools is earmarked for schemes under PFI.[51]

By the early years of the twenty-first century there were clear signs that this was at best a profoundly controversial development. In September 2002 Sir Stuart Lipton, chair of the Commission for Architecture and the Built Environment, warned that 'the majority of PFI buildings are poorly designed and will fail to meet the changing demands of this and future generations'.[52] An Audit Commission report in January 2003 found that PFI schools were 'significantly worse' than those already in existence, particularly in terms of their space, lighting and heating arrangements'.[53] Despite this and the fact that the 2002 Labour Party conference called for a 'full and proper review' of PFI, the government remained (and at the moment of writing remains) determined to press ahead.

But the main objection to the PFI arrangement, and that with the longest term impact on what goes on inside the schools, is the way in which it mortgages the future of those LEAs and schools involved. The funding raised in the private sector to enable these buildings is borrowed at a much higher rate than public sector borrowing, and this charge is, in all cases, passed on to the LEA concerned. Trade unions opposed to PFI produced estimates of the ongoing commitment to PFI projects from the public purse, suggesting that the annual cost might be in total as much as thirty billion pounds, with education accounting for five billion of this figure. Unison General Secretary Dave Prentis commented that 'it cannot be right that huge profits are going into private pockets'.[54] The GMB (Britain's General Trades Union) calculated that the profits accruing to private companies from investment in schools could add up to as much as 3.4 billion pounds over the next thirty years. In 2002 the Conservative Party joined the unions in opposing further PFI schemes without much more careful accounting. The Shadow Chancellor, Michael Howard, said of PFI in the Commons on 27 November: 'there is a black hole in the public accounts ... entirely the making of the Chancellor'.[55] In the health sector, hiding under a cloak of government rhetoric which blames hospital trusts for poor management, large scale programmes of sacking staff have been announced. The same process is beginning in respect of PFI schools.

It is hardly surprising, therefore, that a growing chorus of complaints has been heard in respect of the impact of PFI on the schools. The first head teacher of Highlands School, Enfield (which in 2001 had been the first PFI school to open), resigned in 2006 and told the *Daily Telegraph* that the school was 'crippled' by PFI. She accused the provider (in this case, Equion) of using cheap building materials, of overcharging for various aspects of maintenance work and of failing to provide essential ancillary services. It became clear at this time too that, in many cases, the transfer of employment of ancillary workers in the schools to these private companies meant that agreements concerning pay and conditions of employment no longer applied, with potentially major conse-quences for the employees. Little wonder then that the outgoing head of Highlands reflected in the *Daily Telegraph* that 'it was naive to think that a com-mercial company would have a social conscience ... We could afford only the bare essentials for our pupils because so much of our budget was going on the PFI scheme'.[56] In fact, a Channel Four television programme which investigated PFI during the summer of 2006 claimed that, despite a concordat with the Government about recycling profits from PFI schemes, many of the companies involved were using offshore accounts to avoid taxation of any kind.[57] As a final twist to this ongoing saga of private concerns benefiting from the public educa-tional purse, the *TES* revealed in March 2003 that 'no win, no fee legal firms are costing £200 million a year by encouraging poor parents to sue schools ... one solicitor had contacted his LEA about a claim only fifty minutes after a child had an accident'.[58] Sadly, it appears that there may be many more such comments before these particular initiatives have run their full course. They will certainly continue to have a major impact on the ability of schools to deliver and modify the curriculum for years to come.

'Forward to personalised learning: not back to mass failure'[59]: New Labour and teaching styles

By the autumn of 2003 a new element was discernible in Labour's educational policies, and it was one which involved it in much closer control over what was going on in the classroom. This was its growing insistence on 'personalised learn-ing'. So great was the Government's determination to put this at the heart of its ongoing educational reforms that the headline cited at the start of this section, 'Forward to personalised learning: not back to mass failure', was in fact the intro-duction to the party's 2005 election manifesto commitments on education. This new buzz phrase was first deployed by Charles Clarke at the October 2003 Party Conference where he linked 'personalised learning' to the new 'pupil achieve-ment tracker', although it was then and remains still far from clear exactly what this was meant to involve.[60] By the spring of 2004 the *TES* was ready to gently parody this initiative, commenting that 'the term "personalised learning" might be tumbling out of education ministers' lips every time they make a speech at the moment, but many are struggling to pin down what it means'.[61] By the beginning of 2005 Professor Frank Coffield was pointing out that he had received 'a stream of emails from teachers complaining that inspectors and senior managers con-tinue to recommend (i.e. insist) that they differentiate classes by means of learning styles'. It was an initiative which, in his view, 'might do more harm than good'.[62] Two weeks later a letter from Andy Buck, a Dagenham head teacher, warned of 'the danger of trendy teaching styles', adding that there was 'no clear research basis for the current obsession with learning styles ... For a teacher who may see over 500 students a week, the idea that they can plan for each child's indi-vidual style is nonsense'.[63]

Government interventionism and the school curriculum

If these were some of the main elements of Labour's educational policies since 1997, they were backed by a style of government which was also calculated to ensure that what was planned was implemented as effectively as possible. This, too, is part of any explanation of the impact of New Labour's educational policies on what went on in the schools. First, and perhaps of greatest significance, was the fact that this government, from the outset, proved to be one of the most interventionist in respect of what was going on in the classroom, applying regulations over the heads of civil servants, administrators and head teachers to ensure that their policies had a direct effect on what the teachers were allowed to do in the classroom.

No sooner was Labour in office than this trend was clear. In June 1997 the *Sunday Times* reported that

> plans to eliminate fashionable teaching methods from Britain's classrooms will be announced by the Government this week ... Teacher training colleges which persist in using progressive methods and refuse to go 'back to basics' will lose their government funding and could eventually face closure. Blunkett seeks to transform the culture of classroom education ... The national curriculum will insist on whole class teaching instead of the child-centred system which leaves pupils to learn at their own pace ... There will be more emphasis on the three Rs and an hour a day of reading and the use of the phonics method.[64]

A month later *The Times* reported the publication of *Excellence in schools*, commenting that 'in doing so Labour ministers embrace men and measures they have spent much of the past fighting ... teachers' performance will be monitored by OFSTED under a regime which will be, if anything, more Prussian than before'.[65] This style was soon seen for what it was and became the subject of trade union comment. Nigel de Gruchy, General Secretary of the NASUWT, observed that

> Labour's model is seen by critics as an increasingly interventionist, centralised one, where the Government sets class sizes, imposes literacy and numeracy hours, recommends appropriate hours of homework, gets tough on target setting and talks of 'zero tolerance' of failure.[66]

Similarly, Peter Wilby, writing in the *TES*, commented that

> the literacy and numeracy hours strike me as an extraordinary intervention into teaching methods by central government ... If these policies go wrong, the results will be catastrophic. The flight of both parents and teachers from inner-city schools will become a stampede.[67]

Similarly, a retired HMI, John Slater, commented publicly that

> Labour may have slimmed down the curriculum yet further but they have sur-
> passed the Tories in exerting central control ... Under Labour's numeracy and
> literacy strategies, primary teachers have not only been told what to teach but
> how to teach it.[68]

But, at the same time, it was made clear by members of the new administration
that this was indeed the intention. During the summer of 1998, Margaret Hodge
placed a major article on 'the third way' in the *TES* to explain the Government's
position, pointing out that 'previous Labour governments concentrated on school
structures rather than educational outcomes ... This government has chosen not to
prioritise structures ... The emphasis on outcomes poses new and difficult challenges for teachers ... Assessing outcomes involves opening schools to greater
public account'.[69]

It was to prove an approach to policymaking with which the government persisted. In May 2006 one consultant on the teaching of mathematics, Wendy
Fortescue, was still complaining that

> teachers must be allowed to choose methods that they are not only happy to
> teach but that they are also confident in using ... It was with complete horror
> that I read in the renewal of the mathematics framework that 'Children
> should be taught one standard written method for each operation' ...
> Prescription is a dangerous game for teachers, pupils and for enjoyment of
> mathematics.[70]

Further, it became increasingly clear that not only the initiatives, but often the
details of policymaking, were coming direct from Downing Street itself. In a
telling Radio 4 interview, given shortly after she had left the post of Minister of
Education, Estelle Morris offered a candid account of her annoyance at the
repeated intervention of Downing Street advisers into the details of policymaking and implementation during her term of office. She spoke of the need to win
policy arguments with 'the Andrew Adonises of this world', adding

> it was my job, not their job ... I was elected: they were not ... Number 10 are
> not deliverers, they don't deliver a damn thing. They think of an idea and then
> buzz off and think of another. I always used to say to them, 'Hang on! I am
> still busy delivering the last set of proposals!'[71]

Ted Wragg, whose press comments became a constant thorn in the side of the
Government, amusingly invented a character whom he called 'Tony Zoffis' as a
subtle way of drawing attention to where power in education policymaking actually resided during these years.

Spinning out of control: New Labour and the media

The Labour Party's dependence on public relations and on 'spin' was already widely recognised before it came to office. Once in power, their manipulation of the news became a major preoccupation, and educational policy proved to be one of the more susceptible areas of policy for this treatment. David Blunkett's use of spin to massage his figures for government expenditure on education was ruthlessly exposed by Nick Davies in *The school report* in 2000. Davies showed how Blunkett's announcement of an additional nineteen billion pounds for education on 14 July 1998 was no more and no less than a confidence trick. 'It works like this', Davies reported,

> You take the increase for the first year and you say: 'Well, if I pay this in the first year it will become a permanent part of the budget ... so I should carry on counting it as an increase each year.' This is not the way any previous British government has accounted for its budgets.

Davies showed how the Treasury Accounts Committee quickly spotted what was going on, concluding that 'there is no cash bonanza of the kind the newspaper headlines might suggest'. In fact throughout his first two years in office Blunkett's department was spending less on education than had the outgoing Conservative government, a performance which Blunkett had derided at the time as 'miserable'.[72] It is hardly surprising then that newspapers such as the *Observer* were, by 2001, expressing considerable scepticism about the way in which government education policy was being presented. The *Observer* announced itself 'weary of Mr. Blunkett's notoriously dextrous footwork when making funding announcements. We are understandably sceptical'.[73]

But the full extent of Labour's dependence on a spin machine emerged when Blunkett moved to the Home Office to be replaced by Estelle Morris. Conor Ryan, described as Blunkett's 'spinner in chief', decided to go public on what had been going on in the office. The *TES* reported that

> Education journalists are well aware that ... news management does happen. There is a culture of seeking to bury bad news that pervades Whitehall's information services ... Last month an article entitled 'How to bury the truth' appeared in the *Evening Standard* under the byline of Conor Ryan, special adviser ... to Blunkett throughout his term as Education Secretary.[74]

The article conceded that there had been significant exaggeration of funding levels: 'the apotheosis of this is the £19 billion of new investment Blunkett claimed was being ploughed into education. That was unquestionably triple counting and has continued in the Department's present policy of making several funding announcements a week.'

On behalf of the teachers' unions, John Dunford spelt out the damage all this did to relations with the profession and to their sense of commitment. He claimed that repeated attempts to hide the truth about teacher shortages from 1997 until September 2000, 'when the government finally had to own up', exacerbated the situation by alienating the teachers. Dunford concluded that 'the government is working first and foremost to the political agenda of re-election ... a great pity as the secretary of State has a responsibility to put the interests of the education service – employees and customers – first'.[75]

But this practice was to continue after 2002. The *TES* announced that Estelle Morris was to have three special advisers in her team. It identified them and pointed out that the use of unattributed comments to manipulate public opinion was still going on. The paper commented that

> they tend to think of the media as a Government supporters club ... Now they regard themselves as propagandists ... If it carries on like this it will blow up in their face ... They will get caught out ... They need to be careful.[76]

There can be no doubt that this approach to the presentation and manipulation of the Government's educational performance was a major factor in alienating much opinion within the school staffrooms.

'A toxic mix of educational beliefs and mismanagement'[77]: the significance of Chris Woodhead's rhetoric

The fact that Chris Woodhead remained as chief inspector when Labour came to power was significant, and it allowed the Government to shelter behind the rhetoric of a known polemicist and to invoke 'respectable' opinion in support of its policies during its first few years in office. Certainly, Woodhead continued with his high profile lambasting of the teaching profession and of current practice in schools and his pronouncements received wide publicity in the press. In April 1998, Woodhead addressed Politeia, a right-wing think tank, claiming that schools were failing 'through a toxic mix of educational beliefs and mismanagement ... Common examples include building pyramids out of egg boxes and pupils standing at the roadside counting cars ... pupils' time is being wasted'.[78] It was a view which drew from Peter Smith, the General Secretary of the Teachers' and Lecturers' Association, the comment that 'it is easier for Chris Woodhead to scapegoat teachers than to admit the serious funding difficulties faced by schools'.[79]

Indeed, much of Woodhead's rhetoric appeared to be calculated to support and facilitate government policy. In June 1998 it was the Inspectorate which found itself on the receiving end, as he commented that

> good schools should have more freedom to choose what they teach ... some OFSTED inspectors fall below the standard required ... Schools must 'blow the whistle' on inspectors who bring their own ideological baggage into school. The local authorities should play a smaller role in running schools.[80]

Early in 1999 he returned to his well-known views on the capabilities of the teaching profession, claiming that up to 15,000 teachers were incompetent.[81] A year later he placed another 'teacher-bashing' piece in the *TES*, this time repeating his claim that class size was irrelevant to successful teaching.[82]

The extent to which the Government was happy to hide behind Woodhead's rhetoric became clear in July 2000, following the public suggestion from William Hague that schools should be given more power to set their own policies. Using a GMTV programme, Woodhead commented that these views 'struck a chord' and went on to attack 'the liberal establishment' for ruining the education system. Barry Sheerman, the chair of the Labour Select Committee to which Woodhead was accountable, suggested that Woodhead would do well to stick to 'facts and research' since 'he seems intent on pursuing a reputation as a loveable eccentric. He should be careful it does not detract from his serious purpose as chief inspector'.[83] At the same time both the NUT and the NAHT called for his resignation. But David Blunkett intervened on Woodhead's behalf, using a spokesman to point out that 'Mr. Woodhead has raised concerns about issues of bureaucracy and discipline in schools which the government has already started addressing.'[84] Interestingly, when Woodhead resigned in November 2000 to pursue a career in the media, the Conservative Party let it be known that he was under consideration for a peerage which would grant him the protection of Parliament for an ongoing critique of government policy. This was scotched by a Labour Party leak which made clear that, if this happened, details of Woodhead's private life would be released to the press.[85] There could hardly have been any clearer evidence of the seriousness with which the Government viewed his public comments.

Two years later, when Woodhead's book, *Class war*, was published, the extent of government attempts to control or influence Woodhead's pronouncements during his time as chief HMI became clear. In an interview with the *TES* to publicise his book, Woodhead commented that

> Conor Ryan would phone me ... to offer, ever so nicely, ... suggestions as to what might be included or changed in speeches and reports. Michael Barber would express his disappointment if we criticised one of his cherished initiatives. David Blunkett would, on occasion, fire over a terse little letter ... it was pretty clear which side they felt should be calling the shots.[86]

This reflects, not simply the fact that Woodhead enjoyed his time in the public eye, but that he undoubtedly believed himself to be having an impact on policy-making. During his time as chief HMI, when the Government announced its narrowing down of the primary curriculum so that there could be more time devoted to the core curriculum, Woodhead went on record in the *TES* with the remark that 'I'm not the one saying that my views have led to a Ministerial decision. Let's just say that I'm very, very pleased.'[87]

The expropriation of radical right rhetoric

Not only was it useful to the Government to have figures such as Chris Woodhead available as foil, but some of its leading members were ready to echo his views in their own public statements. In 1999, for example, Tony Blair told a London conference of new head teachers that

> we must take on what I call the 'culture of excuses' which still infects some parts of the teaching profession ... a culture that tolerates low ambitions, rejects excellence and treats poverty as an excuse for failure ... In all reform and change you meet 'small c' conservatives ... who are suspicious of change and who resist change.[88]

In a summary of the performance of Blair and Blunkett made in 2001, *The Times* reflected that

> both men were united against 'trendy' educationists who had let children down. As well as tackling the Department, they targeted LEAs, privatising their services. Fittingly, Islington was the first to lose its education service ... Blunkett's autobiography, *On a clear day*, emphasized that 'I believe in discipline, solid mental arithmetic, learning to read and write accurately, plenty of homework, increasing expectations ... all anathema to modern children.[89]

All this is hardly surprising in view of the extent to which the 'think tanks' from which new Labour drew much of its inspiration were beginning to be influenced themselves by new right and neo-conservative ideas. Alongside the Fabian Society, which remained heavily influenced by those working within the universities, there were by the late 1990s: the New Policy Institute, set up in 1996 and headed by Peter Kenway and Guy Palmer; Demos, established in 1993 by Geoff Mulgan and Martin Jacques; the Social Market Foundation, whose leading figures included Lord Owen and Robert Skidelsky; and the Institute for Public Policy Research founded in 1988.

Demos devoted much of its energies to exploring the possibilities of choice in public services and among its other interests was Education Action Zones. Its director, Geoff Mulgan, went on to a post in the No. 10 policy unit working directly for Tony Blair. The Social Market Foundation was possibly the organisation which did most to bring the charter schools being trialled in the United States to the attention of British policymakers. In 1999 it advocated the extension of EAZs to enable businesses, teachers and parents to become directly involved in the running of schools. But perhaps of all these organisations the one which drew most strident public criticism was the Institute for Public Policy Research. Although it went on to raise questions about the impact of PFI in one of its publications in December 2002, it was itself investigated by Alison Pollock, a leading academic critic of PFI, who pointed out that the IPPR was heavily dependent on backing from corporate sponsors, seeing it as evidence of 'a striking coalition between big business and government'.[90] The organisations from which New

Labour drew its ideas were coming to look more and more like the think tanks on which recent Conservative governments had relied. Thus it is hardly surprising that throughout its time in office, New Labour continued to conform to and to develop the new right rhetoric around schooling which had been such a marked element of the Thatcher and Major administrations. Governments of whatever hue, across the developed world, were coming to sing more and more from the same centre-right hymn sheet, and this determined much of the tone and content of public statements about schooling as well as many aspects of policy.

The issue of teacher morale

The issue of teacher morale was to become increasingly central to the efforts of New Labour to influence what was going on in the classrooms. From the outset, the portents were not encouraging. Within a month of Labour coming to power, the new government was sent an open letter by David Hart, General Secretary of the NAHT, warning that

> the Labour Party's needle seems to have got stuck in a failure groove. I think the teaching profession's morale would be measurably improved if you were immediately to announce a national conference to trumpet success in state schools ... Adhering to the last government's policy on public sector pay ... will not solve the problem ... We must look to a restoration of the enormous damage done to school budgets by 18 years of Conservative government.[91]

A similar plea came from Peter Mortimore, Director of the University of London Institute of Education. He pointed out that

> the 652 pages of job advertisements that have appeared in the *TES* over the past three weeks illustrate the potential crisis facing our education system. You need to act immediately to convince heads and teachers it is worth staying there ... that the Government regards teachers as an asset rather than a problem ... Dropping the emphasis on league tables would show that you are moving away from the last government's 'shame and blame' culture and adopting a more constructive approach.[92]

Yet, during Labour's first year in office, evidence of the Government's failure to convince many members of the profession grew. By September the *TES* was reporting that 'plans to raise educational standards risk being blown off course by a national shortage of teachers which has plunged many inner-city schools into crisis'. The article went on to detail a recent research report from Brunel University which showed that teacher shortages were particularly severe at secondary level in modern languages, maths, science and design and technology, with East Anglia being a particular black-spot.[93] The same report commented that 'everywhere we went we were told that teachers felt oppressed by excessive and ill-informed media criticism which ignored progress made in raising standards'.[94]

In the same month, Peter Wilby, a *TES* correspondent, complained that:

> the insistence on lesson planning, work-schemes, whole-school policies and all the rest of it is turning the classroom teacher into little more than a vehicle for other people's ideas and priorities ... The relentless focus on structured lessons and predetermined outcomes, the pressure created by tests, inspections and appraisals must discourage schools, teachers and, for that matter, pupils, from taking risks. There is no doubt that progressive education generated vast quantities of nonsense. Yet, as the years go on, its underlying philosophy looks more and more to have been ahead of its time ... I think we, as a nation, would be unwise to make it impossible for any teacher ever again to wander off the point.[95]

A month later the *TES* commented that

> the teachers are holding back. At a time when Britain is full of creativity and excitement, they have been left behind. Still struggling away at the chalk face, complaining of overwork and low morale ... What precisely are they waiting for? ... The real problem is that teachers lack recognition. Their difficulties are dismissed as whingeing, and public teacher bashing is still de rigeur if ministers are to retain their image as tough, committed to high standards ... The next step must be a credible strategy of getting the teachers on board.[96]

During 1997, the number of teachers leaving the profession rose by 40 per cent, 21,300 having quit by September, compared with only 15,400 a year earlier. At the same time the GTTR announced a drop of over 10 per cent in applications for teacher training courses, with the shortage subjects hardest hit.[97]

These ongoing pressures were one factor working to sustain the contrasts between schools (and the curriculum) in different locations and in differing types of school. The irony was not lost on the TES, which reflected at the start of 1999 that, although teacher morale remained very low,

> the private sector is more resilient than ever – especially in the affluent south – ... not just because they can command two or three times the level of resources per pupil which state schools get ... The private sector has also steadfastly refused to accept the national curriculum. Almost certainly as a direct result of this ... subjects – particularly those in the arts – which the national curriculum has sidelined now flourish in the independent sector; ... in marked contrast to the 1960s when the arts, creativity and innovation were developing exponentially ... at a time when most public schools were locked into a traditional and unimaginative curricular diet.[98]

But still the question of teacher supply loomed large, and many thought that governmental policies often had the side effect of exacerbating the problems. In October 1999, for example, the TTA announced the first mandatory mathematics tests for all intending teachers, whatever their discipline.[99] At the start of 2000, Janet Pidgeon, the President of the London branch of the NAHT, went public with her claim that 'teacher supply in London is at crisis point ... Many heads rely on teachers from overseas. Many primary classes have no permanent teacher. Recruitment to teacher training is down again ... We cannot succeed without a stable workforce of teachers.[100] A year later the press was reporting that many schools were considering a four-day week for pupils because of teacher shortages,[101] while the Government was encouraging LEAs to bring thousands of retired teachers back into the classroom to cover the gaps. The Headlands School in Swindon was planning to send children home because of staff shortages. Problems were said to be particularly acute in London and Essex.[102] At this time the *Observer* ran a campaign on teacher recruitment and a major article in January 2001 commented that

> as severe staff shortages bite, particularly in London and the South east, anger among teachers and parents over the deteriorating recruitment crisis is reaching boiling point. OFSTED inspectors last week closed another London primary school after they found it 'stretched almost to breaking point' by staff shortages. The school, the inspectors found, lacked even enough staff to teach the national curriculum.

The paper went on to report the comments of a supply teacher from Australia, one of the many working in London:

> It was hard, hard work. Every Australian teacher has a nightmare story to tell from England ... in Britain the teachers seemed to be sick all the time. Us supply teachers didn't even have to wait for a call. We just went to work knowing there would be people off sick.[103]

Before the end of the year Estelle Morris was forced to announce a new ten-year plan which would allow classroom assistants to take charge of classes, despite their lack of proper training and qualifications. The *Observer* pointed out that staff shortages were at a 36-year high, and that the 127,000 aides working in schools who would be affected by this announcement were to be supplemented by 20,000 more by 2006, if the Government had its way.[104] But the issue of support staff did not go away. Whilst the Government became increasingly ready to use the head count of all adults employed in the classroom as a basis for calculation of teacher/pupil ratios, the press highlighted problems of disparities in pay rates and conditions of service for classroom assistants in different parts of the country, and differing policies on the extent that they should take on administrative chores, to flag up that the increasing army of classroom assistants did not, of itself, mean an end to the problems of teacher morale.[105] The extent to which all this represented a 'post-code lottery' was highlighted by the *Observer* in April 2001 in an article which showed that whilst the Manchester LEA spent £35,000 per pupil annually, the comparable figure for Gloucestershire was £26,000, for Tower Hamlets £45,000, and for Redbridge £31,000.[106] These were disparities which spoke for themselves.

In this situation, members of the teaching profession became increasingly prepared to express their anger at what was going on. At the Labour Party
Conference in October 1999, Nigel de Gruchy responded to Tony Blair's 'culture
of excuses' speech by telling him that

> many teachers feel somewhat insulted and patronised by you when you reject
> any criticisms they might make as 'the dark forces of conservatism'. Teachers
> will be incredulous at these comments. We all need to modernise, including,
> perhaps, yourself, in your attitude to teachers.[107]

These reservations were echoed only a week later by Professor Graham Hills,
who, in a letter to *The Times*, argued that

> the good society takes care of its teachers and insists that they be the best that
> money can buy ... This would amount to doubling their salaries, but, within a
> generation or so, the country would have a cohort of teachers to be proud of
> ... The better off know all about these things. Wherever possible they buy or
> manoeuvre their way out of the state system in search of something better ...
> It is an indictment of much of present day state schooling. And who but the
> government is responsible for this? ... It is time that Mr. Blair stopped blam-
> ing others and assumed some responsibility for where we are now.[108]

In June 2002, the *TES* reported on what it called 'a secret government dossier
which reveals 82 ways in which teachers are now being strangled by red tape'.
This document, prepared within the DES for the Cabinet Office, had been leaked
to the press to highlight the impact which government policy was having on
teachers' daily routines. It reported that, in respect of English GCSE coursework,
every teacher had to fill in at least seven pieces of paper for each pupil. A special
needs coordinator with six pupils each taking twelve subjects had to fill in sev-
enty-two forms a term. It was a situation which had led Doug McEvoy, General
Secretary of the NUT, to observe that 'teachers feel they are submerged in a sea of
bureaucracy, most of which is pointless'.[109]

In 2001, one teacher, Sue Palmer, set up her 'time to teach' website, in
response to what she called 'yet another round of challenging new government
targets'. This resulted in so many hits on her website that, by the summer of
2003, the *TES* was reporting that 'other more powerful voices have begun to
take up the cause' of teacher stress in response to continuing policies of target
setting:

> University of Toronto researchers, commissioned by the Government to
> report on the new national strategies, voiced considerable concern about tar-
> gets in their final report. Then David Bell, former chief inspector of schools,
> joined in ... The TES is now launching a campaign to draw attention to what
> has become a national scandal.[110]

Before the end of 2003, the Government was forced to introduce a teachers' work-load agreement, which finally came into full effect in September 2005. Although this was intended to address the issue of teacher stress, the press remained at best sceptical about its impact. At the beginning of 2004 the *TES* reported that over a half of all teachers were receiving no benefit at all from this agreement.[111] In February 2005 the same journal reported that, according to the QCA's annual report, 'primary teachers are spending an hour longer than a year ago as schools struggle to cope with growing curriculum demands'.[112]

As significant as the issue of teacher stress might have been for teacher recruitment and retention, it also had a major impact on the preparedness of the profession to involve itself in public discussion of educational issues, not least curriculum planning. This generated what one observer described in November 2004 as 'the eerie sound of staffroom silence'. This comment came from David Perks, the head of Physics at Graveney School, Tooting, who pointed out that

> teachers' views are seldom asked for and never heard ... a far cry from the 1980s ... Those who deliver education have a responsibility to call the politicians to account ... If teachers refrain from engaging in the debate about the future of education they hand over the responsibility to those least suited to the job, the politicians.[113]

This was an issue highlighted by the *TES* at this time. A week later a lead article stressed that

> the current emphasis on leadership ... risks overlooking teachers, the people who actually improve results but rarely get the glory. Classroom union leader Mary Bousefield is right to worry about a trend to consult heads rather than teachers on possible changes. Policymakers please note: teachers are worth it too![114]

One lead article in the *TES* serves as a fitting if gentle epitaph to teacher influence under a Labour government since 1997. Reporting in May 2005 on the replacement of Ruth Kelly by Alan Johnson as Secretary of State, the *TES* commented on

> suspicions that she had been appointed – with an upcoming general election in mind – to focus on parent power rather than teachers. These were borne out in her first education speech in Manchester in January 2005 ... She used the 'p' word no fewer than 44 times in as many minutes, compared with just six mentions of teachers.[115]

'Duck! Here comes the pendulum!': the impact on the curriculum

The initial impact of Labour in office was to generate the impression, and to some extent the reality, of a school curriculum which was increasingly being pared back to the basics. Yet, within a few years, there were clear signs of a reaction to this trend which involved both educationalists and government spokespersons emphasising the need to move beyond the core curriculum and restricted teaching methods. It is the tension between these two views of curriculum planning which has continued to dominate during the first few years of the twenty-first century.

There can be no doubt, though, that Labour's first few years in power resulted in many teachers calling for a renewed emphasis on the core curriculum, particularly at primary level. The *TES* reported that the literacy and numeracy targets announced by Blunkett in May 1997 were met by a response from primary head teachers that 'the Government's campaign will fail unless the primary curriculum is reformed to concentrate on the 3Rs.' Michael Brookes, the head of Sherwood School in Mansfield commented that 'the national curriculum is too broad. Many teachers at key stage two are struggling to deliver it. As a result children are not spending enough time on the basics'.[116] It was not until the summer of 1998 that the DES published 'long-awaited guidance on how to slim down the primary curriculum'.[117] In May 1999 the *TES* reported that 'teachers' leaders are angry that plans for a revised national curriculum to be announced today will not fulfil Minister's promises to slim the timetable'. The revisions, which were to become effective in 2000 involved primary schools in the resumption of 'a full diet of history, geography, music, art, PE, plus the numeracy and literacy hours', whilst secondary schools were required to give five per cent of their time to citizenship as a preparation for adult life, despite government claims that all this was to be less prescriptive than what went before.[118]

All this was neatly summarised in a special edition of the *Cambridge Journal of Education* in the summer of 1999 offering a critique of Labour's educational record since coming to power. In this collection, Stephen Ball, Director of the Centre for Public Policy Research at the Institute of Education, reflected that

> Labour's reliance on tests and its focus on the 3Rs may defeat its aim of creating a highly-skilled, flexible workforce ... The Government's national literacy and numeracy programmes and the highly-specific targets have encouraged schools to narrow the curriculum at the expense of work that would truly raise the work-skills ... cross-curricular, open-ended, real world problem-solving tasks to encourage group work, creativity, initiative and the application of transfer of learning.[119]

Ball's comments were not only a summary of the immediate impact of the new Labour government on what was happening in the classrooms, but also anticipated the reaction from some teachers and educationalists which was not long in coming. It was heralded by Diane Hofkins, the perceptive *TES* correspondent, who warned her readers in June 2000 to

> duck! Here comes the pendulum! It's swinging back again! It's the one that sweeps back and forth between prescription and freedom, formal teaching and discovery learning, between trusting teachers and telling them exactly

what to do ... The pendulum which traversed a decade through the launch of the national curriculum in 1989; the introduction of league tables; the war against the 'questionable dogmas' of child-centred learning; naming and shaming; test results targets; and the detailed syllabuses for the literacy and numeracy hours has run out of oomph. It will be brought down by its own weight. But not just that ... The mood is changing ... It may not be felt in schools for a while yet, but the signs are there.

Pointing to the call from the Government's new chief adviser on curriculum and examinations, David Hargreaves, for an 'assessment revolution' involving more formative assessment, and a renewed interest among Ministers in thinking skills and social inclusion, she added that

creativity is the buzzword of the moment ... Maybe it is again possible to quote the 1967 Plowden Report 'At the heart of the educational process lies the child' without being vilified ... When Lady Plowden and her committee concluded that 'finding out' was better for children than 'being told', they were writing against a backdrop of boring, highly-formal primary schools geared to the eleven-plus.[120]

It is certainly the case that, during the early years of the twenty-first century, government rhetoric came to focus far more on the need for creativity in the classroom and for teachers to be more innovative. But, in reality, this was never more than a partial swing of the pendulum. Many forces and commentators remained committed to one version or another of the new prescriptive regime. In October 2000, the *Sunday Times* ran an article reporting the research of Nigel Hastings of Nottingham Trent University under the headline 'Children learn better when they sit in lines', claiming that work-rates could be doubled through the use of formal teaching methods. This account was far more disparaging of the impact of Plowden, adding that 'the change from traditional rows to children in groups followed the Plowden report ... It was based on the then 'progressive' idea that children could learn from one another.' The article went on to quote James Tooley, an emerging star of the radical right and a professor at Newcastle University, who had claimed that 'group teaching can be chaos in classrooms and that can stifle pupils' creativity'.[121] The landscape of this particular battlefield seems to have changed little since the 1950s!

But other observers identified another underlying reality of this period. In July 2002, Professors Maurice Galton and John McBeath produced a research report on what was going on in the primary classrooms and this took a far less sanguine view of the changes that had taken place in recent years:

classroom style has changed substantially. Pressure on time meant teachers were 50% less likely to have chats with individual children. Very little one to one immediate feedback took place. Teachers did not have time to go through a piece of work or hear children read. Marking was mostly done away from the children.

John Bangs, a leading figure in the NUT, commented that 'what is shocking about this report is the extent to which arts have been eliminated from primary schools. Tests and targets are wiping out pupil and teacher creativity, the very area that the Government claims to value.[122]

Thus, while many of the public statements emanating from government continued to press for more creativity in the classroom (an emphasis that was reflected by OFSTED inspectors at this time), many within the profession felt and expressed a deep frustration that the demands made of them and the day-by-day working conditions of the classroom made any significant shift towards child-centred methods an impossibility. In March 2003 the Primary Education Alliance was set up, bringing together the Primary National Trust, the National Association for Primary Education and the Primary Headteachers' Association to campaign for the abolition of tests which, in their view, were resulting in an over-focus on the three Rs and squeezing out of art, music and other activities. In the words of one head teacher, 'the tests have narrowed the curriculum quite significantly'.[123] A month later, Ron Evans, head of Havelock Junior School in Northamptonshire, summarised the frustration felt by many teachers in a letter to the *TES:*

> Primary teachers and children have been 'knuckle-dusted' into a curriculum straitjacket; and 'springboarded' and 'boosted' in the inexorable pursuit of higher standards (i.e. test results) in a narrow core curriculum. But now they see a subtle shift: inspectorates ... who were a short time ago cajoling teachers into tunnel-vision targeting of pupils, subjects, parts of subjects, parts of pupils, now seem to be blaming schools for lack of breadth and creativity and for boredom among pupils – as if teachers had instigated the whole sorry business.[124]

Embarrassingly for the Government, a research report from King's College London at this time suggested that whilst Blunkett had promised to ensure that 'children would know their times tables', in reality 'pupils' grasp of multiplication and division has declined'.[125]

At the start of 2004 there was some evidence that those within government were aware of these issues and were seeking to respond. A new Primary Strategy was supported by pronouncements from the QCA and followed immediately by the Government's own *Excellence and enjoyment: a strategy for primary schools.* This stressed that 'we want all schools to offer pupils a rich and exciting curriculum in which all subjects are being taught well'.[126] At the same time the Chief Inspector of Schools, David Bell, was emphasising in his annual report that 'too many schools are not convinced that more creative work will really make a difference to standards. They may be unwilling to take a risk'. Bell went on to cite OFSTED's own publication of the previous autumn, *The curriculum in successful primary schools,* which had also called for more creativity in the classroom.[127] The *TES* commented that 'there is quite a lot of catching up to do in subjects such as art, history and PE because of the neglect since the 1990s', but cautioned that 'standard bearers have worried that encouraging schools to develop a more integrated curriculum will lead to the type of wishy-washy catch-all projects we had in the 1980s, which were condemned for lack of focus and depth'.[128]

But even this intervention provoked strong responses from some teachers. One of them, Tim Peskett from Northamptonshire, expostulated in the *TES:*

> I am genuinely staggered that David Bell said that primary teachers lack the confidence to take control of the curriculum. This is impudence of the very cheapest kind. Can't even the Chief Inspector appreciate the logical legacy of years of prescription, initiatives and imposed priorities ... that he did little to alleviate? What is he going to do now to persuade primary teachers that offering breadth will not result in them being slagged off again?[129]

Meanwhile, other commentators pointed out the self-contradictory elements of policy which were bound to result in this initiative being unsuccessful. Bill Lear, a former chief inspector of London schools, commented in the pages of the *TES* that the continuing OFSTED strategy of focusing on the core curriculum made any possibility of a broadening or freeing up of the curriculum extremely unlikely: 'it is clear from every repost that core subjects have been rigorously inspected. In marked contrast, many of the foundation subjects receive little more than cursory attention'. This, Lear pointed out, was bound to affect poorer children most and result in no lessening of contrasts in performance between schools in different areas.[130] Similarly, a month later, Roy Hughes, the Chair of the Historical Association, wrote to the *TES* with the comment that

> the chief inspector's discovery of a two-tier curriculum is a highly predictable bombshell. The Government's complete eschewal of curriculum thought has created overload pressures and these pull in very different directions. Teaching to the test (English, Maths. And Science) ... is a rational strategy ... No coherent philosophy of education underpins the curriculum and the two-tier curriculum is the result.[131]

At the end of the year Hughes underlined the point:

> The apparently welcome attempts of the Primary National Strategy to add a texture of engagement, excellence and enjoyment to the primary years is a castle built on sand. It will be washed away by the tide of tests, tables and targets. A richer primary curriculum is irretrievably debilitated.[132]

Creating a new historical orthodoxy

What becomes clear from a close reading of policy documents and the educational press during these years is the emergence of what is little short of a new historical orthodoxy. Across the spectrum of educational opinion it became increasingly usual, and even predictable, to find arguments about the school curriculum prefixed by an account of curriculum change since the Second World War which suggested that child-centred approaches and progressive teaching methods dominated the 1960s, but that more recently pressures for whole-class teaching and a focus on standards and targets had involved a new emphasis and that many of the faults of the system during the 1980s and 1990s could be attributed to an over-zealous application of progressivism during that earlier period.

This view was implicit in many letters published in the educational press, such as that from Michael Hurdle in 1998, who argued that

> Chris Woodhead reiterates the view that 'the roots of educational failure lie in poor teaching methods ...' But how did 'poor teaching methods' arise in the first place? Until ten years ago it was common to find school inspectors promoting the view that non-subject based topic teaching was the only valid primary style; that teachers should avoid direct teaching – especially whole-class teaching – and become 'enablers' of pupils managing their own learning. A good many inspectors must now be upholding the opposite of what they preached ten years ago.[133]

A year later, it was this view which underlay a *TES* leader article summarising recent educational change:

> One of the most potent educational myths is the great war between the traditionalists and the progressives ... Certain phrases quickly become code for opposing factions. 'Child centred teaching' or 'real books' act as a red rag to the traditionalists: 'whole-class teaching' or 'learning by rote' raise the hackles of the progressives ... But those days are gone ... the divide is yesterday's agenda.[134]

Similarly, in 1999, Blair's 'forces of conservatism' speech provoked a string of letters to the press. One of them, from Gregory Shenkman, offers a fascinating insight into the way in which discussion of the curriculum was being underpinned by accounts of the recent history of the curriculum. Shenkman wrote:

> Mr. Blair plumbs new depths. The reality is that the sorry condition of many of our schools stems directly from the trendy teaching reforms introduced in the 1960s and 1970s by left-wing idealists in the teeth of resistance by what Mr. Blair refers to as the 'forces of conservatism'. These prudent voices were unable to resist what the Labour Party then considered to be progress. A whole generation of schoolchildren has paid the price ... Therefore, what Mr. Blair is really suggesting is that we should reverse the 'progressive' reforms that were introduced when the forces of conservatism, which he reviles, were overwhelmed. He doesn't have the grace to acknowledge this, but cynically relabels the old progressives as today's conservatives.[135]

A similar perception of the impact of the 1960s was implicit in a letter from one schoolteacher, Alan Kerr, to the *TES* in October 2000:

the effect of Plowden ideology ... has left a generation of children ... short on essential literacy and numeracy skills and insecure in their knowledge of science and the humanities ... A second feature of the legacy is ... the continued reluctance of those involved in primary education to renounce the doctrine of Plowden altogether and view their task with objective clarity untainted by ideology. Group work, cross-curricular themes, seating arrangements, elaborate displays and suspicion of textbooks are examples of issues which go back to Plowden ... The third effect of Plowden lies in where it has led. Such was the confusion in progressive thinking accompanied by low attainment in the classroom that a reaction against the ideas and the practice was inevitable. The national curriculum, the literacy and numeracy strategies, targets and testing are that reaction and represent the true legacy of Plowden in the primary school. Many of us who argue against the progressive ideology legitimised by the Plowden Report broadly, if not unreservedly, welcome the more structured approach to learning which young people experience today. Plowden was a huge mistake and recovering from it has been a long and painful process.[136]

What becomes clear as one reads these emergent histories of curriculum change in recent times is the extent to which this new historical orthodoxy was reliant on what was in essence a version of the radical right rhetoric which had been a constant in post-War educational discourse. Consider, for example, the article written by Stephen Pollard of the Centre for the New Europe in *The Times* in January 2003. Under the title 'Why do we teach this noxious drivel?', Pollard wrote:

[Underachievement at GCSE] confirms the fundamental disease which still rots our education system ... Failed 'child-centred' theories which took hold of education in the 1960s still retain their iron grip on educationalists and still infect teacher-training colleges ... At the root of this drivel are the training colleges, which have ensured that generations of teachers cannot do the one thing they should be doing: teaching.[137]

Similarly, during the same month, in the *Sunday Times* Jenni Russell responded to Charles Clarke's call for education to be made more exciting and attractive with the observation that

this is obvious ... but everything that has been imposed on schools in the past fifteen years has had the opposite effect ... We know how we got here. Once upon a time thousands of children were failed by progressive teachers who used their autonomy as an excuse to teach not much at all. Curriculums [sic!], tests, targets and league tables were brought in by Conservative and Labour governments to produce measurable improvements. The pendulum has swung with a vengeance. It's time to recognise that the system isn't working on anyone's terms ... We have created a structure in which there is almost no space for children to get excited by the ideas they are being taught ... for struggling children from poorer backgrounds, school often becomes a humiliating exercise in bewilderment ... Clarke needs to relax Government central control. He must be brave enough to cut the curriculum back. Most importantly, he should end everyone's dependence on league tables and public tests.[138]

It is worth noting too, in conclusion, that these versions of recent history carried within them, either implicitly or explicitly, the view that these were yesterday's battles, that the contest between 'traditional' and 'progressive' views of the school curriculum had been subsumed within the new educational settlement which had emerged from the period since 1988. As Diane Hofkins put it in 2003:

Where have all the villains gone? ... When the Tories were in power there were big, scary bands of people ... whom their opponents could really hate ... Back in the 1970s, although Cox, Marks, Boyson and fellow authors of the notorious Black Papers seemed well to the right of the standard range of opinion, they still provoked outrage and controversy ... Now, so many of their ideas have been adopted by New Labour (prescription of 3Rs teaching, devolved management, baseline assessment) that they have been neutralised. Instead of fiery, opinionated figures ... we now have worthy managerialists. How can you shake your fist at these people when they are just tweaking the system?[139]

Might it be the case that the new context in which schools find themselves working at the start of the twenty-first century means that for the foreseeable future all discussion of the curriculum is to be set within a radical right framework of ideas? That is one gloomy conclusion towards which this account of the recent politics of curriculum change draws us.

Conclusions and prospects

The first conclusion to be drawn from this account is that the time-honoured tension between those who wanted popular education to be focused on the basics and those who took a more optimistic view of the possibilities of popular schooling has persisted throughout the post-War period. There was nothing new about the Black Paper movement. Its immediate precursor was the McCarthyite rhetoric of the late forties and fifties and it is echoed in much of the more recent radical right rhetoric which remains a feature of the politics of education. And the opposition to these ideas, much of it from within the profession, has also remained constant. As I argued at the outset, these fundamental disagreements about what should go on in school have been a constant in the history of education, certainly since the coming of state-sponsored education, and seem likely to remain so.

What is new is the preparedness of society at large, and of government, to listen to radical right arguments and to respond to them. During the immediate post-War era, commentators such as Geoffrey Bantock and John Garrett had only a limited impact on policy, if any at all, being seen by many (and certainly those responsible for implementing policy) as marginal figures, even if they voiced the aspirations of many within the selective sector. But since the late sixties and 1970s, governments have been increasingly anxious to be seen to be doing something in response to these ideas, and it is the voices of those who would put the needs of the child at the heart of the educational process who have struggled to make themselves heard.

Why is this the case? I believe it is possible to identify several interlinked social and economic transformations which have worked to make this shift in popular perception almost inevitable. First, as a result of the coming of affluence, society has become far more consumerist: people have become accustomed to exercising choice over an increasing range of activities. What began as the ability (and growing readiness) to choose between holiday destinations, consumer goods and aspects of lifestyle, has extended to the point at which those services provided by the State, notably schooling and medicine, have become subject to similar demands and expectations. That is why choice has become such a familiar element in governmental rhetoric around education and health care, relegating a concern for the provision of basic standards to the margins of public debate. The fact that many of the choices on offer are in fact illusory seems hardly to matter. What does matter is that choice itself appears to be available.

This is closely linked to a second major set of changes, namely, the transformation of the mass media during the period since the Second World War. The impact of television, of popular entertainment and of new styles of journalism under the control of multinational corporations has been to transform political discourse for ever. When Clement Attlee was doorstepped by a journalist whilst leaving No. 10 Downing Street, at the height of the 1947 fuel crisis, he was asked: 'Prime Minister, do you have anything to say to the press?' 'Not much, thank you,' was his reply. 'Good night.' In a world now driven by media-induced crises, it would be impossible for any politician to respond in this way today. Perhaps more than ever before the business of government has become a question of responding to yesterday's press scare. Schooling has proved particularly susceptible to this trend and this helps explain the steady incremental increase in government interest in education and in its readiness to legislate and direct with ever-increasing regularity. Since much of this press hysteria is, by definition, a reflection of radical right rhetoric, the general direction of policy in this context becomes inevitable.

Beyond this, the inexorable rise of multinational corporations, with an ever-increasing grip on economies on a world scale, has undoubtedly resulted in a transformation of the workplace. This has happened at a moment when the nature of employment, for many participants, has been itself transformed by the coming of the computer and new systems of mass communication. Ferocious competition, linked to wide disparities in the financial rewards available, have led to a situation in which, increasingly, education systems are expected to produce 'products', namely young people equipped with the qualifications and skills to enter this transformed workplace and to succeed within it. The emphasis has shifted, inexorably, from the experience of schooling as students pass through it, to its outcomes, to the achievement of qualifications. The new media are best served by, and demand, a system in which outcomes are measurable and targets can be set for those involved. Put these three factors together, and it becomes much easier to understand why it is that teachers have lost control of what goes on in the classroom.

Beyond this, it is worth pausing to reflect on the lot of the pupils in this brave new world. It is perhaps not putting it too strongly to suggest that they have become, or are becoming, the victims of the education system in a way that was never previously the case. Childhood itself has been transformed since the Second World War. The final collapse of the extended family, a growing awareness of the dangers and risks of childhood, together with the new isolated lifestyles of youngsters trapped in a nuclear family with television, mobile phone and text message as their constant companions, have meant a new form of childhood. This has all been confirmed as society has become more litigious, leaving those who work with children increasingly looking over their shoulder for potential trouble. Beyond this, and partly as a result of these developments, play has become far more isolated. The range of play of youngsters, which in my case extended several miles from my own home during my schooldays, is diminished beyond measure.

This means that opportunities for social development, the acquisition of social skills and for self-discovery do not exist for most children as they did fifty years ago. But, sadly, at just the moment that the schools might be turned to offer a wider set of experiences to young people, the day-by-day realities of schooling have become narrower than was previously the case. Organised activities and school games suffered irreversible damage as a result of the 1980s teachers' industrial dispute and there is evidence that, under pressure to deliver a new, tightly defined curriculum, teachers are less able to provide the range of out-of-school activities which were a marked feature of the immediate post-War years. Not only have the schools been responding to the changed conditions of childhood, but, through the expectations they now place on children, they have become one element in its transformation. This is the sense in which I write of children as victims.

What then are the prospects before us at the present time? Is there any realistic possibility of the teachers regaining control of what they do and of a genuinely child-centred educational experience becoming the norm in our schools? Given the constraints under which teachers work, and this new context of schooling, it seems unlikely. What I do see as the conclusion from the events outlined in this book, is that our schools can only be as good as the society they serve. The ends of schooling are determined not solely by teachers but also by others outside the schools. They always have been. A society which was prepared to defer to the expertise of the teaching profession has become one in which teachers are subject to constant public scrutiny. This is the transformation I have attempted to describe in this book.

If our society remains one which allows vast disparities between rich and poor, which continues to acquiesce in vast contrasts in lifestyles between regions and between suburbs in individual conurbations, then it will continue to demand particular outcomes from its schools. As parents seek to ensure the best available education for their own children it is inevitable that those with greater social and economic clout will necessarily distort the provision, whether they mean to or not, and whether or not they are aware of this consequence of their aspirations. A society within which power and resources are unevenly distributed cannot expect to generate an education system in which all children go through similar experiences of schooling. At the same time society seems likely to continue to want an education system which can demonstrate to its consumers what it is achieving, even if this is measurable only in ways that diminish the experience of pupils. Teachers will go on being expected to generate examination results which facilitate this situation. The expectations of what goes on in school will remain constrained and focused to one degree or another on that which can be measured and assessed. So long as we have an intrusive press, a consumption-driven society and a government which is in hock to the media, it seems extremely unlikely, even impossible, for things to be otherwise. There is a far better experience of childhood, and of schooling, which we might offer to our children. But it will not be achievable unless we abandon many of our aspirations and beliefs. I believe that our society needs a major rethink of what it considers to be the good life, of the ends towards which social policy is directed. Short of that, I see little prospect of the major redirection of our education system which I believe is needed.

Notes

1 Popular education in England: the historical legacy

1 For the full text see R. Lowe (ed.), *History of Education: major themes*, Routledge Falmer, London, 2000, vol. 2, pp. 9–31.
2 *Hansard*, vol. ix, 798, 13 July 1807.
3 *Report of the commissioners appointed to enquire into the state of popular education in England (the Newcastle Report)*, London, 1861, chapter 4, p. 243.
4 J. S. Maclure, *Educational documents: England and Wales, 1816–1967*, Methuen. London, 1965, p. 79.
5 Ibid., p. 159.
6 See K. J. Brehony, 'From the particular to the general, the continuous to the discontinuous: progressive education revisited', *History of Education*, 20, 5, September 2001, pp. 413–32.
7 H. Kliebard, *The struggle for the American curriculum, 1893–1958*, 2 Edn, London, Routledge, 1995. See also P. Cunningham, 'Innovators, networks and structures: towards a prosopography of progressivism', *History of Education*, 30, 5, 2001, pp. 433–51.
8 J. Latham, 'Pestalozzi and James Pierrepoint Greaves: a shared education philosophy', *History of Education*, 31, 1, January 2002, p. 63.
9 See K. D. Nawrotzki, 'Froebel is dead; long live Froebel! The National Froebel Foundation and English education', *History of Education*, 35, 2, March 2006, pp. 209–23.
10 W. E. Marsden, 'Contradictions in progressive primary school ideologies and curricula in England', *Historical Studies in Education*, 9, 2, 1997, reprinted in R. Lowe, *History of education: major themes*, Routledge Falmer, London, 2000, vol. 3, pp. 142–55.
11 K. J. Brehony, 'Montessori, individual work and individuality in the elementary school classroom', *History of Education*, 29, 2, 2000, pp. 115–28.
12 Ibid., p. 116.
13 Ibid.
14 See H. Silver, *Robert Owen on education*, Cambridge University Press, Cambridge, 1969, and H. Silver, *The concept of popular education*, McGibbon & Kee, London, 1965.
15 B. Simon, *Studies in the history of education, 1780–1870*, Lawrence & Wishart, London, 1960, pp. 241–2.
16 W. A. C. Stewart, *Progressives and radicals in English education, 1750–1970*, Macmillan, London, 1972, pp. 67–72.
17 R. J. W. Selleck, 'The scientific educationist, 1870–1914', *British Journal of Educational Studies*, 15, 2, 1967, reprinted in R. Lowe, op. cit., vol. 3, pp. 239–57.

18 See P. Cunningham, 'The nature of primary education: early perspectives, 1944–1977', originally published in N. Proctor (ed.), *The aims of primary education and the national curriculum*, Falmer Press, London, 1990 and reprinted in R. Lowe, op. cit., vol. 3, pp. 124–41.

19 E. Holmes, *What is and what might be*, Constable, London, 1991. See also C. Shute, *Edmund Holmes and 'the tragedy of education'*, Education Heretics Press, Stapleford, Nottingham, 1998.

20 A. J. Lynch, *Individual work and the Dalton Plan*, George Philip, London, 1924.

21 On this see P. Cunningham, op. cit., p. 125.

22 Report of the Consultative Committee of the Board of Education, *The Primary School*, HMSO, London, 1931, recommendation 30.

23 R. J. W. Selleck, *The new education: the English background, 1870–1914*, Pitman, London, 1968; R. J. W. Selleck, *English primary education and the progressives, 1914–1939*, Routledge & Kegan Paul, London, 1978.

24 P. Cunningham, *Curriculum change in the primary school since 1945: dissemination of the progressive ideal*, Falmer Press, Lewes, 1988.

25 K. Brehony, 'What's left of progressive primary education?' in A. Rattansi and D. Reeder (eds), *Rethinking radical education*, Lawrence & Wishart, London, 1992; K. Brehony (ed.), 'Special issue: progressive and child-centred education', *History of Education*, 29, 2, March 2000; K. Brehony, 'From the particular to the general, the continuous to the discontinuous: progressive education revisited', *History of Education*, 30, 5, September 2001.

26 W. E. Marsden, *Educating the respectable: a study of Fleet Road Board School, Hampstead, 1879–1903*, Woburn Press, London, 1991; W. E. Marsden, 'Contradictions in progressive primary school ideologies and curricula in England: some historical perspectives', *Historical Studies in Education*, 9, 2, 1997.

2 The post-War educational settlement: a conservative revolution

1 Board of Education Consultative Committee, *The primary school*, HMSO, London, 1931.

2 A. D. Lindsay, 'A plan for education', *Picture Post*, 4 January 1941, pp. 27–31.

3 On this see P. Cunningham, *Curriculum change in the primary school since 1945*, Falmer Press, London, 1988, pp. 48–66.

4 Cunningham, ibid., 49.

5 Isobel Irons, formerly headmistress of Blaby Infants School, quoted by D. K. Jones. See his chapter 'Planning for progressivism' in R. Lowe (ed.), *The changing primary school*, Falmer Press, London, 1987, p. 36.

6 *Times Educational Supplement*, 28 October 1949, p. 748.

7 S. Maclure, *Educational development and school building: aspects of public policy, 1945–73*, Longman, Harlow, 1984, pp. 37–60.

8 J. Gagg, *Common sense in the primary school*, Evans, London, 1951.

9 *TES*, 26 July 1947, p. 391.

10 M. Atkinson, *Junior school community*, Longman, London, 1949, p. 54.

11 W. K. Richmond, *Purpose in the junior school*, Redman, London, 1949.

12 M. V. Daniel, *Activity in the primary school*, Basil Blackwell, Oxford, 1947.

13 N. Catty, *Learning and teaching in the junior school*, Methuen, London, 1941.

14 *TES*, 3 November 1950, p. 847.

15 Ministry of Education, *The new secondary education*, HMSO, London, 1947.

16 Public Record Office, files Ed. 147/21, Ed. 147/22 and Ed. 147/23.

17 B. Simon, *Education and the social order, 1940–1990*, Lawrence & Wishart, London, 1991, p. 121–125.

18 PRO, file Ed. 147/22.

19 Ibid.

20 PRO, files Ed. 147/22 and Ed. 147/23.
21 PRO, file Ed. 147/23.
22 Ibid.
23 Ibid.
24 Ibid.
25 Ibid.
26 *TES*, 11 January 1947, p. 23.
27 *TES*, 31 May 1947, p. 267.
28 *TES*, 18 January 1947, p. 36.
29 *TES*, 11 October 1947, p. 541.
30 *TES*, 5 January 1946, p. 3 and 19 January 1946, p. 27.
31 G. H. Bantock, 'Some cultural implications of freedom in education', *Scrutiny*, XV, 2, Spring 1948, pp. 83–97.
32 *TES*, 16 June 1950, p. 470.
33 *TES*, 23 June 1950, p. 493.
34 *TES*, 2 March 1946, p. 123.
35 *TES*, 30 March 1946, p. 147.
36 Ibid.
37 *TES*, 30 May 1952, p. 481.
38 L. Kemp. 'Environmental and other characteristics determining attainment in primary schools', *British Journal of Educational Psychology*, XXV, February 1955, pp. 67–77.

3 A golden age? The sixties and early seventies

1 B. Simon, *Education and the social order, 1940–1990*, Lawrence & Wishart, London, 1991, pp. 388–390.
2 Ibid., pp. 446–51.
3 C. Chitty, *Towards a new education system: victory for the New Right?*, Falmer Press, Brighton, 1989, pp. 135–6.
4 *Times Educational Supplement*, 4 October 1963, p. 449.
5 *Forum*, 1, 2, Spring 1959, p. 52.
6 *Forum*, 2, 2, Spring 1960, p. 45.
7 *Forum*, 3, 3, Summer 1961.
8 C. Daniels, 'Research on streaming in the primary school', *Forum*, 4, 3, Summer 1962, p. 83.
9 *Forum*, 7, 1, Autumn 1964, pp. 3–14.
10 J. W. B. Douglas, *The home and the school*, Macgibbon and Key, London, 1964.
11 Central Advisory Council (England), *Children and their primary schools*, HMSO, London, 1967, chapter 20, pp. 287–91.
12 Simon, op. cit., p. 370.
13 R. Dottrens, *The Primary school curriculum*, UNESCO, 1962. See also *Forum*, 6, 1, Autumn 1963, p. 29.
14 S. Marshall, *An experiment in education*, Cambridge University Press, Cambridge, 1963.
15 L. G. W. Sealey, *Communication and learning in the primary school*, Blackwell, London, 1962.
16 *TES*, 26 February 1965, pp. 579–86.
17 *TES*, 2 December 1960 p. xxiv.
18 P. Cunningham, *Curriculum change in the primary school since 1945*, Falmer Press, Lewes, 1988, pp. 155–160.
19 P. Cunningham, *Curriculum change in the primary school since 1945*, Falmer Press Press, Brighton, 1988, p. 87.
20 B. Simon, op. cit., p. 313.

21 Ibid., p. 317.
22 *Forum*, 1, 1, Autumn 1958, p. 5.
23 *Forum*, 5, 1, Autumn 1962, p. 13.
24 D. Hargreaves, *Social relations in a secondary school*, Routledge and Kegan Paul, London, 1967.
25 C. Benn and B. Simon, *Halfway there*, McGraw Hill, London, 1970.
26 C. Benn and C. Chitty, *Is comprehensive education alive and well or struggling to survive?* David Fulton, London, 1996, p. 253.
27 W. Taylor, 'Changing concepts of the modern school', Forum, 2, 2, Spring 1960, p. 62.
28 *Forum*, 6, 3, Summer 1964, p. 90.
29 *TES*, 17 January 1964, p. 106.
30 *Forum*, 8, 2, Spring 1966, p. 61.
31 Consultative Committee of the Board of Education, *Secondary education* (the Spens Report), HMSO, London, 1938, pp. 352–3.
32 N. A. Flanders, 'Introduction', in E. J. Amidon and J. B. Hough (eds), *Interaction analysis: theory, research and application*, Addison-Wesley, Reading, Mass., 1967 (see also pp. 103–117).
33 *Oxford Review of Education*, 13, 1, 1987, pp. 3–12.
34 *TES*, 20 May 1960, p. 1045.
35 *TES*, 27 May 1960, p. 1090.
36 *TES*, 14 October 1960, p. 486.
37 *TES*, 6 January 1961, p. 11.
38 *TES*, 13 January 1961, p. 53.
39 *TES*, 23 June 1961, p. 399.
40 *TES*, 27 October 1961, p. 570.
41 *TES*, 31 August 1962, p. 217.
42 B. Cox, *The great betrayal: memoirs of a life in education*, Chapman, London, 1992, p. 21.
43 C. B. Dyson, 'Culture in decline', *Critical Quarterly*, Summer 1970, pp. 99–104.
44 B. Martin, 'Progressive education versus the working classes', *Critical Quarterly*, 13, 1, 1971, pp. 297–320.
45 B. Simon, op. cit., p. 390.
46 *Forum*, 4, 3, Summer 1962, p. 92.
47 R. Lowe, *Schooling and social change*, Routledge, London, 1987, pp. 80–95.
48 M. Galton 'Change and continuity in the primary school: the research evidence', *Oxford Review of Education*, 13, 1487, pp. 81–94.
49 Ibid.
50 Ibid.

4 1974–79: the teachers lose control

1 See M. Dintenfass, *The decline of industrial Britain, 1870–1980*, Routledge, London, 1992 and B. W. E. Alford, *British economic performance, 1945–1975*, Macmillan, Basingstoke, 1988.
2 E. Reimer, *School is dead: alternatives in education*, Doubleday, New York, 1971 and I. Illich, *Deschooling society*, Harper & Row, New York, 1971.
3 Centre for Contemporary Cultural Studies, *Unpopular education: schooling and social democracy in England since 1944*, Hutchinson, London, 1981, p. 211.
4 See R. Lowe (ed.), *The changing primary school*, Falmer Press, London, 1987, pp. 1–16.
5 *TES*, 26 July, 1974, p. 16.
6 *TES*, 14 November 1975, p. 4a.
7 *TES*, 10 October 1975, p. 5.
8 *TES*, 21 November 1975, p. 2.

9 *TES*, 28 November 1975, p. 3.
10 The Layfield Report, *Local government finances: report of the committee of enquiry*, HMSO, London, 1976.
11 *TES*, 1 November 1974, p. 14.
12 *The Times*, 18 July 1974.
13 B. Simon, *Education and the social order, 1940–1990*, Lawrence & Wishart, London, 1991, pp. 445–6.
14 James Britten, *The development of writing abilities (11–18)*, published by Macmillan/the Schools Council, 1975.
15 Committee of Inquiry into Reading and the Use of English, *A language for life: report of the Committee of Inquiry under the chairmanship of Sir Alan Bullock*, HMSO, London, 1975.
16 *TES*, 2 January 1976, p. 1.
17 *TES*, 16 January 1976, p. 1.
18 *TES*, 23 January 1976, p. 2.
19 *TES*, 15 October 1976, pp. 16–19.
20 *TES*, 3 September 1976, p. 1.
21 *TES*, 1 October 1976, p. 1.
22 Ibid.
23 *TES*, 8 October 1976, p. 1.
24 *TES*, 15 October 1976, pp. 16–19.
25 *Guardian*, 13 October 1976, p. 1
26 *TES*, 15 October 1976, pp. 16–19.
27 C. Chitty, *Towards a new education system: the victory of the New Right?*, Falmer Press, London, 1989, p. 73.
28 *TES*, 5 November 1976, p. 3.
29 *TES*, 12 November 1976, p. 1.
30 *TES*, 19 November 1976, p. 1.
31 Ibid.
32 *TES*, 3 December 1976, p. 1.
33 *TES*, 14 January 1977, p. 1.
34 *TES*, 21 January 1977, p. 1.
35 *TES*, 27 October 1978, p. 6b.
36 *TES*, 19 May 1978, p. 12b.
37 B. Simon, *op. cit.*, pp. 453–461.
38 National Union of Teachers, *Education in schools: the NUT's response to the recommendations in the 1977 Green Paper*, NUT, London, 1977.
39 *TES*, 6 January 1978, p. 4.
40 *TES*, 14 January 1977, p. 1.
41 *TES*, 23 January 1976, p. 88a.
42 Public Record Office, EJ 1/62.
43 PRO, EJ 3/12.
44 Ibid.
45 *TES*, 4 December 1977, p. 4.

5 1979–89: a decade of change

1 M. Morris and C. Griggs (eds), *Education: the wasted years? 1973–1986*, Falmer Press, London, 1988, pp. 9–10.
2 J. I. Goodlad, *A place called school: prospects for the future*, McGraw Hill, New York, 1984.
3 M. Rutter, *Fifteen thousand hours: secondary schools and their effects on children*, Open Books, London, 1979.

4 S. Maclure, *The inspectors' calling: HMI and the shaping of educational policy, 1945–1992*, Hodder & Stoughton, London, 2000, p. 205.

5 R. Scruton, *The meaning of conservatism*, Macmillan, London, 1984.

6 M. Thatcher, *The Downing Street years*, Harper Collins, London, 1993, p. 51.

7 See Centre for Contemporary Cultural Studies, *Education limited*, Unwin Hyman, London, 1991, p. 47.

8 DES, *Better schools*, HMSO, London, 1985, pp. 11–12.

9 K. Baker, *Turbulent years: my life in politics*, Faber, London, 1996, p. 172.

10 S. Maclure, op. cit., p. 225.

11 Department of Education and Science, *A new partnership for our schools: the Taylor Report*, HMSO, London, 1977.

12 Department of Education and Science, *Education Act (No. 2)*, HMSO, London, 1986.

13 Department of Education and Science, *Local authority arrangements for the curriculum*, DES, London, 1979.

14 Morris and Griggs, op. cit., p. 14.

15 Ibid., p. 221.

16 Department of Education and Science, *A framework for the school curriculum: proposals for consultation by the Secretaries of State for Education and Science and for Wales*, DES, London, 1980.

17 Department of Education and Science, *Better Schools*, HMSO, London, 1985.

18 Department of Education and Science, *School education in England: problems and initiatives*, HMSO, London, 1976.

19 N. Trenamen, *Review of the Schools Council*, Department of Education and Science, London, 1981.

20 Baker, op. cit., p. 168.

21 Centre for Contemporary Cultural Studies, op. cit., p. 66–7.

22 Maclure, op. cit., p. 283–4.

23 Morris and Griggs, op. cit., p. 20.

24 DES, *Better Schools*.

25 Centre for Contemporary Cultural Studies, op. cit., p. 126.

26 Ibid., p. 138.

27 See Morris and Griggs, op. cit., p. 21 or Centre for Contemporary Cultural Studies, op. cit., p. 56.

28 Centre for Contemporary Cultural Studies, op. cit., p. 75.

29 *Daily Mail*, 13 May 1987, p. 1.

30 D. Graham, *A lesson for us all*, Routledge, London, 1993, p. 30.

31 J. Woodhouse, 'Towards central control: government directives on the primary curriculum' in R. Lowe (ed.), *The changing primary school*, Falmer Press, Lewes, 1978, p. 137.

32 D. Jones, 'Planning for progressivism: the changing primary school in the Leicestershire Authority during the Mason era, 1947–71' in Lowe, op. cit., p. 47.

6 'Forging a new consensus in education': the implementation of the Education Reform Act, 1989–97

1 *Times Educational Supplement*, 18 September 1992, p. 5.

2 *TES*, 20 January 1989, p. 4.

3 *TES*, 6 January 1989, p. 16.

4 *TES*, 2 June 1989, p. 16.

5 *The Times*, 24 March 1990, p. 5.

6 *TES*, 6 April 1990, p. 1.

7 *TES*, 29 June 1990, p. 6.

8 *TES*, 22 February 1991, p. 13.

9 *TES*, 10 December 1993, p. 6.

10 *TES*, 29 September 1989, p. 16.

11 *TES*, 22 December 1989, p. 11.
12 *TES*, 24 July 1989, p. 3.
13 *TES*, 29 March 1991, p. 1.
14 *TES*, 24 April 1992, p. 6.
15 *TES*, 3 January 1990, p. 5.
16 *TES*, 20 July 1990, p. 21.
17 *TES*, 5 January 1990, p. 21.
18 *TES*, 4 December 1992, p. 25.
19 *TES*, 6 January 1989, p. 16.
20 *TES*, 24 July 1989, p. 3.
21 *TES*, 15 December 1989, p. 15.
22 *TES*, 13 April 1990, p. 6.
23 *TES*, 25 May 1990, p. 1.
24 *The Times*, 1 May 1989, p. 23.
25 *TES*, 2 June 1989, p. 1.
26 *TES*, 23 June 1989, p. 2.
27 *TES*, 22 September 1989, p. 8.
28 *TES*, 2 June 1989, p. A4.
29 *TES*, 13 July 1990, p. 8.
30 *TES*, 8 February 1991, p. 5.
31 Department for Education, *Choice and diversity: a new framework for schools*, HMSO, London, 1992.
32 *TES*, 31 July 1992, p. 6.
33 *TES*, 31 July 1992, p. 6.
34 *TES*, 25 December 1992, p. 6.
35 *TES*, 23 June 1989, p. 3.
36 *TES*, 9 November 1990, p. 12.
37 *TES*, 8 November 1991, p. 15.
38 *TES*, 13 December 1991, p. 16.
39 *TES*, 18 September 1992, p. 5.
40 Ibid.
41 *TES*, 8 March 1996, p. 2
42 *TES*, 4 February 1994, p. 22.
43 *TES*, 22 January 1993, p. 11.
44 *TES*, 22 December 1989, p. 13.
45 *TES*, 2 March 1990, p. 2.
46 *TES*, 13 April 1990, p. 5.
47 *TES*, 17 August 1990, p. 11 and 14 September 1990, p. 1.
48 *The Times*, 16 April 1990, p. 3 and 17 April 1990, p. 13.
49 *TES*, 9 November 1990, p. 19.
50 *TES*, 4 January 1991, p. 12.
51 *TES*, 22 February 1991, p. 20.
52 R. J. Alexander, J. Rose and C. Woodhead, *Curiculum organisation and classroom practice in primary schools*, HMSO, London, 1992.
53 *Guardian*, 23 November, 1992, p. 1.
54 *TES*, 5 February, 1993, p. 6.
55 *TES*, 9 June 1995, p. 144.
56 *TES*, 31 July 1992, p. 1.
57 *TES*, 21 January 1994, p. 20.
58 *TES*, 6 December 1996, p. 1.
59 *TES*, 1 December 1989, p. 21.
60 *TES*, 29 September 1989, p. 21.
61 *TES*, 17 November 1989, p. 1.
62 *TES*, 16 November 1990, p. 21.

63 *TES*, 24 September 1990, p. 3.
64 *TES*, 6 April 1990, p. 16.
65 *TES*, 8 May 1992, p. 18.
66 *The Times*, 24 December 1990, p. 18.
67 *TES*, 1 January 1993, p. 1.
68 *TES*, 1 January 1993, p. 1.
69 *TES*, 8 January 1993, p. 3.
70 *TES*, 22 January 1993, p. 18.
71 *TES*, 5 March 1993, p. 2.
72 *TES*, 5 March 1993, p. 1.
73 *TES*, 5 March 1993, p. 23.
74 *TES*, 9 April 1993, p. 1.
75 *TES*, 1 October 1993, p. 3.
76 *TES*, 20 January 1994, p. 20.
77 *TES*, 20 January 1994, p. 4.
78 *TES*, 25 August 1989, p. 7.
79 *TES*, 29 March 1991, p. 1.
80 *TES*, 5 March 1993, p. 23.
81 *TES*, 26 March 1993, p. 22.
82 *TES*, 7 June 1996, p. 7.
83 *TES*, 6 September 1996, p. 2.
84 *Sunday Times*, 23 April 1989, p. 8.
85 *TES*, 6 September 1991, p. 9.
86 *TES*, 22 January 1993, p. 18.
87 S. Maclure, *The inspectors' calling: HMI and the shaping of educational policy, 1945–1992*, Hodder & Stoughton, London, 2000, p. 308.
88 *TES*, 27 January 1995, p. 16.
89 *TES*, 3 February 1995, p. 10.
90 *TES*, 29 September 1989, p. 16.
91 *TES*, 24 April 1992, p. 5.
92 *TES*, 3 February 1995, p. 10.
93 *TES*, 31 May 1996, p. 1.
94 *TES*, 29 June 1996, p. 23.

7 New Labour and the curriculum since 1997

1 *TES*, 22 July 2005, p. 20.
2 *Daily Telegraph*, 12 September 2006, p. 1 and p. 23.
3 B. Levin, 'An epidemic of educational policymaking: what can we learn from each other?', *Comparative Education*, 34, 2, 1998, pp. 131–142.
4 *TES*, 9 May 1997, p. 1.
5 Ibid., p. 5.
6 *The Times*, 30 March 2001, p. 16.
7 Ibid.
8 *TES*, 31 October 1997, p. 6 and p. 18.
9 *TES*, 24 March 2000, p. 14.
10 *Sunday Times*, 7 January 2001, p. 1.
11 *TES*, 2 August 2002, p. 9.
12 *TES*, 6 September 2002, p. 18.
13 *TES*, 2 July 2004, p. 14.
14 *TES*, 16 July 2004, p. 6.
15 *TES*, 4 March 2005, p. 2.
16 *TES*, 30 September 2005, p. 14.
17 *The Times*, 25 November 2005, p. 1.

18 *TES*, 23 May 1997, p. 1.
19 *TES*, 5 December 1997, p. 17.
20 *The Times*, 14 January 1998, p. 10.
21 Ibid.
22 *Observer*,19 August 2001, p. 5.
23 *The Times*, 14 January 1999, p. 8.
24 *TES*, 15 January 1999, p. 17.
25 *TES*, 23 July 1999, p. 19.
26 *TES*, 9 May 1997, p. 5.
27 *TES*, 5 September 1997, p. 3.
28 *Sunday Times*, 4 June 2000, p. 1.
29 *The Times*, 30 March 2001, p. 16.
30 Ibid.
31 *Observer*, 18 February 2001, p. 1.
32 *The Times*, 7 January 2001, p. 24.
33 *Observer*, 2 December 2001, p. 29.
34 *Observer*, 14 October 2001, p. 13.
35 *Observer*, 11 November 2001, p. 14.
36 *TES*, 4 December 2004, p. 3.
37 *TES*, 13 January 2006, p. 16.
38 *Education Guardian*, 15 August 2006, p. 1.
39 *TES*, 4 October 2002, p. 16.
40 *TES*, 27 January 2004, p. 12.
41 *Guardian*, 1 March 2006, p. 24.
42 *Sunday Times*, 22 January 2006, p. 16.
43 *TES*, 3 February 2006, p. 26.
44 *The Times*, 22 October 1998, p. 17.
45 *The Times*, 21 October 1999, p. 1.
46 *TES*, 21 January 2000, p. 1.
47 *TES*, 7 January 2000, p. 1.
48 *TES*, 9 March 2003, p. 2.
49 *TES*, 23 May 2003, p. 23.
50 *TES*, 27 January 2004, p. 8.
51 *Observer Business Supplement*, 11 February 2001, p. 5.
52 See Audit Commission, *PFI in schools*, Audit Commission, London, 2003.
53 Ibid.
54 http://www.zyen.com
55 http://www.zyen.com
56 *Daily Telegraph*, 18 August 2006.
57 'Public service: private profit', Channel Four TV programme, 14 August 2006.
58 *TES*, 9 March 2003, p. 10.
59 *TES*, 15 April 2005, p. 5.
60 *TES*, 3 October 2003, p. 10.
61 *TES*, 21 May 2004, p. 17.
62 *TES*, 14 January 2005, p. 28.
63 *TES*, 28 January 2005, p. 25.
64 *Sunday Times*, 22 June 1997, p. 2.
65 *The Times*, 8 July 1997, p. 21.
66 *TES*, 31 October 1997, p. 6.
67 *TES*, 8 May 1998, p. 17.
68 *TES*, 26 November 1999, p. 21.
69 *TES*, 12 June 1998, p. 15.
70 *TES*, 26 May 2006, p. 12.
71 *TES*, 27 February 2004, p. 13.

72 N. Davies, *The school report: why Britain's schools are failing*, Vintage Press, London, 2000, pp. 83–101.
73 *Observer*, 7 January 2001, p. 24.
74 *TES*, 4 January 2002, p. 16.
75 Ibid.
76 Ibid.
77 *The Times*, 29 April 1998, p. 7.
78 Ibid.
79 Ibid.
80 *The Times*, 25 June 1998, p. 15.
81 *TES*, 12 February 1999, p. 1.
82 *TES*, 7 January 2000, p. 5.
83 *TES*, 14 July 2000, p. 11.
84 Ibid.
85 *Sunday Times*, 5 November 2000, p. 1.
86 *TES*, 1 March 2002, p. 28.
87 *TES*, 16 January 1998, p. 5.
88 *TES*, 29 October 1999, p. 6.
89 *The Times*, 30 March 2001, p. 16.
90 Mark Seddon, 'Interests at the heart of New Labour?', *Society Guardian*, 17 August 2001, p. 1 (http:society.guardian.co.uk).
91 *TES*, 9 May 1997, p. 8.
92 Ibid.
93 *TES*, 5 September 1997, p. 1.
94 Ibid., p. 3.
95 Ibid., p. 22.
96 *TES*, 31 October 1997, p. 18.
97 *TES*, 5 December 1997, p. 17.
98 *TES*, 8 January 1999, p. 19.
99 *TES*, 29 October 1999, p. 14.
100 *TES*, 18 February 2000, p. 19.
101 *Sunday Times*, 7 January 2001, p. 15.
102 *Observer*, 7 January 2001, p. 1.
103 *Observer*, 21 January 2001, p. 18.
104 *Observer*, 11 November 2001, p. 7.
105 *TES*, 6 September 2002, p. 6.
106 *Observer*, 29 April 2001, p. 11.
107 *The Times*, 22 October 1999, p. 14.
108 *The Times*, 30 October 1999, p. 23.
109 *TES*, 14 June 2002, p. 1.
110 *TES*, 9 May 2003, p. 20.
111 *TES*, 9 January 2004, p. 1.
112 *TES*, 11 February 2005, p. 2.
113 *TES*, 5 November 2004, p. 21.
114 *TES*, 12 November 2004, p. 13 and p. 22.
115 *TES*, 12 May 2006, p. 4.
116 *TES*, 23 May 1997, p. 1.
117 *TES*, 3 July 1998, p. 23.
118 *TES*, 13 May 1999, p. 4.
119 *TES*, 25 June 1999, p. 11.
120 *TES*, 2 June 2000, p. 15.
121 *Sunday Times*, 8 October 2000, p. 11.
122 *TES*, 5 July 2002, p. 3.
123 *TES*, 21 March 2003, p. 4.

124 *TES*, 11 April 2003, p. 26.
125 *TES*, 9 March 2003, p. 1.
126 *TES*, 30 January 2004, p. 24.
127 *TES*, 9 January 2004, p. 24.
128 Ibid.
129 *TES*, 27 February 2004, p. 25.
130 *TES*, 30 January 2004, p. 24.
131 *TES*, 20 February 2004, p. 25.
132 *TES*, 26 November 2004, p. 29.
133 *TES*, 19 June 1998, p. 18.
134 *TES*, 28 May 1999, p. 14.
135 *The Times*, 25 October 1999, p. 19.
136 *TES*, 27 October 2000, p. 20.
137 *The Times*, 13 January 2003, p. 13.
138 *Sunday Times*, 26 January 2003, p. 19.
139 *TES*, 10 January 2003, p. 19.

Select bibliography

This is a brief list of titles which are central to this topic. The many other sources used in researching the book are identified in the text and in the chapter references. All are readily found using a search engine or a good library catalogue.

P. Addison and H. Jones (eds), *A companion to contemporary Britain, 1939–2000,* Blackwell, Oxford, 2005.

M. Bassey, *Teachers and government,* Association of Teachers and Lecturers, London, 2005.

C. Benn and B. Simon, *Halfway there: a report on the British comprehensive school reform,* McGraw Hill, London, 1970.

C. Benn and C. Chitty, *Thirty years on: is comprehensive education alive and well or struggling to survive?* David Fulton, London, 1996.

Centre for Contemporary Cultural Studies, *Unpopular education: schooling and social democracy in England since 1944,* Hutchinson, London, 1981.

C. Chitty, *Towards a new education system: the victory of the new right?* Falmer Press, Lewes, 1989.

Cultural Studies, University of Birmingham, *Education limited: schooling, training and the New Right in England since 1979,* Unwin Hyman, London, 1991.

P. Cunningham, *Curriculum change in the primary school since 1945,* Falmer Press, Lewes, 1988.

N. Davies, *The school report: why Britain's schools are failing,* Vintage, London, 2000.

K. Jones, *Right turn: the Conservative revolution in education,* Hutchinson, London, 1989.

K. Jones, *Beyond progressive education,* Macmillan, London, 1983.

K. Jones (ed.), *English and the national curriculum,* Bedford Way Series, Institute of Education, London, 1992.

A. C. Kerkhoff, K. Fogelman, D. Crook and D. Reeder, *Going comprehensive in England and Wales: a study of uneven change,* Woburn, London, 1996.

C. Knight, *The making of Tory education policy in post-War Britain, 1950–1986,* Falmer Press, Lewes, 1990.

D. Lawton, *The Tory mind on education, 1979–1994,* Falmer Press, London, 1994.

R. Lowe, *Education in the post-War years,* Routledge, London, 1988.

R. Lowe, *Schooling and social change, 1964–1990,* Routledge, London, 1997.

R. Lowe (ed.), *The changing primary school,* Falmer Press, Lewes, 1987.

R. Lowe (ed.), *The changing secondary school,* Falmer Press, Lewes, 1989.

S. Maclure, *The inspectors' calling: HMI and the shaping of educational policy, 1945–1992,* Hodder & Stoughton, London, 2000.

G. McCulloch, *Educational reconstruction: the 1944 Education Act and the Twenty-First century*, Woburn, London, 1994.

G. McCulloch, *Failing the ordinary child: the theory and practice of working-class education,* Open University Press, Buckingham, 1998.

G. McCulloch, *The secondary technical school: a useable past?* Falmer Press, Lewes, 1989.

G. McCulloch, *Philosophers and kings: education for leadership in modern England,* Cambridge University Press, Cambridge, 1991.

M. Morris and C. Griggs (eds), *Education: the wasted years? 1973–1986,* Falmer Press, Lewes, 1998.

R. J. W. Selleck, *The new education: the English background, 1870–1914,* Pitman, London, 1968.

R. J. W. Selleck, *English primary education and the progressives, 1914–1939,* RKP, London, 1972.

B. Simon, *Education and the social order, 1940–1990,* Lawrence & Wishart, London, 1991.

B. Simon, *Bending the rules: the Baker 'reform' of education,* Lawrence & Wishart, London, 1988.

N. Thomas, *Primary education from Plowden to the 1990s,* Falmer Press, Basingstoke, 1990.

S. Tomlinson, *Education in a post-welfare society,* Open University Press, Maidenhead, 2005.

Index